Culinary Creation

Culinary Creation

An Introduction to Foodservice and World Cuisine

by

JAMES L. MORGAN

ELSEVIER
BUTTERWORTH
HEINEMANN

AMSTERDAM • BOSTON • HEIDELBERG • LONDON
NEW YORK • OXFORD • PARIS • SAN DIEGO
SAN FRANCISCO • SINGAPORE • SYDNEY • TOKYO

Butterworth–Heinemann is an imprint of Elsevier
30 Corporate Drive, Suite 400, Burlington, MA 01803, USA
Linacre House, Jordan Hill, Oxford OX2 8DP, UK

∞ Recognizing the importance of preserving what has been written, Elsevier prints its books on acid-free paper
whenever possible.

Library of Congress Cataloging-in-Publication Data
Morgan, James L. (James LeRoy), 1946–
    Culinary creation : an introduction to foodservice and world cuisine / by James L. Morgan.
        p.   cm.
    Includes bibliographical references and index.
    ISBN 0-7506-7936-0 (pbk. : alk. paper)   1. Food service.   2. Cookery, International.   I. Title.
    TX911.M66 2006
    647.95—dc22

                                                                        2005027673

British Library Cataloguing-in-Publication Data
A catalogue record for this book is available from the British Library.

ISBN 13: 978-0-7506-7936-7
ISBN 10: 0-7506-7936-0

For information on all Butterworth–Heinemann publications
visit our Web site at www.books.elsevier.com

Printed in the United States of America
06 07 08 09 10   10 9 8 7 6 5 4 3 2 1

Dedicated,
with all my love,
to
The Doctor

Contents

Chapter 3

Chapter 4

Introduction to Culinary Techniques and Principles 79

Chapter 5

Planning and Documenting Your Culinary Creations 101

Chapter 6

Chapter 7

Chapter 8

Chapter 9

Chapter 10

Chapter 11

Chapter 12

Chapter 13

Chapter 14

Series Foreword

The Butterworth-Heinemann Hospitality Management Series covers all aspects of the management of hospitality enterprises from an *applied perspective*. Each book in the series provides an introduction to a separate managerial function such as human resources or accounting, to a distinct management segment in the hospitality industry such as club management, resort management, or casino management, or to other topic areas related to hospitality management, such as information technology, ethics, services management, or culinary arts.

The books in the series are written for students in two- and four-year hospitality management programs, as well as entry- and mid-level managers in the hospitality industry. They present readers with three essential features that they are looking for in textbooks nowadays: the books are affordable, they are high quality, and they use an applied and to-the-point approach to hospitality management issues. The authors in the series are selected because of their expertise and their ability to make complex materials easy to understand.

Culinary Creation: An Introduction to Foodservice and World Cuisine by Chef James Morgan is the second text in this series. Because of his passion for food and the art of creating food, his educational experience, his training with Le Cordon Bleu, as well as his incredible "way with words," Chef Morgan is perfectly suited to instill the same passion for culinary creation that he himself is known for in his readers. From the basic omelet to the most elaborate culinary creations, and from basic knife techniques to the most complicated safety and sanitation issues, this book covers it all! Readers will enjoy Morgan's style, and his "joie de vivre," his joy in life, as exemplified in his culinary, and literary, art. The book comes with a wealth of extra information, enough to whet everyone's appetite.

Students and educators alike will find affordability, relevance, and high quality in this and all other texts in the series. As we say in the hospitality industry: welcome and enjoy! Or, in this case, Bon Appetit!

Hubert B. Van Hoof, Ph.D.
Series Editor

Foreword

Chef Morgan has prepared an engaging and *modern* introduction to the world of culinary creation that warmly invites the novice into not only the commercial kitchen, but also the mind of the professional chef—chefs who use the world as their market, chefs who combine the mastery of basic and classic cooking with flavors and traditions from many cultures. Using many lively examples, Chef Morgan illustrates the dangers of "foodism," and emphasizes the need for professionalism, respect, and civility behind the scenes, as well as in the front of the house.

As a long-time author, editor, and customer service analyst in the hospitality industry, and educator at The School of Hotel & Restaurant Management at Northern Arizona University (A Leading Hotel School of the World®), I found myself saying "Yes!" to many of Chef Morgan's points, including the importance of sanitation, technical skills, communication, cost control, menu development, and artful presentation. He urges new culinarians to strive for professionalism from day one, remembering that chefs are given a level of trust granted to few other occupations—to present products that not only enter the human body, but also *change* it. Not forgetting the powerful psychological impact of food, he celebrates how food connects us, creates memories for us, and opens us to the delights of scent, texture, color, and flavor—in a primal yet simultaneously civilized way. His discussion of the universality of the sandwich, in all its cultural permutations, is delightful, as is his matter-of-fact consideration of health, diet, and menu fads.

Hospitality students will enjoy this clear, well-written text, particularly the sidebars dotted with interesting facts and thought-provoking questions. Chef Morgan's book provides a great starting point for future chefs—encouraging them to step into and step up to one of the most challenging, satisfying, and *portable* careers in the world.

Congratulations to Chef Morgan and Elsevier on this refreshing blend of passion, practicality, precision, and polyculturalism.

Dr. Marilyn E. McDonald
School of Hotel & Restaurant Management
Northern Arizona University
September 2005

Preface

Consider the olive, the simple, green, pimiento-stuffed olive, used by the millions each day in martinis, on appetizer platters, and in salads. It seems quite ordinary, doesn't it? A pickled fruit with the strip of another pickled fruit stuffed inside it.

But, think about it. What is the olive? It's a fruit beloved for thousands of years by the people around the Mediterranean Sea. What is the pimiento? It's a strip from a red pepper beloved for centuries by the inhabitants of . . . Mexico?!

Wait! How did this happen? How did a food from one side of the world get stuffed inside a food from the other side? What massive, earth-shaking, historical events occurred that made it possible for these two morsels to meet? And what unsung culinary genius first had the idea of combining the two foods into one immortal creation?

These are types of questions that fascinate me about the world of cuisine. There are so many foods out there on our planet—so many flavors, aromas, textures, colors, shapes, and sizes. We have not yet begun to unlock the possibilities of how all these foods can be combined and recombined into exciting variations.

It's my hope, with this text, to introduce students to the vast array of ingredients that exist in the world of culinary creation. It's also my wish to stimulate the creativity of those who want to pursue a career in the culinary arts by showing them just a few of the foods that people of the world enjoy on a daily basis, so that they might also someday have a brainstorm equal to the pimiento-stuffed olive.

About This Book

Culinary Creation provides you with the basic tools to create foods that will help you implement your own visions and make your own decisions about preparing the style of cuisine you want to serve your customers.

The book does not limit itself to a view of cooking from a strictly European or American perspective. In each chapter, you are not only provided with the classic techniques from the experts in the Western world, but you are also given examples of cuisines and techniques from other regions of our globe to help you appreciate the diversity of tastes and culinary styles in other cultures. As you learn more about how cuisine interrelates, you'll see that there is no such thing as regional cooking; there is only cooking.

A few words about the conventions used in this book. If a word is shown in **bold** type, it is considered important enough for you to learn and understand. Such words may appear on tests.

Although some standard cooking procedures are explained in this text, most of the specific recipes are provided on the *Culinary Creation* CD-ROM in the back of the book. The recipes are all word "searchable" and "printable" in Adobe Acrobat Reader. If you do not have the current release of Acrobat Reader, you may download a free copy at Adobe.com.

This text, for the most part, deals with savory food items like salads, appetizers, sandwiches, entrees, vegetables, and breads. Because the discipline of the *patissier* (the pastry chef) is such a vast field on its own (and usually the basis for an entire curriculum of study), this book does not attempt to cover such topics as cakes, pastries, and sweet fruits. If you are interested in pursuing a career as a pastry chef, you are encouraged to investigate the programs at your local culinary schools.

James L. Morgan

Overview of World Food and Foodservice

Learning Objectives

By the end of the chapter, you should be able to

1. Explain how a culture-bound attitude can hinder your creativity in the kitchen

2. Name major culinary developments in Europe and the people who brought them about

3. Name some of the effects African cultures had on European cuisine

4. Describe some of the major foods of selected African, Asian, Caribbean, and Latin American nations

5. Describe some of the mechanisms by which culinary ideas have crossed national boundaries

6. Name the terms for commercial kitchen personnel and describe their responsibilities

Chapter Outline

The Chef

The Culture-Bound Attitude

A Brief Overview of World Cuisine

1

"The discovery of a new dish does more for human happiness than the discovery of a new star."

—Jean Anthelme Brillat–Savarin (1755–1826), culinary writer

In this, our opening chapter, we will discuss "foodism"—that is, prejudice against the foods of others. We'll also talk about the history of food in various regions of the world and give you some of the details regarding foods in those regions. We'll introduce you to the organization of the modern kitchen, and introduce you to the job titles and duties in the brigade system used in many modern kitchens.

Today, more than at any time in the history of the world, food is a focal point of almost every activity (Fig. 1-1). What's a movie without a buttery tub of popcorn and a nest of cheesy nachos? What's a football game without a carefully planned tailgate party? What's a wedding without the lavish banquet? Admit it. The quantity, quality, and even just the downright availability of food at a function can make the difference between a memorable event and a boring obligation.

With few exceptions, food is beloved by the vast majority of humanity. Food often acts as the central focus for our social interactions; it gives structure to our daily lives. Our

FIGURE 1-1 Food has become an indispensable part of sporting events.

fondest family memories and traditions are most often food related. Eating is something to be anticipated and enjoyed. It is far more than just a means of taking in nourishment. Imagine what life would be like if we just passively absorbed nutrition through our skin as we went about our normal business. Wouldn't that be boring? Instead of such a situation, the human race has developed the ability to distinguish among and enjoy thousands of different flavors, textures, colors, temperatures, and aromas, making food consumption a very stimulating experience.

Furthermore, to most people, food is abundant and affordable—so much so that, for the first time in human history, overeating is a bigger problem than starvation. The business of food is booming.

The Chef

Today, food has become a recognized medium of creativity, an art form in its own right. The **chef**—the person who is able to create and guide the creation of cuisine (Fig. 1-2) at a high degree of proficiency and profitability—is being held in higher and higher esteem around the world.

FIGURE 1-2   The most effective chef must be a culinary artist as well as a manager and a teacher.

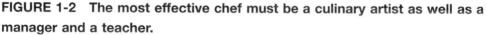

The chef holds one of the highest positions of trust in our society. Think of it. Other than those in the medical field, the chef is the only professional whom we allow to prepare substances that we take into our bodies. Not to put too much of a philosophical spin on it, but what the chef creates actually becomes part of us.

To invent ingenious and beautiful new cuisine, the chef is expected to have a basic knowledge and open-minded curiosity about the foods of all cultures. The successful chef needs to be a total professional, a person who enjoys learning about foods and cooking techniques from around the world and using that knowledge as a springboard to create unique and delicious dishes.

With the growing popularity and availability of foods from every corner of the globe, it is crucial that chefs and managers in the hospitality industry constantly acquire information about cuisines not only from Europe, but Asia, the Pacific Rim, the Middle East, Africa, and the Americas as well. This task is made somewhat easier today with the advent of the Internet, allowing us to travel the world at our desks to get data on any selected cuisine. (But it's still better to visit the places if you can.)

At the end of this chapter, you'll be introduced to the various types of chefs who work in the industry, and you will become acquainted with the responsibilities of each.

The Culture-Bound Attitude

"I want to know if you are genuinely interested in food. I don't want to spend time training someone who has food limitations, who doesn't like this or that. A chef must be open-minded. If you have restricted ideas about food, then this is not the industry for you."

—*Chef Andre Guerrero, Max Restaurant, Los Angeles, California, USA*

Every cuisine in the world has something unique to offer to a menu. Foods of other nations (and even foods from diverse areas within a single nation) are often given little regard by biased students and chefs. Those who have such biases are said to be **culture bound**— that is, they believe everything within their particular culture to be correct and proper, and everything outside their culture to be abnormal. All nations and groups include some members who are culture bound.

Biases are especially strong and hard to overcome in the area of cuisine. Everyone has a tendency to think the food on which they were raised is "right," and everyone else's food is "wrong." Such beliefs might be called **foodism**: prejudice against the foods of other cultures.

How readily do you accept unfamiliar foods? How tolerant are you toward the likes of others if they conflict with your dislikes? Let's find out if you are a foodist. How do you emotionally react to the following dishes?

Boiled peanuts	Head cheese
Peanut butter and jelly	Eel
Rare steak	Well-done steak
Steak tartare (chopped raw steak)	Fried grasshoppers
Lobster	Crawfish
Sushi	Salty licorice
Kraft Miracle Whip®	Mayonnaise

So, what happened when you read this list? Some of you probably reacted with "Yuuukkk!" and some of you said, "Yuuummm!" to the same foods. What does that tell you about being culture bound? Are you a foodist?

When judging others' food tastes, keep in mind that somebody, somewhere finds foods to be delicious that others find repellent. Is food bias the result of reason and knowledge, or more about how and where a person was raised?

To illustrate how perceptions may vary, here are a few observations about some of the items listed.

- Boiled peanuts are an extremely popular snack in the Southeastern United States. They have a completely different flavor and texture than roasted peanuts, but they can be just as addictive.

- Head cheese, a loaf of seasoned shredded meat set in gelatin and sliced as an appetizer or luncheon meat, is a very popular, even beloved, food item in many parts of the world, and in some regions of the United States. In Swedish tradition, for instance, it is called *sylta* (SIL-tuh).

- People in some cultures are repelled by the notion of peanut butter, especially when served with jelly. They find the texture to be disgusting.

- The Pilgrim colonists of New England, a fairly conservative bunch, thought eels were the only fish tasty enough to be worth eating. So why aren't eels more popular today? The major thing working against the eel's popularity as a food item is that it looks like a snake. But it isn't. It's a fish. The flesh of the eel is actually quite rich and delicious.

- People are adamant about how steak should be cooked, aren't they? Furthermore, some people will ridicule those who like steak cooked to any other degree of doneness than what they prefer.

- Lobsters, crawfish, and grasshoppers are all arthropods. What makes one a more legitimate food than another?

- *Sushi* (SOO-shee) is seasoned rice to which things are sometimes added. Sushi is not raw fish. *Sashimi* (sah-SHEE-mee) is raw fish. But some of you said, "Yuuukkk!" based on what you *thought* "sushi" meant, didn't you?

- Salty licorice, called *drop* (rhymes with "rope"), is the number-one snack in Holland. It is available in many varieties, shapes, and colors, and at various levels of saltiness.

- The Miracle Whip/mayonnaise controversy will be debated wherever Americans gather. Mayo proponents find Miracle Whip to be too sweet, whereas Miracle Whip lovers find mayo too bland. Your preference, more than any other, is determined by one thing: which product your family used.

You should fight the tendency to reject foods out-of-hand, regardless of whether you've ever tried them. Open your minds to the diverse possibilities available and consider how any food might fit into an overall, creative culinary plan. Especially, do not openly "disrespect" another person's food tastes. Nothing positive can be gained by doing so.

A Brief Overview of World Cuisine

"In the kitchen, at least, we're in the throes of an unprecedented multinational love affair."

—*Jerry Shriver, USA Today, July 2004*

FIGURE 1-3   The world is a collection of foods to enjoy.

History helps us to understand why things are the way they are. In the culinary industry, it is helpful to know how methods developed so we don't take them for granted, and so that we may continue to improve them. We'll first briefly look at the major European culinary developments throughout the centuries, then we'll look at some aspects of food in the rest of the world (Fig. 1-3).

The Greeks Make Cooking an Art

The ancient Greeks (also known as the Hellenes) are credited with creating **cuisine** (kwih-ZEEN), cooking as an art form, around 1000 BCE. Athenian men spent hours discussing gourmet food items and recipes, including foreign foods as well as native. Greek philosophers at the time of Sophocles, around 400 BCE, discussed food as much as they discussed art, science, or love. As a matter of fact, for many hundreds of years in Greek culture, men were considered to be the only people qualified to cook. Specifically, the priests were the most respected cooks, because they knew how to fabricate meats for sacrificial ceremonies.

The Greeks started, among other things, a tradition of eating four times a day (breakfast, lunch, afternoon snack, and late dinner), a practice still followed in many cultures today. Many of today's common foods were known to the ancient Greeks. For instance, the ancient Athenians knew how to make most of the modern styles of bread, including pancakes, sourdough, and sweet cakes.

When Greece was a powerful nation, from about 800 BCE to 300 BCE, it had colonies in the Mediterranean, the Middle East, Africa, and India. The Greek colonists would bring exotic foreign foods and spices from these foreign lands to their homeland. By the same token, they would introduce Hellenistic foods and cooking standards in the foreign realms. This resulted in wide dispersion of Greek foods such as olives and olive oil, cheese, figs, wine, and wheat. As a result of this, you can easily observe, even today, a strong resemblance between the foods of Greece and the foods of the Middle East.

The Romans Take Over

When Rome became the great force in the world, about 200 BCE, they subjugated the Greeks, but respected them for their knowledge. The Romans eventually learned from their Greek slave chefs and, little by little, adopted their more civilized culinary principles.

The oldest known cookbook was created during the height of the Roman Empire, *De re Coquinaria* (On Cookery), by the Roman gourmet **Apicius** (uh-PEE-see-us) in the first century CE. Among other things, Apicius wrote of force-feeding geese to enlarge their livers, the very method used today in France to produce *foie gras* (fwah-GRAH), a rich duck or goose liver.

Catherine de Medici Goes to France

Even after the fall of the Roman Empire, Italy remained the center of culinary excellence in Europe for about 1000 years. In the 16th century, a teenage Italian princess (Fig. 1-4) named **Catherine de Medici** (MED-i-chee) was wed to Prince Henry, heir to the French throne.

Unwilling to leave the foods of her homeland behind when she moved to France, she imported master chefs called *capi cuochi* (KAHP-ee KWO-chee, "head cooks") from Italy to prepare the culinary treasures of her home—sorbets, macaroons, tarts, and a rich Italian custard called *zabaglione* (ZAB-uh-YO-nee). They also brought new fruits and vegetables— melons, broccoli, truffles (underground mushrooms), green beans, peas, and artichokes. Most important, the *capi cuochi* showed the French chefs how to cook, especially how to move beyond their medieval style of strong flavors and hit-and-miss cooking techniques for more delicate flavorings, textures, and sauces, as well as more refined culinary methods. Catherine de Medici also introduced table manners to the French, including instruction on how to use a fork.

Boulanger Invents the Restaurant

In the 1700s, the first modern restaurant was created in Paris by a man named **Boulanger** (BOO-lon-JAIR). Until that time, guests at a dining establishment ate whatever was put in front of them, but Boulanger felt people deserved a choice. He began offering a variety of food to the customers at his inn. Boulanger said that his varied selections were meant to "restore" the customer. The French word for restore is *restaurer*. The resulting enterprise came to be known as a **restaurant**.

FIGURE 1-4   Portraits of Catherine de Medici hang in foodservice establishments throughout Europe.

Carême and Escoffier Modernize the Kitchen

Another lasting contribution of the French came in the early 19th century when a French chef named Marie-Antoine **Carême** (kuh-REM) refined culinary principles and brought cooking into the modern era. He was the first to organize culinary techniques and to systematize recipes and menus. He is also regarded as the first chef superstar.

But it was Georges Auguste **Escoffier** (ess-KOFF-ee-YAY) who streamlined the commercial kitchen into the arrangement that is still used in major restaurants today. His plan, known as the **brigade system**, is outlined later in this chapter.

Cultural Influences in the Mediterranean

The culinary effects of one culture upon another are more far-reaching than most of us can imagine. Although our condensed version of world food history has so far presented the simplified version of the evolution of cuisine in Europe, there were many more influences upon European cooking, especially from other areas around the Mediterranean Sea, than people normally recognize.

For example, there are very close cultural ties between Africa and Spain. The Moors (Muslims) of North Africa occupied and governed Spain for more than 700 years, from about 700 to the 1400s. As a result, the food of Spain is rich with the influence of their former African rulers, even today. For example, in Morocco, the nation that nearly touches Spain across the Straits of Gibraltar, they have a rich tradition of stews cooked in an earthenware dish called a *tagine* (tah-JEEN). These are normally served over a pasta called *couscous* (KOOS-koos). In Spain, a related dish is called *paella* (pie-AY-yuh), cooked in a similar earthenware dish with rice.

The Moroccans also enjoy a squab-and-almond pie called *b'steeya* (buh-STEE-yuh). An identical dish called *pastilla* (pah-STEE-yuh) is served in Spain and Portugal. It also migrated to the New World and is very popular in South America.

There was also a major influence from North Africa on the foods of Italy and Sicily. The Saracens (Arabs) of North Africa invaded Sicily in the ninth century. They brought not only more sophisticated methods of irrigation that simplified farming, but they also introduced new foods such as dates, rice, melons, raisins, peaches, citrus fruits, and sugar cane, as well as clove, cinnamon, and saffron. The Saracens also introduced more efficient methods of salt production, making salt more available to the Sicilians for the preservation of fish.

Pasta was another probable contribution of the Saracens to Italian cuisine. Yes, yes, conventional wisdom says that Marco Polo first brought knowledge of pasta back from his travels to China in the 13th century, but many culinary experts now say that the Arabs introduced dried pasta, such as couscous, to Italy hundreds of years earlier.

At the eastern end of the Mediterranean, Europeans gained a knowledge of Middle Eastern flavors during the era of the Crusades (1095–1270 CE). During their attempts to conquer the Holy Lands (in what is today, largely, Israel), the armies from England, France, and Italy, among other nations, were introduced to many new flavors that they took back to Europe. Among these taste sensations were basil, fennel, ginger, cardamom, galingale, clove, sorrel, mustard seed, nutmeg, mace, anise, mint, black pepper, and cinnamon.

Africa

"Africa always offers something new."

—*Whoopi Goldberg, Actor, Comedian*

In Western society, there is a notion that, culinarily, Africa is virtually all one nation. To the contrary, Africa has food traditions as complex and diverse as those of Europe. Yet, most people, even chefs, in the United States would be hard pressed to name distinctive foods from the various nations of that huge continent. Let's look at some examples of how the foods of Africa differ from region to region, to give you an appreciation of the potential for using them to diversify a menu.

Morocco

We've already mentioned the tagines of Morocco, the nation in the extreme northwest corner of the continent. Actually, "tagine" refers not only to the dish in which the food is cooked, but the resulting stew itself. Moroccan foods are distinguished by the combination of sweet spices and fresh vegetables and fruits, as well as the use of lamb, chicken, or seafood. **Couscous**, the national dish of Morocco, is a granular pasta made of durum wheat that many people mistake for a grain. Couscous is traditionally steamed in a pan called a *couscousière* (coos-coos-ee-YAY).

Ethiopia

Ethiopia is the only nation in Africa that has never come under foreign rule (except for a brief occupation by Italy during World War II).

 ## Rastafarianism

Of interest to you reggae fans, Ethiopian Emperor Haile Selassie (HI-lee suh-LASS-ee, 1892–1975), was also known as Ras Tafari. He is the Messiah of the Jamaican Rastafarian religion.

Because of its complete independence for thousands of years, Ethiopia developed a rich, unique cuisine. Their *wats* are stews seasoned with peppery *berbere* (BAR-bar-AY) spice mix and eaten with springy *injera* flatbread (Fig. 1-5).

Injera is unlike any bread in the world. It is made by fermenting the local grain *teff* for two days, then cooking the resulting batter into large pancakes. The resulting bread is not only eaten as an accompaniment to food, but it also serves as the dinner plate and the eating utensil. Its supple texture makes it perfect for picking up chunks of meat and vegetables.

Ethiopian is the cuisine of choice among many vegetarians, because of its innovative and flavorful nonmeat dishes, such as *yataklete kilkil* (vegetables with garlic and ginger) and *yemiser selata* (lentil salad).

Not a nation to neglect meat eaters, Ethiopia features one of the world's great dishes for carnivores, *kitfo*, chopped raw beef with oil and berbere spice. (Uh-uh. Watch that culture-bound attitude.)

FIGURE 1-5 In Ethiopia, *injera* flatbread is used as the serving surface as well as the eating utensil.

Ethiopia is also the birthplace of coffee. More than a thousand years ago, Ethiopians noticed they got an energy boost when they chewed red berries of a certain local plant. People began boiling the berries to extract the juice. From that humble beginning, coffee spread throughout the world.

Ghana

Located in West Africa, Ghana offers several culinary treats. The yam is a staple of the Ghanaian menu (not the sweet potato of the Americas, but a starchy white tuber). These are boiled and peeled and pounded into *fufu*, a paste eaten with the fingers, much like *poi* (poy) in Hawaii. Ghanaians enjoy fish stews enriched with bright orange-colored *dendê* palm oil and peanut paste. The **plantain**, a bananalike fruit, is fried and salted as a savory snack, or allowed to ripen and cooked as a dessert.

Plantains

Plantains are enjoyed throughout the tropics, from South America and the Caribbean to Africa, Asia, and Polynesia. Plantains make an excellent garnish for savory entrees because they hold their shape well when fried. A chef can create long, thin strips of fried plantain and use them to add height to a dish.

FIGURE 1-6 Asian cooks appreciate the ability to purchase foods fresh from the source.

Asia

Just as in Africa, the foods of the nations of Asia are individually distinctive (Fig. 1-6). Many non-Asians think of all Asian food as being "Chinese," but in reality there is a wide variety of culinary styles in Asia. Examples of this diversity may be found in two neighboring countries we'll examine: Thailand and Vietnam. We'll also have a look at the Chinese concept of *bao xiang*, the Japanese concept of *umami*, as well as a brief look at the foods of India and Indonesia.

Thailand

The upper classes of Thailand (formerly Siam) developed sophisticated and unique culinary tastes in the late 1800s. King Chulalongkorn, the son of King Mongkut (played by Yul Brynner in *The King and I*), was not only a talented cook himself, but liked to have cooking contests on the Thai New Year among his 32 wives. His entire court joined in the festivities. The cooking competition grew more and more passionate as the years passed. The result of these contests was a complex, ornate, and disciplined array of foods, with subtle tastes and textures that remain today.

The most common cooking technique in Thailand is *kaeng* (kang). *Kaeng* means "liquid," and it covers a range of food, including soups and spicy stews with coconut milk sauce served over rice.

FIGURE 1-7 *Goi cuon* salad rolls are attractive, low fat, and delicious.

Vietnam

On the other hand, neighboring Vietnam developed a unique method of using simple, fresh ingredients to an extent unsurpassed in any other country. This style is best illustrated by the Vietnamese tradition of serving a large platter of greens and herbs to add to your food as you eat. These ingredients are used to their fullest extent when eating *pho* (pronounced like "foot" without the "t"), the clear, rich soups of Vietnam.

The Vietnamese use of fresh greens inspired the lettuce wraps found on the menu in every upscale Asian restaurant in the United States today, such as P.F. Chang's.

Goi cuon (goy-KOON)—fresh, chilled salad rolls usually made with shrimp, pork, greens, and herbs wrapped in translucent rice paper—is another Vietnamese development that has gained popularity during the past decade (Fig. 1-7). You will find some version of rice paper rolls in any of today's popular Pacific Rim establishments.

China and Bao Xiang

The Chinese recognize one part of cooking to which other cultures give less attention, the aspect of aroma. The Chinese term for this is **bao xiang** (BAU-zhee-YANG), meaning "explode into fragrance." It involves the art of exciting people's palates using the aromas generated by the sudden release of volatile oils into the air. This is usually achieved by adding fresh minced ginger, garlic, and onion to a hot *wok* (a large, round pan for stir-frying). As soon as this mixture hits the pan, the fragrance generated prompts an "Mmmm!" from everyone within a 50-foot radius. It's like an appetizer of smells.

Japan and Umami

Just as the Chinese recognize the importance of aroma, so do the Japanese understand the importance of another aspect of flavor that other cultures have been slow too recognize. More than a hundred years ago, the Japanese came to understand that there is a fifth type of taste bud on the human tongue for a component beyond the widely recognized sour, sweet, salty, and bitter. This element can best be called "savoriness" or "richness," the flavor of meat gravy or buttered potatoes. The Japanese named this characteristic **umami** (oo-MAH-mee). Although for many years Western nations largely failed to acknowledge this component, in the late 1990s, scientists at the University of Miami, Florida, confirmed the existence of the fifth type of taste bud.

India and Indonesia

The food histories of India and Indonesia are somewhat similar in that both nations were occupied by European powers for many centuries.

The British had a noteworthy effect on the evolution of Indian cuisine, brought about by attempts to standardize Indian foods for the British colonists' palates. An example of this effect can be found on the shelves of any supermarket, in a product called "Major Grey's Chutney," the British version of the Indian condiment that many Westerners think of as being the only type of chutney, even though there are many different types of *khatni* (Indian chutneys) produced on the Indian subcontinent. These include mint chutney; *raita*, a yogurt sauce; and a tomato/pepper/onion mixture that is, by coincidence, almost identical to Mexican salsa.

Another British influence can be found in the curry powder sold on the spice shelves in many countries today. The flavoring many of us have come to know as "curry" was standardized for British tastes over the centuries of occupation. In reality, there is no single curry flavor. Every region of India has its own distinctive type of curry. It's interesting to visit an Indian grocery store to try some of the curry variations—for example, *garam masala*, a curry from northern India; and Madras (muh-DRAHSS) curry powder, a spicy version from the south.

India contributes several cooking techniques and ingredients to a chef's potential repertoire. The **tandoor**, an oven that cooks at very high heat (700°F/370°C) is used to create a unique style of Indian food that is charred on the outside, yet tender inside. Tandoori chicken, tandoori shrimp, and *naan* (non) flatbread are all popular items cooked in a tandoor.

Another cooking technique that creates a distinctive Indian note is the practice of toasting whole spices to be used in a recipe, greatly intensifying their flavor.

Similar to the British/Indian relationship, the Indonesians were culinarily influenced by their Dutch colonists. The epitome of Indonesian cooking involves a style of service called the *rijsttafel* (REES-tah-full, a Dutch word meaning "rice table"). The *rijsttafel* is a buffet with a centerpiece of decorated bright yellow rice. Surrounding the rice is a variety of dishes intended to satisfy cravings for every texture and flavor of food. Of the dozens of possible selections available, typical dishes at the rijstaffel include

- *Nasi goring*—fried rice
- *Saté babi*—pork grilled on skewers, served with peanut sauce

- *Loempia*—crispy egg rolls usually with a meat filling
- *Sambal*—flavorful sauces ranging from *sambal oeleck*, a fiery chili sauce; to *sambal manis*, a sweet, mild sauce

Today, it is interesting to note that the most popular restaurants in England are Indian, and *rijstaffel* restaurants are among the most popular in Holland.

The Caribbean

"Stir it up!"

—*Bob Marley (1945–1981), Jamaican Reggae Artist*

The food of the Caribbean is a culinary patchwork of fabric from the following peoples: Arawak and Carib natives; British, French, and Spanish colonists; African slaves; and Chinese and East Indian indentured servants. Together, these people gave birth to what may best be termed as "Caribbean Creole" cuisine. **Creole** (KREE-ol) is a term coined 300 years ago by Catholic priests in the Caribbean from the Latin word *creare*, "to create." It was used to refer to people of mixed heritage born (that is, created) in the New World. The word is also applied to the blend of food that evolved from their interaction.

Louisiana Creole

You probably know that the term *Creole* is also applied to the people and food of Louisiana in the United States. Although closely related to the Creole cuisine of the Caribbean, Louisiana Creole resulted from a slightly different collection of people: Native American, French, Spanish, English, African, German, and Italian.

Caribbean Creole cuisine is characterized by the use of

- Fresh tropical fruits, such as papaya, plantain, mango, passion fruit, citrus, ackee (a fruit originally from West Africa; Fig. 1-8), coconut, breadfruit, soursop, and pineapple
- Seafood, especially *conch* (konk, a shellfish), cod (usually dried and salted), dolphin (the fish, not the mammal, also called *mahi-mahi*), lobster, and shrimp
- Roots, including taro root, cassava (from which we get tapioca), and yams (the white tropical kind, not sweet potatoes)
- Spices, such as nutmeg and allspice (called *pimento* by the Jamaicans)
- Peppers, particularly the fiery Scotch Bonnet (called *habañero* in Mexico)

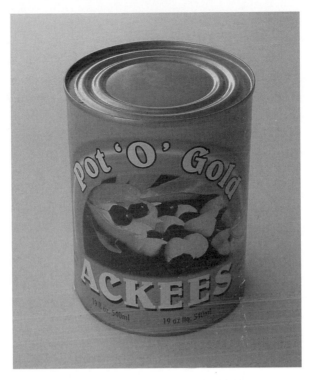

FIGURE 1-8 **Although not widely distributed outside Jamaica, ackee fruit may sometimes be available in other countries in canned form.**

- Poultry
- Meats, including beef, pork, lamb, and, last but certainly not least, kid or baby goat (Hey! Don't be a foodist!)

Outstanding examples of Caribbean cuisine include

- Ackee and saltfish—the Jamaican national dish, salt cod cooked with ackee
- Conch fritters—conch meat, cubed, battered, and deep-fried
- Jerk—usually pork or chicken rubbed with a paste of peppers, onions, and spices (chiefly allspice), then slow smoked
- Cuban *ropa vieja* (ROPE-ah vee-AY-hah, meaning "old clothes")—tender, succulent shredded beef cooked in garlic, tomatoes, and peppers
- Puerto Rican *coquito* (ko-KEE-toe)—the world's best eggnog, made with rum and coconut milk

Latin America

The nations of Latin America feature a wide culinary variety, resulting from a heritage similar to that described for the Caribbean, with the added influence of the Portuguese.

Brazil

Brazil is famous for its national dish, the *feijoada completa* (fay-ZHWAH-duh kom-PLAY-tuh), a festive array of smoked and stewed meats served on a platter with black beans, fresh, sliced oranges, and *farofa*, toasted cassava meal.

Brazilians also make liberal use of the same orange-colored dendê palm oil used in Ghana and most of West Africa.

Nicaragua

Churrasco is the word for grilled meats throughout Latin America, but Nicaragua's version of this taste treat is unique: beef tenderloin sliced in an unusual manner, *with* the grain instead of across the grain. The strips of meat are pounded flat, marinated, then grilled and served with *chimichurri*, a tangy sauce made of parsley, garlic, and olive oil.

Mexico

Often overlooked on the gourmet road map is Mexico, which has a much richer and varied cuisine than the stereotypical something-in-a-tortilla-buried-in-cheese-and-beans you find in most "Mexican" restaurants outside of Mexico.

The caesar salad, for example, instead of being invented in Italy, as everyone thinks, was actually the brainchild of Chef Caesar Cardini in Tijuana, Mexico, in 1924. Celebrities from Clark Gable to Julia Child would periodically make the journey to his restaurant to experience his creation first hand.

Each state in Mexico has a unique style of cuisine. For example, the southern state of *Oaxaca* (wah-HAH-kuh) features an amazing array of **mole** (MOH-lay), complex sauces that sometimes take several people a week to prepare. Most famous is the intense *mole negro* (black mole), an elaborate blend of 30 or more ingredients, including chipotle (chih-POHT-lay) peppers, almonds, plantains, tomatoes, chocolate, sesame seeds, and garlic.

The most unusual aspect of eating mole is that, in the Oaxacan culture, the smooth, silky sauce is considered to be the main component of the meal. Any bits of poultry or meat served with the sauce are there simply to enhance the experience of eating the rich liquid.

 **Going Oaxacan**

To illustrate how a culinary technique can be modified to fit a different cuisine, consider the following example. Chef Paul Prudhomme of K-Paul's in New Orleans has adopted a presentation similar to Oaxacan mole with his gumbo (a type of stew). He spreads the sumptuous pureed gravy from the gumbo on the plate then arranges pieces of chicken, seafood, and sausage artistically to highlight the sauce, in the same way they serve mole in Oaxaca.

The Stations of the Brigade System

Now that we have examined some of the various cooking techniques and flavors that may be found around the world (and hopefully stimulated your curiosity to learn more), let's conclude this chapter by returning to France to examine one of the greatest influences the French have had on modern kitchens: the brigade system.

As we mentioned earlier, in the 1800s Escoffier developed the brigade system used in most large commercial kitchens today. You will encounter the job titles and descriptions he developed (in both English and French) in job ads and on the job in commercial kitchens in the United States, Canada, and other Western nations, so it is helpful to be familiar with their meanings.

It is important to understand that, in the culinary industry, the word *chef* does not mean *cook*. In French, *chef* means "chief" or "boss." The title *chef* is used for those kitchen positions that carry some management or training responsibility and require a certain degree of skill and experience. A worker with no supervisory responsibilities is called a **cook**.

Table 1-1 lists the titles and job responsibilities you might find in a modern kitchen. Obviously, the jobs and duties vary depending on the size and nature of the operation, as well as the country in which the restaurant is located, but this list provides a good basis for what you may encounter.

In addition to the managerial chefs, there are the **station chefs** or **chefs de partie** (par-TEE) who are responsible for particular production areas. Table 1-2 lists and describes these titles. You will see both the English and the French titles in the industry (Fig. 1-9).

Summary and Conclusion

This chapter has touched upon the wide variety of cooking ingredients and techniques that exist on every major continent, and has proposed the concept that there is endless

TABLE 1-1

Managerial Job Titles in the Brigade System

Title	Responsibilities
Executive chef	The manager in a large establishment; handles planning, costing, purchasing, scheduling
Chef or **chef de cuisine**	Oversees food production for an entire establishment, answers to the executive chef
Sous (soo) **chef**	Supervises kitchen employees, reports to the chef
Working chef	Chef in a smaller establishment who not only supervises others but has cooking responsibilities as well

TABLE 1-2

Station Chefs in the Brigade System

English Title	French Title	Responsibilities
Sauce chef	**Saucier** (SAW-see-YAY)	Sauces, stews, hot hors d'oeuvres, and sautéed foods
Fish chef	**Poissonier** (pwah-sahn-YAY)	Fish dishes (except those sautéed by the saucier)
Vegetable chef	**Entremetier** (AHN-truh-met-YAY)	Vegetables, soups, starches, and eggs
Roast chef	**Rotisseur** (ROW-tuh-SOOR)	Roasted and braised meats and their gravies
Grill chef	**Grillardin** (GREE-yar-DAN)	Grilled, broiled, and deep-fried dishes
Pastry chef	**Patissier** (PUH-tiss-YAY)	Bread, pastry, desserts
Pantry chef	**Garde manger** (GARD-mahn-ZHAY)	Cold foods, salads, and dressings
Swing chef	**Tournant** (toor-NAHN)	Works wherever needed

FIGURE 1-9 The grillardin handles some of the most popular items in the restaurant.

potential for culinary inspiration and creativity if you draw upon the cuisines of the entire planet.

This chapter has hopefully convinced you, the student, of the notion that biases against the foods of other cultures and nations are pointless and such attitudes serve only to limit your ability to learn and grow in this industry. Being culture bound can hinder your growth in the business.

This chapter has also defined the role of the chef in the modern world and has introduced you to the various types of chefs that you might find within a modern foodservice establishment.

The next chapter will introduce you to some of the specific facts you need to acquire to be a culinary professional in the foodservice industry. We'll begin by discussing safety and sanitation.

Selected Terms for Review

Brigade system

Chef

Cook

Cuisine

Culture bound

Escoffier

Foodism

Restaurant

Saucier

Sous chef

Station chef

Working chef

Review Questions

1. The Frenchman who "invented" the restaurant was

   a. Escoffier

   b. DeGaulle

   c. Boulanger

   d. Boyardee

2. Match the following dishes to the appropriate chef station:

   a. Baked flounder   1. Grillardin

   b. Caesar salad   2. Saucier

   c. Denver omelet   3. Garde manger

   d. Deep-fried chicken   4. Poissonier

   e. Sautéed pork tenderloin   5. Entremetier

3. The Chinese phrase *bao xiang* means

   a. Explode into fragrance

   b. Savory taste

   c. Very spicy

   d. Sizzling

4. In French, the word *chef* means _____.

5. The brigade system was invented by _____. What do you think are some of the advantages and disadvantages of this system?

6. Name three means by which foods in the cuisine of one culture may travel into another culture.

7. True or false? Africa and Europe have had little effect on each other's cuisines over the centuries.

8. True or false? The foods of Asia are pretty much the same from one end of the continent to another.

9. The high-temperature oven used in India is known as a

   a. Tagine

   b. Tartare

   c. Tandoor

   d. Ras Tafari

10. Coffee first appeared in

    a. Morocco

    b. Ethiopia

    c. Brazil

    d. Ghana

Suggested Readings/Web Sites to Visit

Bourdain, A. (2000). *Kitchen Confidential*. New York: Bloomsbury.

Brillat–Savarin, J. A. (1984). *The Philosopher in the Kitchen*. Middlesex, UK: Penguin Books.

Child, J., Bertholle, L., and Beck, S. (1971). *Mastering the Art of French Cooking*. New York: Knopf.

Culinary Institute of America. (1996). *The Professional Chef*. 7th ed. New York: John Wiley & Sons.

Food Lover's Companion. *Epicurious*. Available at www.epicurious.com/cooking/how_to/food_dictionary/

Food Timeline. *Morris County New Jersey Library*. Available at www.Foodtimeline, org

Food Timeline Culinary Research. *Morris County New Jersey Library*. Available at www.Foodtimeline. org/foodfaqa.html

Gisslen, W. (2003). *Professional Cooking*. New York: John Wiley & Sons.

Hafner, D. (2002). *A Taste of Africa: Traditional and Modern African Cooking*. Berkeley, CA: Ten Speed Press.

Jaffrey, M. (2003). *Madhur Jaffrey's Indian Cooking*. Hauppauge, NY: Barron's.

Labensky, S., Ingram, G. G., and Labensky, S. R. (1997). *Webster's New World Dictionary of Culinary Arts*. Upper Saddle River, NJ: Prentice Hall.

Montagne, P. (2001). *Larousse Gastronomique*. New York: Clarkson Potter.

Root, W. (1980). *Food*. New York: Simon and Schuster.

Trilling, S. (1999). *Seasons of My Heart: A Culinary Journey through Oaxaca, Mexico*. New York: Ballantine Books.

Tropp, B. (1982). *The Modern Art of Chinese Cooking*. New York: Morrow.

Weird Foods from around the World. Available at www.Weird-Food.com

Keeping Your Customers and Employees Safe

Learning Objectives

By the end of the chapter, you should be able to

1. Describe the seven steps for setting up a Hazard Analysis Critical Control Point system in your establishment

2. Name the three major categories of contamination in a foodservice establishment

3. Name and describe the types of pathogens and name the major diseases associated with each

4. Name three types of chemical contamination and describe the purpose of Material Safety Data Sheets

5. Describe and name types of physical contamination

6. Name four ways of eliminating rodents and insects from a foodservice establishment

7. Describe proper food handling

8. Describe proper food storage and define the food danger zone

9. Describe how to sanitize and clean equipment and work surfaces, and how to wash dishes

10. Describe good personal hygiene

11. Describe safe behavior in the workplace

12. Describe the most common sources of allergens in food and how to avoid triggering a customer's allergy

Chapter Outline

The HACCP System

    Background

    The Seven HACCP Principles

Food Contamination

    Biological Contamination

    Chemical Contamination

    Physical Contamination

Allergens

Pest Control

Sanitation and Hygiene

    Sanitizing

    Personal Hygiene

Preparing and Storing Food

    Guidelines for Preparing Food

    Guidelines for Food Storage

Safety in the Workplace

    Professional Behavior

    Management Actions to Promote Safety

    Fire and Burns

    Sharp Objects

    Other Safety Precautions

Summary and Conclusion

Selected Terms for Review

Review Questions

Suggested Readings/Web Sites to Visit

    "First, do no harm."

                               —Hippocrates, 460–377 BCE

The Greek physician Hippocrates' (hip-PAH-kruh-teez) caution to doctors might apply equally as well to chefs. Before all your other concerns in managing your restaurant, your first duty is to make certain that your customers do not become ill or injured as a result of eating your food. This is not a casual concern. Many tragic deaths occur from careless-ness on the part of food workers.

You and your employees must be trained to know how to cook and serve food safely and consistently. Every country has some type of food safety certification. In the United States, you, as a chef or manager, as well as any employee in a supervisory position, should be **ServSafe**® certified (see www.nraef.org for more information) and you should share your knowledge with everyone in your foodservice establishment. You are also required to know your local health department regulations.

This chapter introduces you to the issues involved in food safety and provides you with many of the details necessary to implement a program. However, you must continue to educate yourself in the area of food safety if you wish to be a success in the foodservice industry.

The HACCP System

Background

In the 1960s in the United States, the National Aeronautics and Space Administration (NASA) realized that the possibility of food poisoning onboard a spacecraft was no joke. Astronauts could die or endanger others if they were to eat something tainted during a mission, in a weightless environment, far from medical help. For that reason, NASA teamed up with the Pillsbury Corporation to create the Hazard Analysis Critical Control Point or **HACCP** (HASS-sup) **system**, to reduce the possibility of food poisoning to nearly zero for space missions.

Later, foodservice organizations around the world began to recognize the value of the HACCP system for all foodservice operations. A HACCP program provides the following benefits: decreased possibility of bad publicity and lawsuits, reduced waste, fewer problems and less wasted time, improved standardized processes, higher standards throughout your establishment, and promotion of an attitude of doing things right.

The Seven HACCP Principles

The following seven principles developed in the United States by the National Advisory Committee on Microbiological Criteria for Foods explain how to create a HACCP program in your own business.

Conduct a Hazard Analysis

In a **hazard analysis**, you identify any food safety hazards and the preventive measures you can use to control the hazards. A **food safety hazard** is any biological, chemical, or physical contamination that may cause a food to be unsafe for human consumption. (We'll discuss this in more detail later.) To perform such an analysis you must

- Examine all the ingredients used in all your menu items and determine which of them may be potentially hazardous (Table 2-1)
- Identify where hazards may occur (for example, in undercooking an egg)
- Identify which equipment may contribute to food hazards (for example, a cutting board may become contaminated)

TABLE 2-1

The Most Hazardous Foods (per the U.S. Department of Health and Human Services)

Animal Origin	Plant Origin
Dairy	Cooked starches
Fresh eggs	Cooked vegetables and fruits
Meats	Cut melons
Poultry	Soy protein (for example, tofu)
Seafood	Garlic-in-oil mixtures
Shellfish	Raw sprouts and seeds

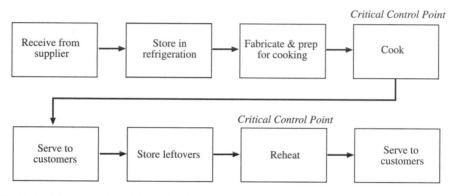

FIGURE 2-1   Flow of food for chicken.

- Determine which customers are most at risk to food hazards (for example, young children, senior citizens, and people with food allergies and deficient immune systems)

Identify Critical Control Points

A **critical control point** (CCP) is a place in the flow of food at which an action can be taken to prevent, eliminate, or significantly reduce a food safety hazard. The **flow of food** is the path a food item takes from receiving to storage, preparation, and serving. Each food item has a unique flow (Fig. 2-1). The actual cooking of an item is often a CCP.

Establish Critical Limits for Each CCP

So, you've decided what the control points are. Now what? Now you've got to decide to what level the hazard is to be controlled to make it safe. A **critical limit** is the value to which a hazard must be controlled to prevent, eliminate, or reduce it to an acceptable level. For example, you have to know how hot a food item must be to prevent the growth of bacteria, and for how long it must be maintained at that temperature.

Establish CCP Monitoring Requirements

Now you have to decide how to monitor what you've set up. You've got to decide the method for monitoring the CCP, what instrument to use, who is going to monitor the CCP, and how often the CCP needs to be monitored. Monitoring is necessary to make certain the process is under control.

Determine Appropriate Corrective Actions

So, let's say you discover that an item is not within the limits you've set up. What now? You have to decide what needs to be done to correct the problem. This might involve simply reheating an item to the proper temperature or it may be throwing it away. Corrective actions are intended to make certain that no harmful product is served in your establishment.

Set up Record-Keeping Procedures

Next, remember: you've got to keep track of everything. You've got to maintain certain documents, including your hazard analysis and written HACCP plan, and records documenting the monitoring of CCPs, critical limits, verification, and how you handled corrective actions.

Establish HAACP Procedures

This step ensures that the plans do what they are supposed to do—that is, they ensure the production of a safe product. To make certain your plan is working, on a regular basis (not just once, because things change), you must review your HACCP plans, your CCP records, and your critical limits. You've got to make sure your employees are following procedures, your monitors are alerting you to hazards, and that the appropriate corrective actions are being taken. (If you work in a corporately owned kitchen, HACCP procedures will already be standardized. However, you still need to be aware of the process involved.)

Food Contamination

Food contamination occurs when food contains hazardous substances that can make people ill. Food contamination falls into three categories: biological, chemical, and physical. We'll spend most of our time discussing the most common (and the most hazardous) category: biological contamination. **Food-borne illness** is any sickness resulting from food contamination.

Biological Contamination

Microorganisms are living things so small they can only be seen through a microscope. When microorganisms cause food-borne illness it is called **biological contamination**. Please understand that not all microorganisms are harmful; many foods such as cheese and yogurt not only contain beneficial living organisms, but are created by them. Microorganisms that produce disease are called **pathogens** (PATH-uh-juhnz). They fall into the categories of bacteria, viruses, parasites, and fungi.

Bacteria

Bacteria are microscopic, single-celled animals. They are everywhere. Even after you take a shower, the bacterial population on the surface of your skin is greater than the human population of the United States. However, don't be too shocked. Most bacteria are harmless or even beneficial. But many bacteria cause food spoilage or are pathogens.

Bacterial pathogens spread by food handlers are the number one cause of food-borne illness. These pathogens are spread chiefly by unclean hands or by coughing and sneezing. Therefore, it is important that food workers educate themselves about bacterial pathogens.

The following is a list of some of the most common food-borne illnesses caused by bacteria:

- **Staph** (staff)—caused by the bacterium *Staphylococcus aureus* (STAFF-uh-low-KAHK-us OR-ee-us). The source is most often sick food workers. Staph is the most common food poisoning. Symptoms include nausea, fever, cramps, and diarrhea. To avoid spreading staph, use good personal hygiene and sanitation practices, store foods properly, and don't allow sick employees to handle food.

- **E. coli** (EE KOHL-aye)—Caused by the bacterium *Escherichia coli*. It is most often found in undercooked red meats and unpasteurized dairy foods. Symptoms include abdominal pain, vomiting, and diarrhea. To avoid *E. coli* contamination, cook foods thoroughly, especially ground meats, and practice good personal hygiene and sanitation.

- **Salmonella** (SAL-muh-NEL-uh)—Caused by the bacterium *Salmonella*. It is most often found in meats, eggs, poultry, and fecal matter from workers' unwashed hands. The bacterium is very common; *most chickens carry salmonella*. Symptoms include nausea, fever, cramps, and diarrhea. To avoid spreading salmonella, use good personal hygiene and sanitation practices, and store and cook foods (especially chickens and eggs) properly.

- **Strep**—Caused by the bacterium *Streptococcus* (STREP-toe-KAHK-us). Sources are sick food workers or customers. Symptoms include sore throat and fever. To avoid spreading strep, protect buffets from sneezes and coughs, and don't allow sick employees to handle food.

- **Listeriosis** (liss-TEER-ee-OH-sis)—Caused by the bacteria *Listeria monocytogenes* (lis-TEER-ee-uh MAH-Noh-sy-toh-JEN-eez). Sources are soil, water, humans, and animals. Symptoms include nausea, vomiting, diarrhea, cervical infections, and miscarriage in pregnant women. To avoid spreading listeriosis, cook foods to proper temperatures, serve only pasteurized dairy foods, and practice good hygiene and sanitation.

- **Campylobacteriosis** (KAM-pil-oh-bak-teer-ee-OH-sis)—Caused by the bacteria *Campylobacter jejuni*. Sources are domestic animals and raw milk. Most poultry carries this bacteria. Symptoms include diarrhea, abdominal cramps, fever, and vomiting. To avoid spreading, thoroughly cook food, avoid cross-contamination, and use pasteurized milk.

- *Clostridium perfringens*—Caused by the bacteria *Clostridium perfringens*. Sources are food workers, meats, and soil. Symptoms include nausea, fever, cramps, and diarrhea. To avoid, keep foods out of the food danger zone (FDZ).

- **Botulism** (BAH-chuh-liz-um)—Caused by the bacterium *Clostridium botulinum*, an anaerobic (nonoxygen-breathing) bacteria. The source is usually home-canned foods and infection usually results in death. To avoid botulism, always use commercially canned foods. Never open a can or jar if it is swollen. Never taste or even smell suspect foods.

Viruses

A **virus** is much smaller than bacteria and is much simpler in form, because it has no cells. A virus cannot grow or multiply outside a living cell. Unlike bacteria, all viruses are pathogens. The following are two of the most common food-borne illnesses caused by viruses:

- **Hepatitis A** (HEP-uh-TIE-tuss AY)—Caused by the virus hepatitis A. Sources include human feces and seafood from water contaminated by feces. Symptoms include jaundice (yellow skin and eyes), abdominal pain, and fatigue. To avoid spreading hepatitis A, practice good hygiene and sanitation, and use only seafood purchased from reputable suppliers.

- **Norwalk gastroenteritis** (NOR-wok GASS troh-en-tur-AYE-tiss)—Caused by the virus Norwalk. Sources are human feces and seafood from water that has been contaminated by feces. Symptoms include nausea, vomiting, cramps, and diarrhea. To avoid spreading, practice good hygiene and sanitation, and use approved seafood.

Parasites

Parasites are organisms that live on or in another organism called a *host*. They extract their nourishment from the host. Some human parasites are harmless, such as the microscopic demodicid mites that live in our hair follicles and eyelashes. However, other parasites can cause severe diseases. The two most common diseases caused by food-borne parasites are the following:

- **Trichinosis** (TRIK-in-OH-sis)—Not as common as it once was, trichinosis is caused by a roundworm, *Trichinella spiralis*, that embeds itself in the host's muscle tissue.

The source is pork. Symptoms include nausea, abdominal pain, and muscle soreness. To avoid trichinosis, cook pork to a minimum of 150°F (65°C).

Rare Pork?

Pork from Canada is now considered to be trichinosis free. It may be cooked to lower than the recommended safe temperature. As a result, rare pork may now appear in some restaurants, even though that may be difficult for some people to accept.

- **Anisakiasis** (AN-nih-SAHK-ee-ah-sis)—Caused by the roundworm *Anisakis simplex*. The source is saltwater fish, usually herring. Symptoms include nausea, abdominal pain, and vomiting worms. To avoid, obtain fish only from approved sources. If fish are to be eaten raw, freeze to –4°F (–20°C) for a minimum of seven days or –31°F (–35°C) for a minimum of 15 hours in a blast chiller before serving.

Fungi

A **fungus** (plural, "fungi") is a plantlike organism that comes in many varieties. Like bacteria, fungi are found everywhere—in the air, water, and soil. Also like bacteria, there are beneficial and harmful fungi. Beneficial fungi include **yeasts**, which are used to produce bread and alcoholic beverages; **mold** (Fig. 2-2), used in cheese making; and **mushrooms**.

FIGURE 2-2   Mold may appear on foods as they spoil, as seen on these olives.

FIGURE 2-3   Wild mushrooms may look tempting, but should be picked only by experts.

Fungi that are harmful from the human standpoint include *Aspergillus flavus* and *Aspergillus parasiticus,* which produce the **aflatoxin** poison sometimes found in grains. Aflatoxin can cause lung damage or even death.

Many mushrooms growing in the wild are extremely toxic to humans, even though they may resemble edible varieties (Fig. 2-3).

To avoid harmful effects from fungi, use the following guidelines:

- Discard any moldy food unless the mold is part of the food, as in bleu or brie cheese.

- Discard any food (for example, jelly) that shows the symptoms of yeast infestation, unless the infestation is natural to the food, as in bread dough. Spoilage creates a distinct alcoholic odor and bubbles.

- Serve only mushrooms obtained from a reputable source.

Who is FAT TOM and How Can He Help?

No, FAT TOM is not the star of the latest slacker movie. It's a name to help you remember how microorganisms grow.

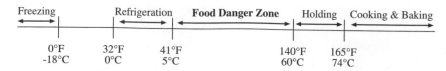

| Freezing | | Refrigeration | | Food Danger Zone | | Holding | Cooking & Baking |

| 0°F | 32°F | 41°F | | 140°F | 165°F |
| -18°C | 0°C | 5°C | | 60°C | 74°C |

FIGURE 2-4   Important food temperatures.

Most microorganisms (other than viruses) need six things to live that can be remembered by the acronym **FAT TOM**: food, acidity, temperature, time, oxygen, and moisture.

- **Food**—Usually, microorganisms' food consists of protein and carbohydrates.

- **Acidity**—They require more or less a neutral pH—that is, neither a very acidic nor a very basic environment.

- **Temperature**—Microorganisms like a temperature between 41°F and 140°F (5°C and 60°C; Fig. 2-4). This is called the *food danger zone* (or FDZ).

- **Time**—Of course, the more time they have, the more they grow. If hazardous food remains in the FDZ for a *total* time longer than 4 hours, it may cause illness. A half hour here and there can make a difference.

- **Oxygen**—Most microorganisms are **aerobic** (air-ROH-bik)—that is, they need oxygen. Some, like botulism (described earlier), are **anaerobic** (AN-uh-row-bik)—that is, they don't require oxygen.

- **Moisture**—Like most life on earth, microorganisms need water.

With the help of FAT TOM, you can set out to fight the growth of pathogens in your establishment. Use these steps to get started:

- Raise the acidity of your foods with an acid like lemon juice or vinegar.

- Limit the time foods spend in the FDZ.

- Keep the environment and foods as dry as possible, especially during storage.

Chemical Contamination

Chemical contamination occurs when any toxic substance from chemicals or toxic metals in the kitchen finds its way into food.

- **Chemicals**—May include pesticides, lubricants, cleaners, and sanitizers. To avoid contamination, use only according to the manufacturer's directions and store away from food. Pesticides should be used only by a professional pest control agent, not kitchen personnel.

- **Toxic metals**—May be found in utensils used in the kitchen. Common toxic metals include lead, zinc, antimony, and copper. To avoid contamination, use only approved food-grade utensils.

In the United States, to minimize harm from chemical contamination, the Occupational Safety and Health Administration (OSHA) requires that manufacturers provide a material safety data sheet (**MSDS**) on every hazardous chemical to the purchaser of the chemical. The sheet provides information on such things as safe use, precautions, protective gear, and first-aid. The MSDS is to be kept in a location in the workplace accessible to all employees, to provide full information about any hazardous materials the employees must handle.

Physical Contamination

Physical contamination results when actual foreign objects get into food. Such objects may include broken glass, bits of metal shavings from can openers, bandages, fingernails, or staples. To minimize harm from such objects, make certain your employees closely inspect all food at every step during the flow of food.

Allergens

Allergens are substances in food that cause allergic reactions in some people when eaten. People who have these reactions are said to have a **food allergy.** About one in 30 people has a food allergy.

Allergic reactions may range from rashes to swollen glands, tightening of the throat, shortness of breath, or vomiting. The most severe reaction is called **anaphylactic** (AN-uh-fill-AK-tik) **shock,** a condition in which the victim may become unconscious, have difficulty breathing, or even die.

The most common food allergens are

- Dairy products
- Eggs
- Fish
- Shellfish
- Tree nuts
- Peanuts
- Wheat
- Soy products

You, as a restaurant worker or foodservice manager, are responsible for, among other things,

1. Memorizing the list of common food allergens
2. Knowing *all* the ingredients in *all* the items on your menu, so that you can answer any question about a particular ingredient.

MATERIAL SAFETY DATA SHEET

SECTION 1 - PRODUCT IDENTIFICATION AND USE

PRODUCT IDENTIFIER ⇨		PRODUCT IDENTIFICATION NUMBER (PIN)
PRODUCT USE ⇨		

MANUFACTURER'S NAME		SUPPLIER'S NAME	
STREET ADDRESS		STREET ADDRESS	
CITY	PROVINCE	CITY	PROVINCE
POSTAL CODE	EMERGENCY TELEPHONE NO.	POSTAL CODE	EMERGENCY TELEPHONE NO.

SECTION 2 - HAZARDOUS INGREDIENTS

HAZARDOUS INGREDIENTS	%	CAS NUMBER	LD_{50} OF INGREDIENT (Specify species & route)	LD_{50} OF INGREDIENT (Specify species)

SECTION 3 - PHYSICAL DATA

PHYSICAL STATE	ODOUR AND APPEARANCE			ODOUR THRESHOLD (ppm)
VAPOUR PRESSURE (mm Hg)	VAPOUR DENSITY (AIR = 1)	EVAPORATION RATE	BOILING POINT (˚C)	MELTING POINT (˚C)
pH	SPECIFIC GRAVITY	COEFF. WATER/OIL DIST.		

SECTION 4 - FIRE AND EXPLOSION DATA

FLAMMABILITY
YES ❑ NO ❑   IF YES, UNDER ⇨ WHICH CONDITIONS?

MEANS OF EXTINCTION

FLASHPOINT (˚C) AND METHOD	UPPER FLAMMABLE LIMIT (% BY VOLUME)	LOWER FLAMMABLE LIMIT (% BY VOLUME)
AUTOIGNITION TEMPERATURE (˚C)	HAZARDOUS COMBUSTION PRODUCTS	
EXPLOSION DATA ⇨ SENSITIVITY TO IMPACT	SENSITIVITY TO STATIC DISCHARGE	

SECTION 5 - REACTIVITY DATA

CHEMICAL STABILITY
YES ❑ NO ❑   IF NO, UNDER WHICH CONDITIONS?

INCOMPATIBILITY WITH OTHER SUBSTANCES
YES ❑ NO ❑   IF SO, WHICH ONES ⇨

REACTIVITY, AND UNDER WHAT CONDITIONS

HAZARDOUS DECOMPOSITION PRODUCTS

A

FIGURE 2-5A and 2-5B   (A, B) An MSDS, shown here front (A) and back (B), is invaluable for preventing chemical injuries on the job.

PRODUCT IDENTIFIER

SECTION 6 - TOXOLOGICAL PROPERTIES

ROUTE OF ENTRY

    SKIN CONTACT ☐   SKIN ABSORPTION ☐   EYE CONTACT ☐   INHALATION ☐   INGESTION ☐

EFFECTS OF ACUTE EXPOSURE TO PRODUCT

EFFECTS OF CHRONIC EXPOSURE TO PRODUCT

EXPOSURE LIMITS	IRRITANCY OF PRODUCT	SENSITIZATION TO PRODUCT	CARCENOGENICITY
TERATOGENICITY	REPRODUCTIVE TOXICITY	MUTAGENICITY	SYNERGISTIC PRODUCTS

SECTION 7 - PREVENTATIVE MEASURES

PERSONAL PROTECTIVE EQUIPMENT

GLOVES (SPECIFY)	RESPIRATOR (SPECIFY)	EYE (SPECIFY)
FOOTWEAR (SPECIFY)	CLOTHING (SPECIFY)	OTHER (SPECIFY)

ENGINEERING CONTROL (SPECIFY E.G., VENTILATION, ENCLOSED PROCESS)

LEAK AND SPILL PROCEDURE

WASTE DISPOSAL

HANDLING PROCEDURES AND EQUIPMENT

STORAGE REQUIREMENTS

SPECIAL SHIPPING INFORMATION

SECTION 8 - FIRST AID MEASURES

SPECIFIC MEASURES

SECTION 9 - PREPARATION DATE OF MSDS

PREPARED BY (GROUP, DEPARTMENT, ETC.)	PHONE NUMBER	DATE

B

FIGURE 2.5A and 2.5B *Continued*

As a cook, you must be able to prepare a customer's specially ordered item and make certain that it is free of any particular allergen. For example, if a customer is allergic to shellfish, you must be certain that the chicken they order is not fried in the same oil as shrimp.

Servers must be able to describe fully any menu item and tell how it is prepared. If not, the server must honestly tell the customer he/she isn't sure and go ask a chef, or suggest the customer try something else.

 ## Seafood Allergies and Southeast Asian Cuisine

Here's an example of how a minor ingredient can be important to someone with an allergy. In southeast Asian restaurants, most recipes include fish sauce, an anchovy-based seasoning. From the menu, it would be impossible for the customer to tell that the chicken dishes, the pork dishes, the vegetarian dishes, the soups, the sauces, the marinades, and even many of the salads contain this ingredient. Therefore, it would be important that the managers, servers, and cooks all understand that most of their dishes would be hazardous to someone with a seafood allergy.

Pest Control

Pests such as rats, cockroaches, and flies spread disease. It is a major health violation to have an infestation of such animals in your establishment. The following guidelines for controlling pests are based on eliminating their food, water, and shelter:

- Keep the area outside your building clean and free of garbage and debris.
- Make certain that outside doors close completely and automatically.
- Eliminate hiding places, both inside and outside.
- Use heavy-duty garbage containers and dumpsters, and keep them tightly sealed.
- Keep your kitchen clean and sanitized. "Clean as you go" is a good rule of thumb.
- Keep all foods in the kitchen tightly sealed when not in use. Store food off the floor.
- Inspect all incoming deliveries for pests.
- Keep your kitchen in good repair. Seal holes and cracks in the wall, and gaps around pipes and electrical outlets.
- Repair leaky pipes and dripping faucets.

- If necessary, hire a qualified exterminator who can professionally apply appropriate chemicals such as pesticides. It is hazardous to try to apply pesticides yourself.

Sanitation and Hygiene

The two major paths to preventing food-borne illness involve proper sanitation in the kitchen and good personal hygiene. In this section, we look at the details of each of these important topics.

Sanitizing

Sanitizing means washing with enough heat and/or chemicals to kill pathogens. **Cleaning** means just getting rid of visible dirt. Dishes, utensils, work surfaces, and equipment must be sanitized.

Manually Sanitizing Dishes, Utensils, and Small-Equipment Parts

There are six steps to sanitizing items manually in a three-compartment sink in a commercial kitchen (Fig. 2-6). The following procedure may be used when washing dishes, kitchen utensils, equipment, and parts of equipment that can fit into the sinks (the temperatures and times may vary according to local regulations):

1. **Scrape** pieces of food from the items into the garbage.

2. **Prerinse** the items, usually using a sprayer.

3. **Wash** items in warm water at 110 to 120°F (43–49°C) in the first sink compartment with a good detergent. Change the water frequently.

4. **Rinse** the items in clean water in the second sink compartment. Change the rinse water frequently.

5. **Sanitize** in the third compartment by immersion for at least 30 seconds at a water temperature of 170°F (77°C) or higher, or in an appropriate sanitizer solution (following the manufacturer's directions).

6. **Air-dry** in a rack, so items will not be recontaminated by towels, fingers, and so forth. Inspect the dishes as you place them on the rack.

Mechanically Sanitizing Dishes, Utensils, and Small-Equipment Parts

There are five steps to sanitizing items in a mechanical dishwasher. This procedure may be used when washing dishes, kitchen utensils, equipment, and parts of equipment

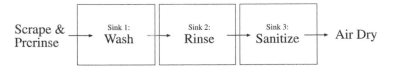

FIGURE 2-6   The flow of dishes in a three-compartment setup.

FIGURE 2-7   A typical three-compartment setup in a commercial kitchen. Note the dispensers for soap and sanitizer.

that can fit into the washer (The temperatures and times may vary according to local regulations.):

1. **Scrape** pieces of food from the items into the garbage.

2. **Prerinse** the items, usually using a sprayer.

3. **Place** items onto the rack in the dishwasher. Do not overload.

4. **Run** the machine. Make certain the sanitizing temperatures are set at 180°F (82°C) for heat sanitation or 140°F (60°C) for chemical sanitation.

5. **Air-dry** in a drying rack, so items will not be recontaminated by contact with towels, fingers, and so forth. Inspect the dishes as you place them on the rack.

Sanitizing Large Equipment and Work Surfaces

Bacteria can grow rapidly on equipment and work surfaces that have been contaminated by residue from cooking. To prevent this from happening, observe the following principles for cleaning your work area and equipment:

- Clean and sanitize tables, counters, and work surfaces frequently during the day with a cloth soaked in sanitizer. Again, follow the rule "clean as you go."

- Dismantle, clean, and sanitize large food preparation machines at least daily. Hint: To make this task easier, purchase equipment that can be easily dismantled and cleaned.

- For parts that cannot be dismantled, sanitize all surfaces with a sanitizing solution and wipe with a clean cloth. Especially make certain to sanitize the cutting blade on the can opener, which is notorious not only for harboring bacteria, but also for being the first place the health inspector checks.

- Clean hoods, grease filters, vent pipes, ranges, and grills daily.

- Clean empty food bins and containers before refilling them.

- Do not use chipped, cracked, or split meat blocks, cutting boards, or tables, which can harbor dirt and bacteria.

Personal Hygiene

As stated earlier, poor personal hygiene is the main cause of food-borne illness. Isn't that ridiculous? Ask yourself the following: How careless does an employee have to be to neglect washing his or her hands after using the bathroom? There is no excuse for such behavior. The few seconds it takes to scrub up can save the lives of customers and millions of dollars in lawsuits.

The following is a list of rules everyone in the foodservice industry should follow to minimize the risk of food-borne illness:

- Always wash your hands and forearms with plenty of soap and hot water for 20 seconds after using the restroom, eating, smoking, drinking, or touching any possibly contaminated item. Also, wash your hands after you are finished preparing each type of food item (for example, after prepping chicken).

- Don't sit on work surfaces.

- Bandage cuts according to your local regulations. For example, a cut on a finger usually must be covered with a brightly colored bandage, *and* a finger cot (a tight-fitting latex covering), *and* a plastic glove.

- Don't touch your hair, scalp, face, or arms while handling food.

- Take a bath or a shower *every day*.

- Wear a clean uniform and apron *every day*. Change aprons that become soiled during work. Remove your apron before entering the bathroom.
- Don't wipe your hands on your apron while working. Use a sanitized cloth.
- Wear a hat or hairnet while in the kitchen.
- Cut your fingernails short and do not use polish.
- Don't handle food if you are sick with a communicable disease.
- Men should be clean shaven or have neat beards or mustaches.
- Remove jewelry; it harbors bacteria.
- Don't eat (other than legitimate tasting), smoke, or chew gum while in the kitchen.

Preparing and Storing Food

Food preparation and storage must be carried out to keep bacterial contamination and growth to a minimum. The main two goals of the following guidelines are (1) keeping food out of the FDZ and (2) preventing **cross-contamination**, the transfer of pathogens or allergens from one food to another. Such contamination can take place by direct contact with the another food, or by contact with contaminated surfaces, equipment, hands, or clothing.

Guidelines for Preparing Food

To reduce risks from food hazards, use the following guidelines when preparing food for your customers:

- Purchase only wholesome ingredients from trustworthy suppliers.
- Remove only as much food from the refrigerator as you can prepare at one time.
- If you drop a piece of unwrapped food on the floor, discard it, even if it's a filet mignon.
- Don't let hazardous foods remain in the FDZ longer than one hour at a time, or longer than four total hours.
- Clean and sanitize work surfaces, cutting boards, and utensils after each type of item has been prepared.
- Thaw frozen food in a refrigerator at 41°F (5°C) or lower, or under running water at 70°F (21°C) or lower, or in a microwave if it is to be served immediately.
- Wash fruits and vegetables before use.
- Don't combine leftovers with newly prepared foods.
- Cover foods except while using them.

- Wear gloves when handling ready-to-eat (RTE) foods—in other words, food that is to be served to the customer without further cooking (salads, sandwiches, plated entrees, and so on). Use tongs or spatulas instead of your fingers when possible.

- Cool hot foods such as soups or stocks as quickly as possible. According to the U.S. Food and Drug Administration, to minimize bacterial growth, hot foods must be cooled from 140°F (60°C) to 70°F (21°C) within two hours, then from 70°F (21°C) to 41°F (5°C) in the next four hours. The technique used to cool large amounts of liquid is called *venting*. To vent a container of soup, place the container into a sink on blocks, to allow circulation under the container. Fill the sink with ice water to the level of the soup. Stir occasionally. (Use an ice wand to stir, if available, a long plastic rod filled with ice.) When the soup has reached 70°F, cover it and place it in the refrigerator.

Guidelines for Food Storage

To provide an environment that is inhospitable to pathogens, use the following guidelines when storing food:

- Store dry foods in tightly closed containers; in a cool, dry place; off the floor; and away from the wall.

- Store frozen foods at 0°F (−18°C) or lower, tightly wrapped, labeled, and dated.

- Refrigerate potentially hazardous foods at 41°F (5°C) or lower, tightly wrapped or sealed in storage containers, labeled, and dated. (Exception: Store refrigerated fresh meats loosely wrapped to prevent bacterial growth.)

- Keep refrigerators, freezers, and storage shelves clean.

- Store cooked items separately from raw items. If this is not possible, store cooked items above raw items to prevent potentially hazardous raw liquids from dripping onto cooked foods.

- Store foods in the following order on the refrigerator shelves, top to bottom:
  - Top shelf: cooked and RTE foods
  - Second shelf: whole fish
  - Third shelf: whole meats
  - Fourth shelf: ground meats
  - Bottom shelf: raw poultry

- In general, store raw foods at the following temperatures (specific temperatures and storage methods are discussed later in this text):
  - Uncooked fruits and vegetables: 40 to 45°F (4–7°C)
  - Eggs: 38 to 40°F (3–4°C)

- Dairy liquids (milk, cream, buttermilk, yogurt): 36 to 40°F (2–4°C)

- Meat and poultry: 32 to 36°F (0–2°C)

- Seafood: 30 to 34°F (−1–+1°C)

- When holding hot foods for service, hold the food at or above 140°F (60°C) throughout service.

- When holding cold foods on a refrigerated table or similar equipment for service, make certain that all portions of the food are held at 41°F (5°C) or less throughout service.

Safety in the Workplace

Kitchens are dangerous places. They are crammed with two of the most dangerous categories of items known to humans: very hot things and very sharp objects. Add urgent activity to this situation and you have an environment ripe for accidents to happen.

Professional Behavior

"[In the kitchen of New York's three-star Veritas Restaurant] during the middle of the rush on a Friday night, with a full dining room, the pace was positively relaxing—more a seriously focused waltz than . . . the mosh-pit slam-dancing I live with. No one was screaming. Nobody was kicking any oven doors closed . . . or hurling pots into the sink. [Chef] Scott . . . never raised his voice."

—Chef Anthony Bourdain, *Kitchen Confidential*

The most important action you can take to minimize danger in the commercial kitchen is to *behave professionally*. **Professionalism** means having an attitude that emphasizes responsible behavior and self-control:

- Avoid anger. Maintain a consistently courteous attitude.

- Defuse conflicts between others as quickly as possible.

- Eliminate horseplay and rowdiness. People get hurt when they are distracted by such behavior, when they should be paying attention to their tasks.

- Avoid unnecessary noise. Noise only adds to an already stressful environment.

- Always make your presence known when you are approaching someone who can't see you. Call out "Behind!" Or, if you are carrying something hazardous, call out "Knife behind!" or "Hot pan behind!"

- Walk. Don't run.

- Carry only as much as you can handle. Otherwise, get help.

- Use equipment only if you are trained in its use.

- Use all safety devices that are provided on the equipment.

- Wear sturdy nonskid shoes and a long-sleeved, double-breasted chef's jacket.

Management Actions to Promote Safety

As a manager of a foodservice establishment, you must minimize the risks in your workplace by making certain that the environment is as safe as possible.

- Train your managers and workers to behave courteously. Anger only adds to the potentially dangerous environment in the kitchen.

- Make sure the electrical system is in good working order.

- Install adequate lighting.

- Make certain the work area is logically designed, providing a smooth work flow and few bottlenecks.

- Make sure the floors are skid proof.

- Provide a sufficient number of exits.

- Provide a system to extinguish fires automatically, and provide a sufficient number of clearly visible manual fire extinguishers.

- Keep equipment in good repair.

Fire and Burns

Because most cooking involves controlled heat, fire is always present in the kitchen. The trick is to manage the fire so it never causes serious injury or damages your building.

Unfortunately, burn injuries occur constantly during cooking activity. No matter how careful or well-trained the employees are, they are going to suffer minor burns from time to time. However, it is of absolute importance that you prevent major burn injuries. The following are guidelines for preventing fires and serious burns:

- Make sure you have fire extinguishers readily available for every type of fire. The three types are class A (for common items like cloth, wood, and paper), class B (for liquids like grease, oil, and gasoline), and class C (for electrical equipment). Make certain all employees know how to use the extinguishers.

- Don't block exits.

- Don't walk away and leave hot fat cooking on the stovetop.

- Always assume everything is hot. Don't grab a pan handle with your bare hand. (You will do this anyway, and get burned, but at least we warned you.)

- Use a *dry* towel or pad to handle pans. Wet cloth conducts heat.

- Don't leave handles of pans sticking out into the aisle. Position them over the stove, but not over an open flame.

- Don't stand in the path of escaping steam when you open a pan or a steam cooker.

- When reaching into an oven, make sure your forearm is protected from contact with the racks. (You'll ignore this advice and burn your forearm anyway, but, again, we told you so.)

- Be careful when using a deep fryer. Don't let liquids sit near the fryer; liquids spilled into a fryer can erupt violently. Don't put wet foods into the fryer. When placing foods in hot oil, let them fall away from you, to prevent splashing.

- When lighting a gas appliance, strike matches before you turn on the gas.

- Don't overfill pans.

Some Don't Like It Hot

Jokes about the elderly and hot coffee aside, flaming food plates and scalding water *do* constitute physical hazards in the foodservice industry. Make certain that your employees are fully trained to serve those sizzling platters, flaming desserts, and steaming liquids safely to customers, and that customers are sufficiently cautioned when being served such items.

Sharp Objects

There are numerous ways to get cut working in a kitchen. In addition to knives of every shape and size, there are slicing blades, shears, garnishing tools, bone saws, peelers, graters, and food-processing cutters, not to mention bones, fins, scales, claws, and thorns in and on the food items themselves. If you follow these rules, you can minimize the number of cuts you might receive:

- Most important, pay attention to what you are doing. As we said earlier, lack of concentration is one of the primary causes of injury.

- Don't clown around with knives. It's amateurish and dangerous.

- Keep your knives sharp. Sharp knives have less tendency to slip or cut crookedly than dull ones. In addition, don't use your knives for jobs like prying or hammering. They are strictly for *cutting*.

- Cut on a cutting board. Do not cut on the countertop. Place a piece of rubber shelf liner under the board for stability. (Shelf liner is available in rolls at any discount mart.)

- Don't put knives or glass in the dishwater. There is too much danger of somebody getting cut as they feel around for things in the water.

- Keep glass out of the kitchen entirely. Use food products packaged in plastic or metal containers.

- When a knife falls, step back immediately. The instinctive (wrong) reaction is to try to catch it with your abdomen or leg. Let it fall!

- When cleaning large fish, remember that there are many sharp objects (fins, bones, scales, spines) on the fish. Use shears to remove the fins and spines before you begin. Use a sharp tool for scaling. Scale with a motion that moves away from any sharp objects. Again, pay attention to what you are doing.

- When carrying a knife, hold it with the point down. Use a sheath if possible. As stated earlier, warn people that you are near them.

- If you do break glass, sweep it up. Don't try to pick it up. Put broken glass in a separate container from the other trash.

- Throw away any chipped or cracked glassware.

Other Safety Precautions

Here are a few other safety tips that may save you from injury:

- To prevent back injuries when lifting heavy objects, squat using your knees, and lift using your leg muscles. Don't bend from the waist.

- Unplug electrical equipment before cleaning or disassembling it.

- Use a ladder to reach high storage areas. Don't stand on a chair or box.

- Stack items such as pots or supplies in a safe, stable manner on a shelf or rack.

- Clean spills immediately.

Summary and Conclusion

Your first duty as a restaurant manager is to make certain that your customers do not become ill or injured as a result of entering your establishment and eating your food. Most of the rules for preventing customer illness are based on common sense: Keep the kitchen sanitized, make certain all workers maintain good personal hygiene, buy your supplies from trustworthy sources, and keep food out of the FDZ.

Setting up a HACCP system in your place of business is the most important step toward maintaining food safety. By doing so, you'll be compelled to identify the CCPs in your business and to define the actions necessary to correct problems.

Maintaining professionalism, and encouraging others to behave in a professional, courteous manner, are the best means for preventing injuries on the job site. Anger and horseplay only add to the already unsafe conditions in the kitchen environment.

Selected Terms for Review

Anaphylactic shock

Biological contamination

Chemical contamination

Cleaning

Cross-contamination

FAT TOM

FDZ

Food allergy

Food-borne illness

Food safety hazard

HACCP

MSDS

Physical contamination

Professionalism

Sanitizing

ServSafe

Review Questions

1. What are the seven steps to designing a HACCP system?

2. True or false? If you drop a knife, you should do everything you can to prevent it from hitting the floor, because its point might break off.

3. Which of the following is not a category of food contamination?

   a. Chemical

   b. Nutritional

   c. Physical

   d. Biological

4. Name the four types of pathogens and name a disease or toxin associated with each type.

5. What is FAT TOM? Why is it important and how is it used?

6. MSDSs are related to what type of contamination?

7. _____ is an example of physical contamination.

8. Name the seven most common food allergens

9. True or false? One employee should be designated to spray pesticides in the kitchen frequently during the day to reduce the number of cockroaches and flies.

10. _____ means to remove visible dirt. _____ means to kill bacteria.

11. Which of the following is not a step in manually sanitizing dishes?

   a. Rinse in clean water.

   b. Scrape off pieces of food.

   c. Wipe dry with a clean towel.

   d. Sanitize in hot water or a sanitizer solution.

12. Define cross-contamination. Give two examples.

13. True or false? If you drop a piece of unwrapped food on the floor and pick it up within five seconds, it's OK to clean it off and use it.

14. When should you wear gloves while preparing food?

15. Stocks should be cooled from 140°F (60°C) to _____° within _____ hours and then to _____° within the next _____ hours.

16. How should foods be arranged, from top to bottom, on refrigerator shelves?

17. Describe three types of professional behavior in the kitchen. Describe three types of unprofessional behavior.

18. Describe the three categories of fire extinguishers. Which type would you used on burning cardboard? Bacon?

19. True or false? You should only use a dry towel or pad to pick up a hot pan. Why or why not?

20. True or false? Stainless-steel countertops are fine cutting surfaces.

Suggested Readings/Web Sites to Visit

National Restaurant Association Educational Foundation. *Food Safety Program*. Available at www.nraef.org/

National Restaurant Association. (2002). *ServSafe Essentials*. Chicago: National Restaurant Association Educational Foundation.

Reddy, S., and Waliyar, F. *Properties of Aflatoxin*. Available at www.aflatoxin.info

Santa Barbara County Public Health Department. *How Do I Prevent Bug and Rodent Infestation?* Available at www.sbcphd.org/ehs/howdoi.htm

Schlosser, J. (2001). *Serving the Allergic Guest*. Scottsdale, AZ: Scottsdale Press.

Your Tools

Learning Objectives

By the end of the chapter, you should be able to

1. Name the various types of cooking equipment

2. Describe the equipment used in the commercial kitchen for processing, mixing, and slicing

3. Name the types of pots, pans, and other containers

4. Describe the materials used for making pots and pans, and their characteristics

5. Name the basic types of knives used in foodservice, and be able to use a steel

6. Describe other equipment and utensils used in the kitchen

Chapter Outline

Cooking Equipment

Ranges and Cooktops

Ovens

Steam Appliances

Broilers, Grills, and Griddles

Deep Fryers

The Shape of Things to Cook: Food Processors, Mixers, and Slicers

Food Processors

Mixers

Slicers

Cold Storage

Pots, Pans, Bakeware, and Other Containers

Characteristics of Cooking Materials

"Without the culinary arts, the crudeness of reality would be unbearable."
—*From the film* Kate and Leopold, *paraphrasing playwright George Bernard Shaw*
(1856–1950)

The first foods didn't require much in the way of equipment; they were eaten raw. Nuts, berries, meats, tubers, insects, and plants were eaten in a totally unadulterated form by early modern humans 40,000 years ago. However, as time passed, humans began to discover (sometimes intentionally, sometimes accidentally) various means for modifying foods, both to preserve them and to change their appearance and flavor. These methods included cooking (heating), cooling, salting, pickling, smoking, drying, and fermenting. In addition, early humans began to combine foods in imaginative ways to add flavorings and seasonings and to alter their form to make them more appetizing or attractive.

 **Give 'Em a Hand**

The human hand was the first human tool and it remains the most important. The vast majority of what we call *tools* are intended simply to increase the range of functions our hands can perform.

As foods became more diverse and complex, humans needed new, more elaborate tools for their collection, preparation, and storage. Open fires gave way to adobe ovens; animal skins and baskets made way for earthenware pots and metal pans; stone points evolved into knives and cleavers; and wooden branches evolved into chopsticks, skewers, spoons, forks, and spatulas.

Today, there are hundreds of tools, ranging from simple to sophisticated, available for use in the commercial kitchen. Some, such as combi ovens, are intricate, computerized, and require training to use. Others are as straightforward as a chef's knife, which simply requires practice.

This chapter provides an overview of the essential tools used in a 21st century commercial kitchen. This equipment roughly falls into these categories: cooking equipment, fabricating appliances, cookware, and handheld utensils.

Cooking Equipment

There is a great variety of methods and appliances around the world for heating food to cook it. In this section we discuss ranges/cooktops, ovens, steamers, broilers, grills, griddles, and fryers.

Ranges and Cooktops

Ranges (cooking appliances with surface burners) vary according to their cooktops. There are essentially four types of cooktops on ranges in today's commercial kitchens: open burners, closed tops (also called flat tops or hot tops), induction, and wok burners.

Open Burner

The **open burner** (Fig. 3-1) consists of a simple metal grate over a heat source, which may be either gas or electric, although most cooks prefer gas. In general, open gas burners provide the fastest heat response and may be turned on and off as needed. Such burners also have the advantage of providing the best visual indication of heat; the cook can tell at a glance how high the flame is. The chief drawback to this type of burner is that the cooking area is limited to one pot per burner.

Closed Top

The burners on a **closed top** range are covered with a light-to-heavy metal covering. Pans may be set anywhere on the top and, depending on the features of the particular model, the heat may be adjusted so the entire surface is uniform or so the heat varies from one area to another.

Induction Burners

The third type of cooktop is like something from a sci-fi story. They are still fairly uncommon, but do have their advantages. **Induction burners** use magnetism to excite the atoms

FIGURE 3-1   An open-burner range top.

in an iron or steel pan, causing the pan to heat, but the cooktop itself doesn't heat. This keeps the kitchen cooler and reduces the risk of burns. The disadvantages are (1) you must use cookware that is at least partially iron or steel and (2) it is sometimes difficult to tell if an induction burner is working.

Wok Burners

Wok burners are gas units that accommodate stir-frying (known also as sautéing, a cooking technique we'll discuss later) in the Asian pan known as the *wok*. Woks are large and hemispherical, and require high heat to function most effectively. The wok burner is an oversized open burner that is built to provide extra heat. This burner may be included as part of an array on top of a range or it may be installed as a stand-alone unit. Wok burners are sometimes fitted with a knee-operated gas valve that provides a burst of high heat on demand.

Ovens

There are many types of ovens available for the modern kitchen—some simple, involving ancient cooking methods, and some modern, intricate, and computerized. Types of ovens include conventional, convection, ovens in motion, infrared, microwave, smoker, low temperature, and high temperature.

Conventional Ovens

Conventional ovens operate in the simplest manner possible, by surrounding food items with hot air in a closed area. These may be **rack ovens** (large versions of home ovens), which consist of a single, enclosed area with one temperature control in which pans may

FIGURE 3-2   A deck oven has separate heat controls for each level.

be placed on wire racks; or **deck ovens** (Fig. 3-2), in which each level of the oven is a separate, enclosed deck with its own temperature controls.

Convection Ovens

Convection ovens cook more quickly and uniformly by circulating hot air or steam around the food with blowers. Normally, such ovens require cooking temperatures of 25 to 50°F (15–30°C) lower than conventional ovens.

However, *convection* is also a term used regarding steam cookers. See the discussion of steam cookers later in this chapter for a more complete explanation.

Ovens in Motion

Some ovens move food about in different ways to ensure the product is cooked evenly. Such ovens are most often used in bakeries. They include **rotating ovens** that contain several shelves upon which items are placed to be baked. As the food cooks, the shelves rotate around an axis. A **revolving oven** is similar, except the food is moved up and down, as if on a Ferris wheel. A **conveyor oven** moves a food item (for example, a sandwich) along a conveyor belt from one end to the other, cooking it on the way.

Infrared Ovens

High-intensity **infrared** (in-fruh-RED) **ovens** use special quartz tubes to produce even, controllable infrared radiation. Infrared ovens can quickly heat large quantities of foods.

The Truth about Radiation

Some people confuse "radiation" with "radioactivity" and become fearful that an infrared or microwave oven will mutate them or their food. However, such fears are groundless. Radiation simply refers to projecting waves. Sound, light, and heat are all examples of waves that are produced by the process called *radiation*.

Microwave Ovens

Microwave ovens are the targets of some of the worst prejudices in the food industry because of a long-standing and unwarranted belief that they lack versatility. Although they are quite good at reducing the time, heat, and labor involved in producing such basic food items as caramelized onions, roux, and duxelles (dooks-ELL, which we'll discuss later), they are largely snubbed by the chef community for doing any "real" cooking.

In **microwave ovens**, microwave radiation is produced by a mechanism called a *magnetron*, which is the same device used in radar. The microwaves bounce around inside the oven and excite water molecules, producing heat, which in turn heats nearby molecules (for example, protein and starch). In the commercial environment, microwave ovens are used mostly for quick, simple heating of previously prepared foods.

Smoker Ovens

Smoker ovens heat wood to produce smoke. The smoke surrounds foods to produce a distinctive flavor and color. Smoker ovens are used especially in American barbecuing and in sausage production. Smoker ovens may operate with cold smoke, which does not cook the food, or hot smoke, which does.

Low-Temperature Ovens

It has been proved that the best way to retain the juiciness of roasted meat is *not* to sear it (more on this later), but to cook it slowly and continuously for many hours at temperatures as low as 200°F (95°C). There are now sophisticated, computerized **low-temperature ovens** (Fig. 3-3) that can precisely maintain low temperatures to cook large cuts of meat (for example, a prime rib roast) over long periods of time. These ovens also sense when the meat is done and reduce the temperature to a holding mode at that time. Meat cooked in this manner is intensely succulent and tender.

High-Temperature Ovens

Today's **high-temperature ovens** have evolved from the adobe or clay ovens that have been used for hundreds of years by various cultures the world over. In these ovens, food is cooked very quickly by being subjected to intensely high heat. As mentioned in Chapter 1, in India the *tandoor* is used to cook such foods as tandoori chicken and the flatbread

FIGURE 3-3   Low-temperature ovens hold a steady, low heat level for long periods.

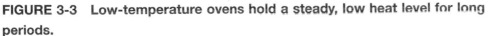

naan. On the other side of the world, in Manhattan, the traditional thin-crust New York pizzas are baked in wood-, coal-, or gas-fired pizza ovens, usually made of brick or clay, that reach temperatures ranging from 600 to 1000°F (315–540°C). Bakers also use the same type of oven for creating artisan breads with crispy, deeply caramelized crusts.

Steam Appliances

Steam is a versatile and efficient medium for cooking food and it can be used in a wide range of appliances. For example, the Chinese have used bamboo steamers (round, covered baskets in which food is cooked over boiling water) for hundreds of years. The British have cooked plum pudding for generations by suspending it in a container over boiling water.

About Steam and Safety

The word *steam* actually refers to two things. The first, true steam, is invisible. Steam is water that has been heated to the point where it becomes a gas. This is the very hot substance that powers steam engines and circulates inside steam cookers. What most of us commonly call *steam*, the fluffy white stuff, is actually water vapor—tiny droplets of water that have cooled to a liquid state. You can see the difference between steam and water vapor if you heat a teapot until it starts to whistle. Look closely at the spout. Notice that the water vapor doesn't appear until it is about an inch or so above the hissing spout. The first inch of invisible substance is true steam.

It is important to understand this distinction, so you can appreciate that true steam is hotter than boiling water, and can cause severe, scalding burns. For this reason, it is important to be very careful when using steam appliances, especially when opening them.

Today, some of the most sophisticated cooking devices in the kitchen involve the use of steam. In this section, we'll discuss steam cookers, including combi ovens, and steam-jacketed kettles.

Steam Cookers

Steam cookers are metal chambers, like ovens, in which steam comes into direct contact with food. They allow efficient cooking of vegetables and other foods, with reduced loss of vitamins.

Pressure steamers are tightly sealed units that allow pressure to build up to acclerate cooking. Modern pressure cookers are safer that older units, because they do not allow themselves to be opened until the pressure inside is at zero. These units also come equipped with pressure release valves to prevent pressure from accidentally building too high.

Pressureless convection steamers circulate steam in the cooking compartment without pressure. These may be opened at any time, but users must be cautious when opening the door, because the hot vapor does often billow out.

Convection Confusion

The word *convection* can be misleading if you are purchasing a commercial oven. Convection can refer to the circulation of hot air or steam *or both* inside the oven. Make certain that you understand which features you want and which type is being described when the vendor uses the term *convection oven*.

A **combination steamer oven**, or **combi oven** (Fig. 3-4), can be operated in three modes: as a pressureless convection steamer, as a dry-air convection oven, or (with both functions operating) as a high-humidity oven that reduces drying when roasting meats.

Steam-Jacketed Kettles

Steam-jacketed kettles (Fig. 3-5) are free-standing large pots, usually fixed to the floor or a tabletop, ranging in size from a few gallons to hundreds of gallons, that have a hollow

FIGURE 3-4   A combi oven uses steam or dry heat, or both.

FIGURE 3-5   Steam-jacketed kettle.

body through which steam circulates and heats the product. Some are emptied by tilting, and some are emptied through a spigot. Steam-jacketed kettles heat food very efficiently and quickly, with no danger of scorching the food.

Broilers, Grills, and Griddles

There is often confusion in the use of the terms *broiler, grill,* and *griddle.* In this section we discuss the characteristics of each of these and some of their variations.

Embroiled in History

Many cultures around the world have used simple forms of broiling for thousands of years. The Tillicum tribe of the Pacific Northwest in the United States props salmon on a cedar post in front of (not above) an open fire, using the fire's radiant heat to cook the fish. Similarly, the Cajuns of Louisiana slow roast their *cochon de lait* (KOH-shawn-duh-LAY, whole suckling pig) by mounting it on a framework in front of a fire, thus preventing the fat from dripping onto the flames and igniting, possibly scorching the meat.

Broilers

Most **broilers** use heating elements (gas or electric) that generate infrared heat from *above* or *beside* the food item. Typically, broilers are used for cooking things like steaks, pork chops, fish, or chicken breasts, or for browning food items (for example, those topped with cheese or buttered breadcrumbs) just before service. A **salamander** (Fig. 3-6) is an open-front broiler, usually installed above the range, that can be accessed quickly and easily.

A **rotisserie** is a broiler with a rod called a *spit*. The food item (for example, a turkey) is placed on the spit, which rotates in front of or beneath the heat source. Although most rotisseries hold the item in a horizontal position, some spits hold the food vertically, like the Indian *shawarma* broiler or the Greek **gyros** (YEER-ose) broiler. In each of these, a loaf of seasoned meat is placed on a vertical spit and rotated in front of the heat source.

Grills

A **grill** serves essentially the same function as a broiler, except it generates heat from *beneath* the food (Fig. 3-7). Unlike a broiler, a grill imparts a distinctive flavor by producing smoke from fat dripping on to the heat source from the food. More flavor can be obtained by adding wood chips or other plant matter (corncobs are popular) to the fire, or by using a particular kind of wood or charcoal as the heat source for cooking.

Griddles

Griddles (Fig. 3-8) are large (sometimes six-feet across), heavy polished plates upon which food, typically burgers, pancakes, bacon, and eggs, can be directly and efficiently cooked. They have the advantage of retaining heat very well, and provide an even, reliable cooking temperature.

FIGURE 3-6   A salamander is an indispensable piece of equipment in most commercial kitchens.

FIGURE 3-7   Grills heat from beneath the food.

FIGURE 3-8   Griddle.

Tilting skillets are essentially free-standing hinged griddles with high sides and a lid in which food can be cooked and then tilted out into a receptacle. Tilting skillets, also called *tilting fry pans* or *tilting braziers*, are extremely versatile and can be used for frying, sautéing, boiling, braising, or steaming large amounts of food.

Deep Fryers

"[Deep-fried] doughnuts . . . have been around so long that archaeologists keep turning up fossilized bits of what look like doughnuts in the middens of prehistoric Native

American settlements."—*David A. Taylor*, Smithsonian Magazine (MARCH, 1998,) Vol 28, Issue 12.

Deep-fat frying has been a popular cooking technique since the invention of pottery 7000 to 10,000 years ago. Meats, breads, and vegetables cooked in fat have been enjoyed by humankind for millennia.

Deep fryers are basically boxes for heating fat into which foods are submerged in wire baskets. Today's commercial deep fryers are sophisticated, computerized tools that not only control the temperature of the fat, but also automatically control the time the food is submerged.

Pressure fryers fry foods under pressure, substantially speeding up the cooking process.

The Shape of Things to Cook: Food Processors, Mixers, and Slicers

Cooks have always looked for more creative and efficient ways to change the characteristics of their food. For this reason, tools that alter the shape, texture, and size of edible raw materials are constantly being invented and improved.

Throughout history, ingenious methods and devices have been created for the purpose of fabricating food. In ancient times, it was discovered that if wheat seeds were pulverized, mixed with water, and baked, they became more appetizing and digestible in the form of bread. So, grinding stones were developed and continuously improved to perform the task of turning wheat into flour. It was likewise discovered that if tough pieces of meat were chopped into small bits, the meat became more tender and edible. At first, this function was performed with crude knives, but, as time passed, meat grinding became more efficient. As a result, today we have a never-ending supply of sausage and hamburgers.

 ### Try a Little Tenderness, Hun

There is a legend that the Tartar horsemen of Russia rode all day with raw meat under their saddles to tenderize it for each night's meal. This practice supposedly originated the modern-day raw-beef dish steak tartare. (Uh-uh. Don't be a foodist!)

This section introduces you to some of the current technology available for the modern commercial kitchen for the purpose of changing the shape and texture of your food.

Food Processors

Most homes currently have small versions of the food processors used in the commercial environment (Fig. 3-9). A **food processor** consists of a canister or bowl with a rotating blade in the bottom that chops or purees food. Large food processors, called *vertical cutter/mixers*, can hold up to 80 quarts of food.

Blenders are taller, narrower processors that may be used for such chores as mixing sauces or for blending drinks at the bar. A portable hand-held model, the **immersion blender** (Fig. 3-10), may be used to mix items as they are cooking in a pot. Immersion blenders range in size from small units the size of an electric toothbrush to large, two-handed models.

FIGURE 3-9   A commercial food processor.

FIGURE 3-10   A large Immersion blender.

 ## Safety Note

Many injuries are caused each year because foodservice workers disable the safety features on processors, mixers, and slicers in the belief that doing so will speed up production. As tempting as it may be, *don't do it*. Those features are there for *your* safety.

Another large food processor, commonly called the *buffalo chopper* (because its cover looks like a buffalo's hump; Fig. 3-11), consists of a big tube pan that rotates food through spinning blades. The buffalo chopper, also called the *food cutter*, has many available attachments (for example, grinders, slicers, and shredders) that fit into a drive on the side of its motor.

Mixers

Mixers chiefly perform the task that their name describes: They mix foods together to produce a uniform blend. Mixers range in size from the small countertop model (similar

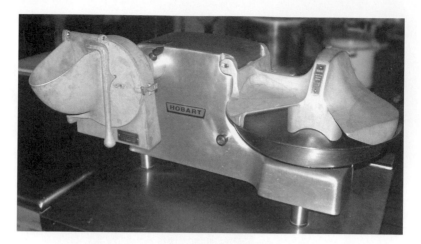

FIGURE 3-11   Buffalo choppers are versatile, but require training to use safely.

to home models) that holds a few quarts to large floor models (Fig. 3-12) that can hold up to 140 quarts.

Typically, there are three types of attachments (Fig. 3-13) used to mix the food to produce different results: The **wire whip** attachment beats air into such materials as egg whites and cream to produce a fluffy meringue or whipped cream, the **dough hook** kneads bread dough to the right consistency, and the **paddle** performs general, all-purpose mixing.

Slicers

Slicers are electric appliances designed to cut food items, chiefly meat, into slices of uniform size and thickness. Most have a circular blade of noncorrosive metal and can be adjusted to cut various thicknesses. The blades of modern slicers are set at an angle, so the slices fall naturally into a stack as they are cut. Some basic machines require that the operator push the food back and forth manually, whereas other more elaborate models can be set to slice automatically.

Cold Storage

There are two basic types of cold storage: freezers and refrigerators. **Freezers** are insulated boxes that hold foods for long periods, ideally at or below 0°F (–18°C). They work most efficiently when packed full. **Refrigerators** hold foods for shorter periods of time, below 41°F (5°C)—that is, out of the FDZ, but above freezing. They work most efficiently when there is plenty of air around the shelves and food items for circulation.

Either piece of equipment comes in various shapes and sizes. A **reach-in** model is a smaller size unit, whereas a **walk-in** model is large enough to allow a person to enter it.

FIGURE 3-12   Floor-model mixer with wire whip attachment.

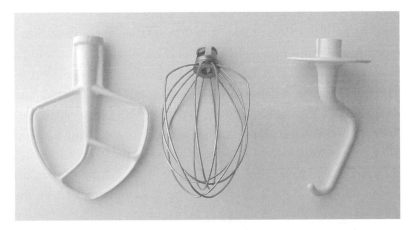

FIGURE 3-13   Paddle, wire whip, and dough hook attachments for a countertop mixer.

Pots, Pans, Bakeware, and Other Containers

This section presents the various types of cookware available, and the materials from which they are made.

Characteristics of Cooking Materials

There are many materials from which cooking vessels may be manufactured, and just as many reasons why one material should be used over another in various circumstances. In general, heavier, thicker pans are superior to lighter ones. Nonreactive pans (made of a material that does not chemically react to acids or alkali, are considered superior to reactive pans.

There are various advantages and disadvantages to each of the common cookware materials (Table 3-1). Most commercial pots and pans are steel, aluminum, or a combination of the two.

Round Pots and Pans

Pots and pans vary according to size, shape, and purpose. Most of the various pots and pans have specific names that you must know so you are able to refer to them precisely and consistently in your recipes and among the employees in your establishment.

The largest size (range, 8–200 quarts) is called the *stockpot*. It is deep and straight sided, and has loop handles on each side. As its name implies, it's used for making large quantities of stocks, soups, and other liquids. Some stockpots, called *marmites*, are equipped with a tap at the bottom to make them easier to empty.

The **saucepot** is similar to the stockpot, but is smaller, ranging in size from 6 to 60 quarts. A **rondeau** (ron-DOE) or **brazier** (BRAY-zhur) is a large, shallow pan with loop handles on each side, ranging in size from 10 to 30 quarts. These are good tools for braising large quantities of meats. A **saucepan** is a smaller pot with a straight, single handle, ranging in size from 1 to 15 quarts. A **sautoir** (saw-TWAHR), also called the *straight-sided sauté* (saw-TAY) *pan*, is like a shallow saucepan, used for sautéing and cooking sauces. More on this later. A **sauteuse** (saw-TOOSS), also called the *slope-sided sauté pan*, is a fry pan with sloping sides and a straight, single handle. It allows the cook to use the characteristic tossing motion to make food jump and flip. (As a matter of fact, the word sauté means "jump" in French.) A **wok** is a deep sauté pan with a rounded bottom and curved sides that make it easy to toss food as it cooks. This pan has either a single, straight handle or two loop handles.

Rectangular Pans

Rectangular pans are usually used for baking or roasting. A common rectangular pan is the shallow **sheet pan**, an indispensable item in any kitchen, which is used for baking,

TABLE 3-1

Common Cookware Materials

Material	Advantages	Disadvantages	Comments
Stainless steel	Easy to clean, durable	Poor conductor of heat, scorches	Best used for low-temperature cooking or storage containers, may be clad with aluminum or copper to improve conductivity
Copper	Excellent conductor; copper bowls are classically used for beating egg whites	Very reactive, can produce toxic chemicals with some foods, extremely expensive	Copper cooking pots and pans must be lined with a nonreactive material; may be clad in stainless steel to improve the steel's heat conductivity
Aluminum	Good conductor, inexpensive	Reactive, not very durable, not good for storage	May be clad in stainless steel to improve the steel's heat conductivity
Anodized aluminum	Good conductor; has nonreactive, electrochemically treated interior surface	More expensive and even less durable than standard aluminum; dark interior makes some foods hard to see	Very popular type of cookware, sold under brand names such as Anolon and Calphalon
Cast iron	Very good conductor, heats evenly, retains heat well, good for high temperatures	High maintenance, must be carefully dried and oiled or quickly rusts	The material of choice for much traditional "heirloom" cooking in the United States and Europe
Nonstick coatings (for example, Teflon or Silverstone)	Easy to clean, nonreactive	Requires gentle handling, easily scratched	The best material for omelet and crepe pans
Glass	Nonreactive	Breakable; shards of glass dangerous in kitchen	Limited use in commercial applications
Earthenware	Attractive, nonreactive	Poor conductor of heat, breakable	Good for rustic-looking serving containers for items like French onion soup or paella
Enamel lining	Attractive when new	Harbors bacteria when chipped; can be toxic	Do not use; banned for commercial use in many areas

roasting, transport, and storage. Sheet pans are either full size, $1 \times 18 \times 26$ inches ($2.5 \times 46 \times 66$ cm); or half size, $1 \times 18 \times 13$ inches ($2.5 \times 46 \times 33$ cm). **Bake pans** are 2 inches (5 cm) deep and come in various sizes. Bake pans are fitted with a folding loop handle at each end. The deeper **roasting pans**, also fitted with folding handles, are used for roasting large cuts of meat or poultry. Stainless steel **hotel pans** are made to fit standard slots in holding tables, and come in a range of sizes from the standard $2.5 \times 12 \times 20$ inches ($6.25 \times 33.5 \times 53$ cm) to various smaller sizes referred to in fractions of the standard size (for example, one-sixth pans).

Earthenware Cooking Containers

There are essentially three earthenware cooking containers that are used in foodservice, not because they are better at cooking, but because they are traditional vessels in their respective countries and they make attractive, attention-getting serving containers.

As mentioned in Chapter 1, the Moroccan **tagine** (tah-ZHEEN) is a shallow earthenware dish with a conical lid that is used to cook the characteristic stews of the same name in that northwest African nation.

The Spanish **paella** (pie-AY-yuh) **dish** (Fig. 3-14) is used for creating the traditional rice casserole of saffron, seafood, shellfish, and chicken that is well loved around the world. Likewise, the unique French **cassoulet** (cass-oo-LAY) bowl, with its sloped sides, is recognized as the only true vessel for creating and serving the sumptuous traditional concoction of white beans, duck, and sausage.

FIGURE 3-14   Spanish earthenware paella dish, approximately 12 inches. (30.5 cm).

It may be well worth your time to obtain and use these containers if you want to create a memorable presentation for your customers.

Other Containers

Stainless steel is the material of choice for various miscellaneous containers because it's nonreactive and durable. Stainless steel also allows foods placed in it to chill quickly, because of its excellent conductivity. This is especially important when you want to reduce the temperature of a heated food quickly to minimize its time in the FDZ.

The **bain-marie** is a tall stainless-steel container used to set into a water bath to keep food items warm. It's also a popular container for storage, because it's nonreactive and durable.

Stainless steel bowls of all sizes are used for food mixing and preparation, as well as storage.

Knives

Knives can be an intimidating subject. There are so many sizes and shapes and materials. Everyone feels as though they have to buy dozens of specific knives for specific chores. This isn't true. There are just a few basic knives you need to get the job done.

Materials

First, let's discuss materials. These days, blades made of high-carbon stainless steel are the choice for most professionals, because they don't corrode and they are relatively easy to keep sharp. However, certain knife blades made of lightweight, soft stainless steel can also be a good choice.

Handles are typically made of wood, plastic, or metal. Handle shapes range from straight and simple to curved and "ergonomic" that is, fitted to the human hand. The handle material and shape are largely a matter of personal preference.

The main thing to remember is that price is no indication of quality in a knife. Some of the least expensive knives are among the most popular among professional foodservice workers. For instance, in a recent comparison test by *Cook's Illustrated* magazine (November/December, 2002, Number 59), some brands of inexpensive knives won out over more expensive brands. Do some research and try knives before you decide. Don't be bullied by "prestige" brands.

Types of Knives

The **chef's knife** (Fig. 3-15) is the star of the cooking profession. It is by far the most versatile and frequently used, for everything from slicing and dicing to julienning, chiffonading, and carving. It will, after some practice, feel like part of your hand. Chef's knives, also called *French knives*, normally have blades of about 10 inches (26 cm), but the best size is more dependent on the user's personal comfort level.

 ## Chinese Chef's Knife

In Asian kitchens, the all-purpose cutting tool is the Chinese chef's knife (Fig. 3-15), a broad-bladed square-tipped knife that resembles a cleaver, but is actually much lighter and quite suitable for delicate slicing and cutting. Chinese chefs use this versatile knife in exactly the same way as Western chefs use the chef's knife.

The **boning knife** has a blade of about 6 inches (16 cm). It can be either rigid or flexible. It's used to cut flesh away from the bones of meat, fish, or poultry.

The **paring knife** has a short blade, 2 to 4 inches (5–10 cm), and allows delicate cutting of fruits and vegetables. Variations include the **tourné knife** (tor-NAY) with its hooked tip.

The **utility knife** has a narrow blade of 6 to 8 inches (16–20 cm). It is used for various cutting and carving chores.

Slicers are knives with long blades of up to 14 inches (36 cm). The regular slicer is used for carving meats; the serrated slicer is used for slicing bread or cutting cake.

FIGURE 3-15 A 9-inch (23-cm) chef's knife (top) and an 8-inch (20-cm) Chinese chef's knife (bottom).

Cleavers are heavy square knives with broad blades. They are used for cutting heavy bones or large, tough vegetables. Do not confuse them with the Chinese chef's knife (see sidebar).

The **truing steel** (usually called *the steel*) is a long rod used for "truing" knives that have already been sharpened. Using the steel realigns the edge of the knife, but doesn't sharpen it.

The **pizza cutter** or **pastry wheel** is a sharp, rotating blade with a handle, and is used for cutting pizza or delicate doughs like puff pastry.

Dough knives (or **bench scrapers**) are square pieces of flat metal with a handle along one edge. It is used to cut dough or to scrape work surfaces.

The **mezzaluna** (Fig. 3-16) is an Italian two-handed, crescent-shaped knife that you might also add to your collection. It is used in a rocking motion for chopping and mincing vegetables. A smaller, one-handed Native Alaskan version, the **ulu** (OO-loo) **knife**, is also quite handy for mincing.

On Sharpening and Truing

Sharpening refers to removing part of the metal of the blade to reshape it into an effective edge. **Truing** refers to realigning the tiny irregularities that develop on the edge over time, without removing any of the blade material.

If you true your knives regularly with your steel, knives do not have to be sharpened often. When you do sharpen knives, have them sharpened by your local sharpening professional (a company that specializes in sharpening, *not* the clerk in the knife store in the mall), then keep them sharp by truing them with your steel a few times each day. Pro sharpening is inexpensive and well worth the effort. You can locate a pro in the phone book.

To true your knife with your steel, follow these steps:

1. Hold the heel of the blade against the tip of the steel.

2. Holding the edge of the blade at a 20° angle to the steel, move the knife downward in an arc, holding it lightly against the steel.

FIGURE 3-16 Mezzaluna knife.

3. Make certain you cover the entire length of the blade, from heel to tip.

4. Move the knife to the other side of the steel and repeat.

5. Repeat a maximum of five times on each side of the knife.

Cutting Boards

Next to the chef's knife, the cutting board is the most important piece of cutting equipment in the kitchen. It's the first thing you get out when you begin work, and it's the last thing you put away. Cutting boards may be made of plastic, rubber, or hardwood. Wood is the material of choice for many chefs. However, health regulations in many communities forbid wooden boards in commercial environments because of the belief that they are more unsanitary than plastic or rubber. Read the article at www.reluctantgourmet.com/cutting_boards.htm, then decide for yourself. Make sure you always follow your local health regulations, however.

Other Equipment

There are other various pieces of equipment that are indispensable in the kitchen. This section covers various examples of hand tools, measuring devices, and some international equipment.

Basic Hand Tools and Measuring Devices

Spatula (SPAT-choo-luh) is a loosely used term for utensils with straight handles and unsharpened blades. The most important are *straight spatulas*, with long metal blades, used mostly for spreading icing; *offset spatulas*, with broad metal blades bent to keep your knuckles from touching the surface of a griddle when turning pancakes, eggs, and so forth; and *rubber spatulas*, with flexible rubber or plastic blades, used for scraping bowls or folding delicate mixtures.

Wire whips (not "whisks") are loops of crisscrossed wire with a handle. They are used for beating sauces, egg whites, or cream. Whips come in various sizes and degrees of flexibility.

Strainers are used to separate solids from liquids, or large solids from small solids, and come in various shapes and sizes. The standard strainer is bowl shaped with a handle. The **China cap** is a cone-shaped strainer with a handle. It has a fairly wide mesh. The point allows straining into a small container. The **chinois** (shin-WAH) is a China cap with a finer mesh. The **colander** is a large, perforated stainless steel or aluminum bowl with a handle on each side, used for straining pasta, greens, and so forth.

The **sieve** (siv) is a round screen with a solid, cylindrical frame. It is used chiefly for sifting flour.

The **food mill** is like a strainer, but it has a hand crank that turns a paddle that forces food through a mesh to puree it.

Tongs have two attached handles that let you handle foods without touching them. They are made in two versions: the V-shaped spring type or the X-shaped scissors type.

Graters are metal boxes with sharpened holes in the side. They are used to shred or grate vegetables or cheese.

Zesters are small tools used for removing the zest (the colored part) of citrus peel to use for flavoring.

A **pastry bag** is a plastic or canvas bag with an interchangeable metal tip. It is used to apply items decoratively like mashed potatoes or icing.

Scales are important in the professional kitchen, because many recipe ingredients are referred to *by weight* instead of by volume. Scales are used constantly for measuring ingredients, as well as for portion control.

Volume measures of various sizes are for measuring liquids. They look like metal pitchers.

Measuring cups and spoons are used for measuring exact small volumes of liquid or dry ingredients.

A **ladle** consists of a bowl attached to a long handle, and it is hooked at one end for storage. Ladles come in various sizes (for example, 8 ounces, 4 ounces), with the size marked on the handle. They are used to pour liquids, and are especially handy in quickly measuring precise amounts.

Scoops look like ice-cream scoops, but in the commercial environment they come in various sizes and are used for quickly measuring precise amounts of soft foods. The sizes are numbered based on fractions of a quarts or liters. For instance, a number 4 scoop would contain $1/4$ of a quart (8O2). A number 14 would contain $1/16$ of a quart (2O2).

Thermometers come in various types. The most common is the **meat thermometer**, which is used to indicate the internal temperature of meats. The **instant-read thermometer** (preferably digital) is a handy thermometer that chefs carry like a pen in their pockets and use for quick temperature checks. The **candy** or **fat thermometer** is used for reading high-temperature liquids.

A Few International Devices

The **pasta machine** (Fig. 3-17) is a hand-cranked stainless-steel device that is used to roll pasta dough into long flat pieces, then are cut into noodles, if desired.

The **spiral shredder** (Fig. 3-17) is a hand-cranked plastic device with steel blades used to shred vegetables (like carrots) into long, decorative strips.

The **sushi mat** is a bamboo mat used to roll sushi into its characteristic tube shape, which can then be sliced.

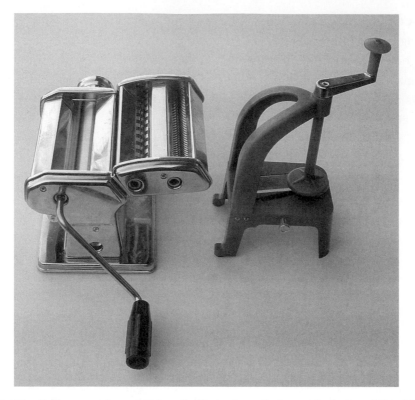

FIGURE 3-17 **Italian pasta machine (left) and an Asian spiral shredder (right).**

The **mortar and pestle** is a two-piece utensil consisting of a rough stone, ceramic, or wooden bowl called the *mortar*, and a club-shaped object, the pestle (PESS-uhl). It's used for grinding many types of foods, from spices to vegetables and meats. The mortar and pestle is used in countries from Mexico, where it's called the *molcajete* (MOHL-kuh-HET-tay), to Italy, where it's used to grind basil for pesto. (The word *pesto* comes from "pestle.")

Summary and Conclusion

Humankind has developed a vast array of foodservice tools over the centuries. It would take many books and a lifetime of instruction to learn them all. This chapter has introduced you to some of the more common equipment used in the foodservice world today. It is important that you develop a working knowledge of this equipment if you expect to be successful in the industry.

Selected Terms for Review

broiler
chef's knife
combi oven
convection oven
conventional oven
deep fryer
food processor
freezer
grill
hotel pan
mixer
range
refrigerator
spatula
steam-jacketed kettle
stockpot
strainer
sushi mat
wire whip

Review Questions

1. Name two types of cooktops.

2. True or false? Deck ovens consist of separate, enclosed levels with separate controls.

3. The term *convection oven* may refer to which type of cooking?

    a. Circulated hot air

    b. Circulated steam

    c. Microwave radiation

    d. None of the above

    e. Both a and b

4. Low-temperature ovens are best for retaining the _____ of large cuts of meat.

5. True or false? The white clouds produced when water is heated consist of water vapor, not steam.

6. What type of device should you use if you want to create flavor from smoking fat? Why?

7. True or false? Most safety devices are added because of government regulations. After you become an expert on a particular piece of machinery, it is acceptable to disable the cutoff switches and remove the shields to increase productivity.

8. Which of the following pan materials is best for high-temperature cooking?

   a. Stainless steel

   b. Cast iron

   c. Copper

   d. Enamel

9. Nonstick pans are best for cooking _____ and _____.

10. The most important knife in professional cooking is the _____ knife.

11. Define sharpening. Define truing. Which is performed more often?

12. What's the basic difference between a China cap and a chinois?

Suggested Readings/Web Sites to Visit

Albert, A. *Choosing Pots and Pans to Improve Your Cooking*. Taunton Press. Available at www.taunton.com/finecooking/pages/c00007.asp

Cutting Boards, Wood Versus Plastic. *The Reluctant Gourmet*. Available at www.reluctantgourmet.com/cutting_boards.htm

History and creation of cassoulet in France: www.cassoulet.com

Information regarding cooking products: www.cooksillustrated.com

Lodge Manufacturing Cast Iron Pots: www.lodgemfg.com

Vulcan Hart Product Center: www.vulcanhart.com/productcenter.cfm

4

Introduction to Culinary Techniques and Principles

Learning Objectives

By the end of the chapter, you should be able to

1. Describe mise en place

2. Understand the process for meeting the challenges of mise en place

3. Know how to hold a knife and how to hold food being cut

4. Describe the basic knife cuts

5. Define nutrients

6. Name the nutrients in the food we prepare

7. Describe how nutrients react to cooking

8. Define the difference between seasonings and flavorings, and provide examples

9. Describe the importance of salt

10. Name and describe the three ways heat is carried into food

11. Define the two broad categories of cooking, and the cooking techniques within those categories

Chapter Outline

Mise en Place

    The Basic Challenge Regarding Mise en Place

    Determining the Answer to the Mise en Place Question

No matter what type of cuisine you cook, you need to understand certain information related to food and cooking before you can be successful in the kitchen. For example, you have to know how to hold a knife and how to cut basic shapes consistently. You also must know what food is made of, how heat works, and the different basic ways food can be prepared. You also need to have a firm grasp of the importance of organization and advance preparation. This chapter gives you a starting point regarding some of this basic culinary knowledge.

Mise en Place

"Mise en place means far more than simply assembling all the ingredients, pots and pans, plates, and serving pieces needed for a particular period. Mise en place is also a state of mind."

    —*Mary Donovan*, The New Professional Chef (1996, John Wiley & Sons, New York)

FIGURE 4-1 **Even a simple dish like beef and broccoli requires a certain amount of preparation before cooking begins.**

Let's begin this chapter with an explanation of the most basic, important concept in cooking: organization. **Mise en place** (MEEZ en plahss) is a French phrase that literally means "setting in place." The phrase is used nearly universally in the restaurant industry, in all types of restaurants, to refer to (1) the overall concept of having everything prepared, organized, and ready before you begin cooking; and (2) the resulting ingredients you prepare during the mise en place process. The term is often shortened to slang terms such as "meez" (as in the sentence "Does everyone have their meez ready?").

Chinese cooks are masters of mise en place. It may take just a minute or so to stir-fry, say, beef and broccoli, but all the ingredients must be partially prepared in advance to make efficient, final preparation possible (Fig. 4-1). If the cook were to heat the wok to very high temperature, throw in the oil, ginger, garlic, onions, and sliced beef, then say "Hey! I need broccoli!" the dish would be ruined, because the beef and other ingredients would overcook while the cook took time to chop the broccoli.

Mise en place often involves precooking food items. For instance, to prepare French fries properly, you must first cook them ahead of time at a low temperature until tender before finally frying them crisp at a higher temperature.

Partially precooking foods in oil or water before their final preparation is called **blanching**. **Blanch and shock** refers to cooking a food item partially, then plunging it into ice water to stop its cooking. The chilled food item is then reheated briefly just before service. Tomatoes and peaches are often blanched and shocked so their peels may be easily removed.

The Basic Challenge Regarding Mise en Place

If you give it even a little thought, you'll realize that there is a challenge regarding the concept of mise en place. The basic question is: How far do you go in partially preparing your items? In the previous beef-and-broccoli example, the chef cannot fully cook the dish until it is ordered by the customer. If it were fully cooked in advance and held, it would become limp and soggy. The broccoli only retains its flavor and texture for a short time after stir-frying. (You've probably noticed this if you've eaten at a Chinese buffet where the food has been held too long.) Therefore, the chef must ask the following mise-en-place question for every item on the menu: How far in advance can the ingredients be prepared before there is a significant loss of quality in the final dish?

Determining the Answer to the Mise en Place Question

The next step is difficult work. To determine the answer to our question, the chef must resolve the following related questions for every item on the menu:

- *What steps can be performed ahead of time?* In our beef-and-broccoli example, the beef could be sliced ahead of time.

- *How long do those steps take?* It may take the cook 30 minutes to slice enough beef for each evening's service.

- *How can the partially prepped items be held for final prep?* The sliced beef could be held in a hotel pan in a reach-in refrigerator at the cook's station.

- *How could the steps be improved to make the prepping process more efficient?* The chef may decide that there would be enough time savings to justify purchasing an electric slicer for the kitchen. Instead of spending time slicing the beef by hand, the cook would be free to perform other necessary tasks. A lower level employee could be trained to slice the beef using the machine.

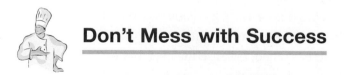 **Don't Mess with Success**

If you happen to be a cook in a commercial kitchen and you think you have a great idea to speed things up at your station, don't change your procedure unless you first ask the chef. You may not realize the full impact of your change.

Basic Knife Use

We all think we know how to use a knife. We've used them most of our lives, right? But we've never really been instructed how to use them properly. We're self-taught. The following is a brief primer on correct knife use.

The Grip

To grasp a chef's knife with optimum power and control, grip the base of the blade with the thumb and forefinger, then grip the handle with the last three fingers (Fig. 4-2). After a while, this grip will seem like second nature to you and you'll wonder how you ever held a large knife in any other manner. (You'll now cringe when you see TV "chefs" gripping knives with very ineffective techniques, like putting the forefinger on the top edge of the blade.)

To cut items effectively, use your other hand to guide the food toward the knife blade. Hold the item against the cutting board firmly, and let the knife blade slide against the knuckles of your guiding hand as you push the food toward the blade. Make certain to keep the fingertips of your guiding hand curled under to protect them from cuts (Fig. 4-3).

Basic Cuts

Consistent knife cuts are important not only because they enhance the appearance of the product, but because they enable the product to cook evenly. There are certain knife cuts and cutting techniques that you are expected to know to be able to work in a professional kitchen. Table 4-1 describes these cuts.

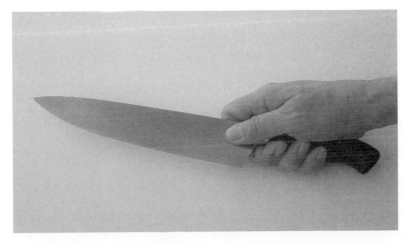

FIGURE 4-2   The proper knife grip gives the user greater power and control.

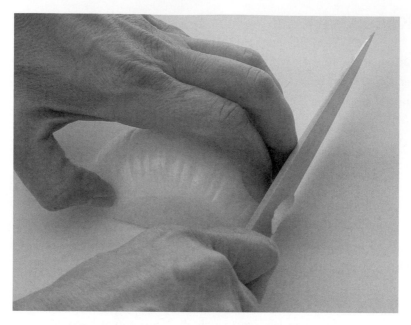

FIGURE 4-3   Holding food items correctly while cutting ensures speed, safety, and accuracy.

The Components of Cooking

Now that we've discussed two of the most important topics in the culinary world—mise en place and knife cuts—let's look at some of the components of food and cooking, and the role each plays in the cooking process.

Nutrients

Nutrients are the substances in your food that provide energy, promote growth, or generally regulate processes and maintain your body. The categories of nutrients are

- Fats
- Carbohydrates
- Proteins
- Vitamins and minerals

Food Energy

The energy provided by fats, carbohydrates, and proteins is measured in Calories. A **Calorie**, with an uppercase "C," also called a *kilocalorie*, is the amount of energy needed to raise the temperature of a kilogram of water by 1°C. This is the common "calorie"

TABLE 4-1
Common Knife Cuts and Cutting Techniques

Name of Cut	Description	Method
Batonnet (French fry cut)	A stick $2\frac{1}{2} \times \frac{1}{4} \times \frac{1}{4}$ inch ($60 \times 6 \times 6$ mm)	Trim food item into an even block $2\frac{1}{2}$ inches (6 cm) long; slice into $\frac{1}{4}$-inch (6-mm)-thick slices or **planks**; cut planks into $\frac{1}{4}$-inch-wide (6-mm) sticks.
Julienne (allumette potato cut)	A stick $2\frac{1}{2} \times \frac{1}{8} \times \frac{1}{8}$ inch ($60 \times 3 \times 3$ mm)	Trim food item into an even block $2\frac{1}{2}$ inches (6 cm) long; slice into $\frac{1}{8}$-inch (3-mm)-thick planks; cut planks into $\frac{1}{8}$-inch-wide (3-mm) sticks.
Large dice	A cube $\frac{3}{4} \times \frac{3}{4} \times \frac{3}{4}$ inch ($20 \times 20 \times 20$ mm)	Trim food item into an even block; slice into $\frac{3}{4}$-inch (2-cm)-thick planks; cut planks into $\frac{3}{4}$-inch (2-cm)-wide sticks; cut sticks into $\frac{3}{4}$-inch (2-cm) cubes.
Medium dice	A cube $\frac{1}{2} \times \frac{1}{2} \times \frac{1}{2}$ inch ($12 \times 12 \times 12$ mm)	Trim food item into an even block; slice into $\frac{1}{2}$-inch (12-mm)-thick planks; cut planks into $\frac{1}{2}$-inch (12-mm)-wide sticks; cut sticks into $\frac{1}{2}$-inch (12-mm) cubes.
Small dice	A cube $\frac{1}{4} \times \frac{1}{4} \times \frac{1}{4}$ inch ($6 \times 6 \times 6$ mm)	Trim food item into an even block; slice into $\frac{1}{4}$-inch (6-mm)-thick planks; cut planks into $\frac{1}{4}$-inch (6-mm)-wide sticks; cut sticks into $\frac{1}{4}$-inch (6-mm) cubes.
Brunoise (broon-WAH)	A cube $\frac{1}{8} \times \frac{1}{8} \times \frac{1}{8}$ inch ($3 \times 3 \times 3$ mm)	Trim food item into an even block; slice into $\frac{1}{8}$-inch (3-mm)-thick planks; cut planks into $\frac{1}{8}$-inch (3-mm)-wide sticks; cut sticks into $\frac{1}{8}$-inch (3-mm) cubes
Tourné (tor-NAY)	Similar in shape to an American football; a seven-sided (don't ask why) tapered oblong, 2 inch (5 cm) long, $\frac{3}{4}$ inch (20 mm) thick in the middle, with flat ends	Everyone has their favorite method for this. One way is, using a tourné knife or paring knife, roughly cut food item into a 2-inch (5-cm)-long shape with seven sides. Then trim it until the seven sides are even and the required size is achieved.

TABLE 4-1

Continued

Name of Cut	Description	Method
Chop	To cut into pieces of roughly the same size but of irregular shapes	Place the food item on the cutting board. With a rocking motion, move the blade back and forth until the desired size is achieved.
Concasser (KON-kuh-SAY)	To chop coarsely. (Note: The terms *concasser* and *concassée* are used differently in different kitchens. Check with your chef.)	Place the food item on the cutting board. With a rocking motion, move the blade back and forth until the desired size is achieved.
Concassée (KON-kuh-SAY)	Peeled, seeded, and diced tomatoes or, depending on the chef, a coarsely chopped tomato	Remove peel and seeds; dice or chop the tomato per instructions.
Mince	To chop finely	Place the food item on the cutting board. With a rocking motion, move the blade back and forth until the desired size is achieved.
Shred	To cut into thin strips; more irregular than julienne	Use a hand grater or cut roughly with a chef's knife.

(popularly spelled with a lowercase "c") used to measure food energy. Technically, a calorie with a lowercase "c" has only 1/1000 the energy of a kilocalorie. This type of calorie is not used for everyday measurement. The calorie count used on product packaging is in kilocalories.

Fats

The excess energy in the food you eat is stored in your body as fat. **Fats** are nutrients that provide energy and structure to cells. They are produced in animals, chiefly as stored energy, and in some plants, especially nuts and grains.

Fats called **oils** are liquid at room temperature. These fats are called *unsaturated*. Fats like butter or shortening are solid at room temperature. These are called *saturated*.

Fats are important in cooking, because they not only are used as a cooking medium, as in deep-fat frying, but they provide flavor and texture as an ingredient. Fats break down when subjected to heat. When they become hot enough, they begin to smoke, indicating they have completely broken down and will give a bitter flavor to food. The temperature at which this occurs is called the *smoke point*. Some fats, such as peanut oil, have a very high smoke point and function well in high-temperature cooking.

Carbohydrates

Carbohydrates, commonly called *carbs*, are the primary source of energy in the human body. They are found mostly in plants, such as beans, vegetables, grain, and fruit. They are found in small amounts in fish or meat as well.

There are three categories of carbohydrates: sugars, starches, and fiber. **Sugars** are commonly used in forms such as refined sugar and corn syrup. They are also found naturally in such foods as fruits, grains, and honey. **Starches** are most commonly found in the Western diet as flour, potatoes, and beans. In Asia and some other regions of the world, rice is the most common form of starch. **Fiber** is the term for indigestible carbohydrates found in beans, fruits, and vegetables. Fiber aids in maintaining regularity in the digestive tract.

Carbs provide two of the most important functions in the cooking world:

1. When sugars are heated, they turn brown, creating the golden color of French fries, for example. This is called *caramelization*.

2. When starches are added to liquid, they swell. This process, called *gelatinization* (juh-LAT-in-ih-ZAY-shun), makes possible, for example, the thickening of gravy and the creation of bread and pastries.

Proteins

Proteins are pretty much the basis of all animal life. They provide the structure to cells and regulate the functions of the body. Proteins are present in all animal products, including meat, poultry, eggs, milk, and fish. They are also found in some plants, like nuts and grains.

To a chef, the main concern when cooking proteins is controlling their **coagulation**— the stiffening that occurs when proteins are heated. In general, if proteins (such as meat or eggs) are heated too long, they become tough and dry. However, some proteins in meats, called *connective tissues*, the proteins that join muscles and bones together, are naturally tough. One type of connective tissue, called *collagen*, dissolves if cooked for a long time over low heat, making the meat in which it is found more tender. Another connective tissue, called *elastin*, does not dissolve and remains tough.

An important by-product of proteins is **gelatin**, a jellylike substance that results when bones and connective tissues, especially collagen, are cooked. Gelatin is naturally present in well-made stocks (see Chapter 6) and is also the main ingredient in gelatin desserts. (Yes! Fruity, sweet Jell-O® is an animal by-product!)

Let Your Thoughts Jell

Yes, it's a cruel and confusing joke on culinary students that the word "gelatin" relates to a product of proteins, and the very similar word "gelatinization" relates to starches. You just have to learn that the two words are similar but different. Sorry.

Vitamins and Minerals

Vitamins and minerals are nutrients that provide no calories (energy) when consumed, but are important for regulating bodily functions. **Vitamins** are substances essential in small quantities in maintaining growth, reproduction, and other processes. There are some vitamins in practically everything we eat, but they are found in higher quantities in fresh fruits, vegetables, grains, meats, and dairy products.

Some of the major vitamins include

- **Vitamin A**—found in dairy, eggs, liver, leafy dark green vegetables; necessary for vision, growth, and healthy skin

- **Vitamin B$_1$ (thiamine)**—found in pork, liver, whole grains, and nuts; necessary for carbohydrate use and maintaining the nervous system

- **Vitamin B$_2$ (riboflavin)**—found in dairy, eggs, leafy green vegetables, cereals; necessary for forming cells, enzymes, and maintaining vision and tissues

- **Vitamin B$_3$ (niacin)**—found in liver, poultry, lean meats, fish, cereals, nuts; necessary for using fat and functioning of skin, and nervous and digestive systems

- **Vitamin B$_6$**—found in liver, fish, poultry, cereals; necessary for enzyme production and metabolism

- **Vitamin B$_{12}$**—found in dairy, liver, lean meats; essential for using fats and carbohydrates

- **Vitamin C (ascorbic acid)**—found in fruits, green leafy vegetables, potatoes; necessary for preventing scurvy, healing wounds

- **Vitamin D**—produced in the human body in sunlight; also found in eggs, fish oils, and fortified milk; necessary for forming bones and regulating calcium

- **Vitamin E**—found in plant oils, green leafy vegetables, whole grains, nuts; essential as an antioxidant

Some vitamins are water soluble and may be cooked out of foods. In addition, certain vitamins may also be destroyed by the plant's own enzymes when the food is chopped. See Chapter 12 for a further discussion of minimizing vitamin loss.

Minerals are elements or compounds that are required for specific needs, such as building bones and teeth or providing iron for red blood cells. For the most part, minerals cannot be cooked out of foods, but it is important that chefs be aware of mineral content of specific foods. Some major minerals include

- **Calcium**—found in dairy, beans, sardines, chard, kale; important for bones and teeth

- **Iron**—found in red meat, leafy green vegetables, raisins, whole grains; important for red blood cells

- **Potassium**—found in bananas, green leafy vegetables, grains, potatoes; necessary for transmission of nerve impulses, muscle use, and protein use

- **Sodium**—found in salt, soy sauce; necessary for transmission of nerve impulses; see "On Salt" later in this chapter

Seasoning and Flavoring Your Food

Seasonings and flavorings are important paints in the chef's palette. Using them is as much an art as a science. To become a truly creative chef, it is important that you understand how specific ingredients affect flavors in different ways.

Familiarize yourself with every type of herb and spice. In addition to sampling all the spices in your own kitchen, visit local supermarkets and ethnic grocery stores and get examples of a wide variety of items. (For example, large Asian markets will normally feature several different types of fresh mint, not just one.) Learn how each ingredient smells, tastes, and looks. Use them in various dishes to discover how they affect flavors. Learn how ingredients differ when they are fresh and when they are dried, or when they are whole and when they are ground. Also, learn which flavorings are prevalent in various international cuisines, like curries in India or sambals in Indonesia, and familiarize yourself with their characteristics.

Because all five senses are involved in this learning process, a book cannot give you all the possible information you'll need. It's knowledge you have to acquire on your own.

What Are Seasonings?

Seasonings are ingredients that *enhance* existing flavors without changing them. The chief example of a universal seasoning is salt (more on salt later). In addition to salt, certain ingredients are considered to be seasonings when used in small amounts. These include black pepper, nutmeg, and lemon juice. In addition, around the world chefs use such diverse ingredients as monosodium glutamate (MSG, an umami enhancer that occurs naturally in many foods and it may cause an allergic reaction in some people), fish sauce, soy sauce, and wine in small quantities to enhance, not alter, flavors.

FIGURE 4-4   Fresh ginger is an important flavoring in Asian dishes.

What Are Flavorings?

Flavorings are ingredients that *change* the flavor of the food (Fig. 4-4). Flavorings not only include classic examples like oregano, onion, garlic, basil, ginger, and cinnamon, but also some of the same ingredients we mentioned as seasonings, such as lemon juice (as in a lemon pie), wine (as in beef burgundy), nutmeg (as in an apple pie), or black pepper (as in steak *à la poivre* [pwahv]).

Two of the major categories of flavorings are herbs and spices. **Herbs** are flavorings using leafy portions of plants. Common international herbs (Fig. 4-5) include basil, dill, cilantro, mint, parsley, tarragon, and rosemary. However, there are many regional herbs in international cuisine. For instance, Asian cooks commonly include the citrus-flavored *lemongrass* and *kaffir lime leaves* in their dishes, and Mexican cooks are fond of *epazote* (EH-pah-ZOH-tay), a strong-flavored herb native to the Americas.

Spices (Fig. 4-6 and 4-7) are flavorings using seeds, bark, fruits, roots, flowers, or other components of plants. Spices include black pepper, cinnamon, capers, nutmeg, saffron, ginger, garlic, cumin seeds, juniper berries, allspice, vanilla beans, and star anise.

FIGURE 4-5   Common herbs: (top), lemongrass; (bottom, left to right) cilantro, mint, dill, and parsley.

The Most Expensive Spice

You'll often hear the factoid that saffron, the stamen of the crocus flower, is "the world's most expensive spice." Although it is a fact that saffron costs hundreds of dollars a pound, you need so little of it (just a pinch) to flavor and color a dish, that it's actually fairly inexpensive. On a per-recipe basis, vanilla beans, for example, are more costly, requiring several dollar's worth just to make one batch of pastry cream.

When adding flavors to foods, it is easier to add a little at first then add more if necessary. If you add too much, it's impossible to remove. Keep in mind that, ordinarily, flavorings shouldn't be the predominant flavor in a dish, except in certain exceptional cases like garlic mashed potatoes or basil pesto.

On Salt

Nutritionally, **salt** or NaCl, sodium chloride, is necessary for not only the proper absorption of water by your body, but it is also an electrolyte. It's critical for creating the proper environment for signals to travel along your nerves.

Salt is the superstar of flavor enhancers, because most humans naturally associate its taste with pleasure. If a food, even a sweet food, is lacking salt, there seems to be something bland and unexciting about it.

FIGURE 4-6   Whole spices, such as (left to right) star anise, nutmeg, cinnamon, cloves, and allspice (called *pimento* in Jamaica), retain flavors in storage longer than ground versions.

FIGURE 4-7   Capers, the pickled buds of a seaside shrub, are a key flavoring in many Mediterranean dishes.

Keller's View on Salt

In the culinary world, the word *seasoning* is virtually synonymous with *salt*. Thomas Keller, the creator and owner of The French Laundry restaurant in Napa Valley, California, has often been named the finest chef in the United States. In an interview conducted in 2000, he was asked by food writer Michael Ruhlman, "What is the single most important skill you value in a cook?"

He responded, "Salt—the ability to season food properly."

Salt was the most important commodity traded among early civilizations. Many battles were fought over control of salt production areas. Why? Because salt was (and still is) important as a preservative. If a nation possessed an abundance of salt, it had the ability to preserve food (fish, meats, and vegetables) that could then be used for military purposes to feed an army, or economically to trade with other nations.

According to some experts, especially Mark Kurlansky in his book *Salt: A World History*, the Confederacy may have lost the American Civil War because the Union army captured its major salt supply at Avery Island, Louisiana, early in the war. This left the South with limited means to preserve food for its army, resulting in widespread malnutrition among its soldiers. As recently as the 1930s, the British used military force in India to prevent Mahatma Gandhi and his followers from making their own sea salt, because salt production meant power.

Many modern words come from words for *salt*. In ancient Rome, salt was used to pay the military. So, today, not only does the word *salary* come from the word *salt*, but so does the word *soldier*. The words *salad*, *salami*, *sauce*, *salsa*, and *sausage* also come from *salt*. In England, a town name ending in "-wich," like Greenwich or Norwich, indicates it was a salt production area. Elsewhere in Europe, the letters "hal" in a town's name—for example Hallstatt, Austria—indicate it was a source of salt.

There are many textures and colors of salt (Fig. 4-8) available to the creative chef. Kosher salt, for example, has a coarser grain and some say a more satisfying flavor than ordinary table salt. Other varieties include costly Hawaiian pink sea salt, sulfur-tasting Indian black salt, French gray sea salt, and intense Korean bamboo salt. The most cherished salt to many chefs is the delicate *fleur de sel* ("flower of salt"), harvested from the surface of still tidal pools along the coast of France. *Fleur de sel* is often used as a garnish, even on desserts.

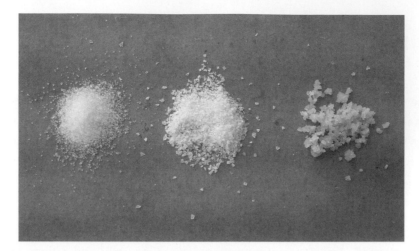

FIGURE 4-8   The texture of salt varies widely, as seen in this comparison of (left to right) table salt, slightly coarser grain kosher salt, and French gray sea salt.

A Salty Fact

Despite the fact that salt has been popularly demonized in recent years, there is no evidence to suggest that eating less salt increases your life span or decreases your risk of disease.

Types of Heat

There are three basic ways that heat may be carried into food: conduction, convection, and radiation. You must understand these three types of heat to make informed decisions about appropriate cooking methods.

Conduction is heat transfer from one object to another (as from the surface of a pan to a roast cooking in the pan), or from one part of an object to another (as from the outer part of a roast to the inner part of the roast). As discussed in the previous chapter, copper and aluminum are examples of rapid conductors of heat, whereas glass and air are relatively poor conductors of heat.

Convection is the circulation of heat in a gas or liquid. For example, when a pot of water heats, the hot water at the bottom rises to the top and the cooler water falls to the bottom, causing a constant circular motion. The same effect occurs in a deep-fat fryer or in the air in an oven. Although convection occurs naturally, it can be sped up by electric fans or other devices, as in a convection oven.

Again, as stated in the previous chapter, **radiation** simply refers to anything that is generated as waves, such as sound, light, and heat. In cooking, radiation refers to any heating process that doesn't require direct contact between the heat source and the item being heated. Two examples of radiation in the kitchen are infrared heat (for example, heat emitted by electrical elements) and microwaves.

Types of Cooking

There are essentially two cooking techniques: moist-heat cooking and dry-heat cooking. This section discusses the differences between the two.

Cold Cooking

Although cooking is usually defined in terms of heating food, there are cold-cooking methods that work with proteins. One involves marinating the food in an acid, usually vinegar or lemon juice, until it appears and tastes cooked. This technique, used when preparing the classic Latin American seafood dish *ceviche* (suh-VEE-chay), creates a product with a very delicate, but not raw, texture. Another method involves curing fish in salt and sugar until it becomes opaque and seems "cooked." An example of this technique is used to make the Swedish salmon dish *gravlax*.

Moist-Heat Cooking

Moist-heat cooking is cooking using water in the form of steam or a heated liquid. **Steaming** means cooking food by exposing it to steam in a special, pressurized steam cooker (as discussed in the previous chapter) or by heating it in a tightly covered pan or other container. Steaming is preferred when you want to cook delicate food items, such as vegetables, without agitating them. The French technique *en papillote* (AWN pah-pee-YOHT) involves steaming food in paper folded like wings. (Although most people, even chefs, will tell you *en papillote* means "in paper," it literally means "in butterfly.")

Cooking food in heated water may be done at four temperature levels. The highest temperatures are achieved in a pressure cooker, where water may be heated to temperatures in excess of 212°F (100°C). Cooking in a pressure cooker greatly speeds the cooking process. **Boiling** involves cooking food in water heated to 212°F (100°C) at sea level, unpressurized. Boiling is used chiefly to cook starches like pasta and potatoes.

You Say High; I Say Low

Boiling occurs at much lower temperatures at higher elevations. For example, at 7000 feet (about 2100 m), the altitude of Flagstaff, Arizona, water boils at less than 200°F (93°C). This means chefs in such areas have to adjust for significantly longer cooking times when cooking with moist heat.

Simmering means to cook food in water that is heated to less than a full boil, usually to a temperature range of 185 to 205°F (85–96°C). This is an appropriate method for most foods, because boiling tends to agitate foods and break them apart.

Poaching means to cook food gently in water that is heated to a temperature range of 160 to 180°F (71–82°C). This is an appropriate method for very delicate items such as Dover sole or eggs.

Braising involves cooking a food item in a covered pan, partially submerged in a liquid at a very low temperature for a long period of time. The item is normally browned first. The liquid usually becomes the basis for a sauce. Veal shanks and pot roasts are commonly cooked by braising.

Stewing is similar to braising, but the food is normally cut into smaller pieces and more water is used.

Microwave Cooking Takes Practice

Because it chiefly uses excited water molecules (in other words, moisture) to cook food, microwave cooking is technically also a moist-heat method of cooking. However, because microwave ovens are unique in the cooking world, and because each microwave oven differs in features and power from others, it is a good idea to practice using them before attempting any major cooking.

Dry-Heat Cooking

Dry-heat cooking involves cooking without water, with or without fat. As counterintuitive as it may seem, cooking in fat is considered to be dry cooking. Oils and fats are simply a medium for transferring heat. If used properly, they don't actually wet the food, as water does.

Sautéing, pan frying, and deep frying all are dry-heat methods involving fat. **Sautéing** (saw-TAY-ing) is cooking smaller pieces of food (for example, fish fillets) very quickly on

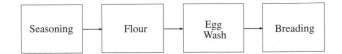

FIGURE 4-9   Standard breading procedure.

high heat using a small amount of fat. This technique is used extensively in both French and Asian cooking.

Pan frying is similar to sautéing except it uses more fat and lower heat. The food items cooked in this method (for example, chicken pieces) are normally larger than in sautéing and take longer to cook.

Deep-fat frying involves totally submerging food in a fat. Foods cooked in this manner (for example, fried shrimp) are attractive and crisp. Deep frying should be done at 350 to 375°F (175–190°C). Don't fry dissimilar foods, especially seafood and other foods, in the same oil, because of the risk of flavor distortion and allergen contamination. All frying should be performed immediately before service. For safety reasons, keep liquids away from the deep fryer to avoid the risk of steam "explosions" if liquid is spilled into the fryer.

Deep-fried and pan-fried savory foods such as meats, poultry, or seafood, are often breaded according to the **standard breading procedure** (Fig. 4-9). This procedure involves, first, seasoning the item, usually with salt and pepper; second, lightly coating the item with flour; third, coating the item with beaten eggs; and, fourth, rolling the item in a coating like bread crumbs, corn meal, or crushed nuts. *Panko*, or Japanese bread crumbs, has become the breading of choice in many restaurants today, for its distinctive, light, crispy texture and even, golden color.

Batters—mixtures of starch, eggs, a liquid, seasonings, and flavorings—are popular coatings for deep-fried sweet and savory foods. These range from very light and crispy Japanese tempura batter to Western batters that are thicker and more heavily flavored.

Dry-heat cooking without fat includes the categories of baking, roasting, grilling, griddling, and broiling. **Baking** and **roasting** are essentially the same thing: cooking a food item uncovered in hot, dry air, usually in an oven. The term *baking* is normally used when cooking pastry, vegetables, fruits, and fish. The term *roasting* is used when cooking meats and poultry. (The terms are sometimes used interchangeably, as in "roasted chestnuts" or "baked lamb.") **Barbecue** refers to roasting slowly with heat and smoke generated from burning coals or hardwood. Items to be barbecued are often seasoned and flavored before cooking.

As stated in Chapter 3, **grilling** refers to generating heat from *beneath* a food item through a metal grate, imparting a distinctive flavor from fat dripping on to the heat source. **Griddling** is cooking on a flat, solid surface. **Broiling** cooks with heat generated from above or beside the food. When broiling, no flavor is imparted from smoking fat.

Summary and Conclusion

Certain skills and knowledge are required to become a professional chef or even to understand the chef's role. The most important of the chef's skills is organization, the ability to prepare mentally and physically for the tasks ahead. *Mise en place* is the term used in the culinary profession for the necessary preparation that has to be performed. It will benefit you to begin to get into the habit of thinking in terms of mise en place regarding everything you do, always thinking and planning ahead.

You've acquired other crucial knowledge in this chapter that will lay the foundation for understanding food and cooking, including knife handling, knife cuts, herbs and spices, vitamins and minerals, types of heat, and the type of cooking used with various foods.

Selected Terms for Review

Calorie

Caramelization

Carbohydrate

Dice

Dry-heat cooking

Fats

Flavorings

Gelatinization

Grilling

Heat transfer

Julienne

Minerals

Mise en place

Moist-heat cooking

Nutrient

Proteins

Roasting

Seasonings

Standard breading procedure

Vitamins

Review Questions

1. Why not cook everything in the morning and keep it warm until you serve it that night? Wouldn't that save a lot of stress?

2. True or false? The primary reason for shocking food in ice water is to replenish fluid it loses during cooking.

3. Which of the following is a dice cut?

    a. Julienne

    b. Brunoise

    c. Tourné

    d. Batonnet

4. True or false? If you hold your index finger on the top of the knife blade, it gives you the most control.

5. _____ in the human body are stored energy.

6. Define smoke point.

7. The three types of carbohydrates are _____, _____, and _____.

8. Define gelatinization. Define caramelization.

9. True or false? Coagulation is the stiffening that occurs when proteins are heated.

10. Gelatin comes from

    a. Vegetables like potatoes

    b. Fruits like strawberries and cherries

    c. Bones and connective tissues

    d. Dissolved minerals

11. Name two nutrients that do not provide calories when eaten.

12. What is the difference between seasonings and flavorings?

13. What is the difference between herbs and spices?

14. The most important seasoning is

    a. Pepper

    b. Salt

    c. Nutmeg

    d. Mint

15. Cooking a veal shank slowly partially covered in liquid is an example of _____. This falls into the general category of _____ cooking.

Suggested Readings/Web Sites to Visit

Cook, S. (2003). *Salt & Pepper.* San Francisco: Chronicle.

Donovan, M. (1995). *The New Professional Chef.* New York: Van Nostrand Reinhold.

Kurlansky, M. (2002). *Salt: A World History.* New York: Penguin.

McGee, H. (2004). *On Food and Cooking.* New York: Scribner.

Norman, Jill. (2002). *Herbs & Spices: The Cook's Reference.* New York: DK.

Penzeys spices Web page: www.penzeys.com

Salt Institute Web site: www.saltinstitute.org

Stout, P. Salt in the Oceans and in Humans. *Rhode Island Sea Grant Fact Sheet.* Available at www.seagrant.gso.uri.edu/factsheets/salt.html

Yan, M. (1998). This is your knife! *Asian Connections.* Available at asianconnections.com/food/how_to/cutting/

Planning and Documenting Your Culinary Creations

Learning Objectives

By the end of the chapter, you should be able to

1. Describe a standardized recipe

2. Write a recipe using the block form

3. Describe metric units of measure, U.S. units of measure, and be able to convert from one to another

4. Determine what items to offer on your menu

5. Describe the different types of menus

6. Add variety to a menu

7. Use ingredients efficiently

8. Describe the USDA dietary guidelines

9. Describe the Mediterranean food pyramid and how it differs from the USDA guidelines

10. Allow for flexibility in your menu with regard to alternative diets

11. Design a printed menu

12. Determine the selling price of menu items

Chapter Outline

The Basics about Recipes

    Standardized Recipes

    The Block Form for Standardized Recipes

    Measuring

        Measuring Ingredients

Recipes and menus are the focal points of your foodservice establishment. Through your recipes, you communicate to your staff how the product is to be created, in what quantities, and with what equipment. The menu is the actual list of your products, and it affects every part of your operation, from purchasing to production to sales. This chapter explains the basics of creating recipes and menus, and the factors to consider for each.

The Basics about Recipes

The word *recipe* comes from the Latin word "to take." As a matter of fact, recipe originally meant "prescription." The letters "Rx" that you see on a prescription today actually are an abbreviation for the word *recipe*. This reinforces the statement in the first chapter of this book, that chefs are given the same trust in our society as doctors, doesn't it?

Recipes are written documents that describe the creation of a particular food item. Recipes are also the records of your creativity. Accurate recipes are necessary for various reasons:

- To document CCPs for your HACCP program

- To provide information for ordering supplies

- To provide a baseline for creating new, improved items

- To train new personnel

- To provide a refresher for experienced personnel

- To provide a documented list of ingredients if, for instance, allergy questions arise

- To control the quality and quantity of products prepared

If cooks are expected to create a dish precisely every time, time after time, written recipes are absolutely necessary. Moreover, customers should expect to get exactly the same dish each time it is ordered, regardless of the time of day or day of the week. "The food is always spicier when Charlie is on duty" is not an acceptable scenario for a professional foodservice establishment. It is important that you, as a chef or a hospitality manager, know how to write or at least recognize, complete, clear, detailed recipes for your establishment.

However, no matter how detailed a recipe is, it only provides the guidelines for preparing a dish. Why? Because circumstances change. Ingredients are unavailable, humidity changes, or oven temperatures vary. Any number of factors can require a chef to use personal judgment in creating a dish. After you gain knowledge and experience in the field, you should be prepared to step in and alter a procedure if you think that things are not going as planned.

Standardized Recipes

A recipe that is used in a commercial kitchen is called a *standardized recipe*—that is, a set of instructions for preparing a particular product in your establishment. Standardized recipes usually include some or all of the following information:

- The **title**, usually in bold type at the top of the page, that precisely describes the product (for example, not just "mint sauce" but "Indian Mint-Cilantro Sauce")

- The **yield**, given in weight, number of pans, number of servings, or some other easily understandable measurement

- The **portion size** by count, weight, or some other measurement

- **Cooking times** and **temperatures**, described as accurately as possible (for example "simmer for 10 to 15 minutes" or "bake at 350°F (177°C) for 1 hour")

- **Ingredients**, arranged in order of appearance in the recipe. Ingredients should be described as follows: descriptive terms relating to the condition of the food at purchase should appear first, as in "dehydrated onions" or "frozen broccoli"; descriptive terms relating to an operation the cook has to perform should appear after the name of the item, as in "onions, chopped" or "garlic, minced."

- **Quantities** of ingredients, such as "1 cup" or "2 kilos." The quantities can appear either before the ingredients or after, as long as you are consistent. See the discussion later in this chapter for a description of quantities and conversions.

- **Directions** for preparation, arranged in steps, *in order*, each starting with a verb, such as "Add sugar" or "Sauté mushrooms." Directions should include an indication of which steps are CCPs. They should also include, as necessary, a description of any required equipment, using the correct term for the equipment.

- Other optional information may include nutritional data and recipe variations.

The Block Form for Standardized Recipes

The **block form** of recipe writing, illustrated in Figure 5-1, has several advantages. Most important, it clearly lines up the ingredients and the steps, making it easily understood by the cook. This format also forces the writer to think clearly about the entire recipe. Any inconsistencies in your thought processes are evident when they are written in this format. Another advantage to this format is that it may be easily designed in popular word processors using the table function, or it can be set up easily in HTML for use on a Web page.

Measuring

Measuring ingredients and portions accurately is extremely important to the success of a foodservice operation.

Measuring Ingredients

Ingredients may be measured by weight, by volume, or by count. Solid food items, such as meats or vegetables, are normally measured by weight, usually on a portion scale. When following a recipe that measures by weight, it is important that you know the difference between **AP weight** (as purchased, before an item is trimmed), and **EP weight** (edible portion, after an item is trimmed; Fig. 5-2). For example, in a recipe such as the one illustrated in Figure 5-1, you must know whether the weight of the potatoes is AP or EP. Because it says that the potatoes need to be peeled, you know that the stated weight is AP. Especially for items such as shellfish, the AP weight may be as much as 50% or 75% greater than the EP weight.

Volume measurement is used for liquids. An example would be a pint of milk. Certain small quantities of solids, such as a teaspoon of sugar, are also measured by volume. **Measurement by count** is used for items that can easily be counted and are of fairly standard size, such as bananas or eggs.

Whipped Potatoes		
Yield: 25 portions	Size of portion: 5 oz (150 g)	
Ingredient	**Quantity**	**Directions**
Russet potatoes	9 lb (4 kg)	1. Peel the potatoes and cut into a large dice. 2. Simmer potatoes covered in water approximately 15-20 minutes until they are tender. 3. Drain potatoes. 4. Put potatoes into a mixer with a paddle attachment; mix until they are broken into small pieces.
Butter, diced Cream, heated	8 oz (230 g) 1 cup (250 ml)	5. Add butter and cream to potatoes. 6. Change to a wire whip attachment. Beat until cream and butter are completely absorbed.
Milk, heated	as necessary	7. Mix in milk until potatoes are smooth and firm, but not runny.
Salt White pepper Nutmeg, grated	2 tbsp 1 tsp ½ tsp	8. Mix in salt, pepper, and nutmeg.
		9. **CCP** - Hold covered at 140°F (60°C) or higher.

FIGURE 5-1   A block form standardized recipe.

FIGURE 5-2 Trimming a vegetable can make a significant difference in its weight.

Bakers and Accuracy

Although most foodservice organizations and home cooks happily measure dry ingredients like flour and sugar by volume, professional bakers require greater accuracy to ensure consistent results. For example, the weight of a measured cup of flour may vary by brand, by the type of flour (for example, whole wheat or all purpose), or by the amount of settling that has occurred. A baker requires a precise amount of flour. For this reason, in bakeshops, dry ingredients are always weighed or scaled, not measured (Fig. 5-3).

Here's another related fact: To emphasize the precision of their craft, bakers refer to their recipes as formulas.

Portion Measurement

Portion control (the amount served to the guests) is another critical item of measurement in a restaurant. **Portions** are measured by five different methods: by **count** (6 scallops), by **volume** (8 ounces of soup), by **weight** (a 6-ounce fillet of salmon), by **division** (an eighth of a pizza), or by **fill** (a half-full cup of espresso).

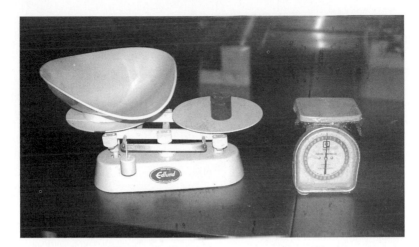

FIGURE 5-3 Scales like these are commonly used to weigh ingredients in commercial kitchens.

Units of Measure

Ahhh! Now to the math. You knew it was coming eventually. Because of the nature of our modern, shrunken, wide Web world, no matter where you work, you have to deal, at some time or another, with both metric measurements and U.S. measurements in a recipe. So you have to know both systems and be able to convert from one to another, preferably in your head.

Metric measurements (Table 5-1), used in most countries of the world, are based on the number ten. For each type of measurement, there is a base unit that is multiplied by ten to get the next higher unit.

U.S. measurements (Table 5-2), are, let's face it, a kind of hodgepodge of various units, some from colonial times, some from England, some from elsewhere. They simply have to be memorized.

Units of Temperature Measurement

Throughout most of the world, the **Celsius** (SELL-see-uss) system (abbreviated C) is used for temperature measurement. In the Celsius system, 0°C is the freezing point of water, and 100°C is the boiling point of water. The United States uses the **Fahrenheit** (FAIR-en-hite) system (abbreviated F), in which 32°F is the freezing point of water and 212°F is the boiling point of water. To cook in a modern restaurant, you will be expected to understand both systems and to be able to convert from one to the other.

Until it becomes second nature to you, use the following formulas to convert from one system to another.

Converting from Fahrenheit to Celsius:

$$C = \frac{5}{9}(F - 32)$$

TABLE 5-1
Common Metric Measurements

Volume

Unit	Abbreviation	Number of Liters	U.S. Equivalent
Liter	l or ltr	1	33.8 ounces
Deciliter	dl	0.1 (1/10)	3.38 ounces
Centiliter	cl	0.01 (1/100)	0.338 ounces
Milliliter	ml	0.001 (1/1000)	0.0338 ounces

Weight

Unit	Abbreviation	Number of Grams	U.S. Equivalent
Gram	g	1	0.035 ounces
Kilogram	kg	1000	35.3 ounces (2.2 pounds)
Decigram	dg	0.1 (1/10)	3.53 ounces (0.22 pounds)
Centigram	cg	0.01 (1/100)	0.353 ounces (0.022 pounds)
Milligram	mg	0.001 (1/1000)	0.000035 ounces (very small)

Length

Unit	Abbreviation	Number of Meters	U.S. Equivalent
Meter	m	1	39.37 inches
Decimeter	dm	0.1 (1/10)	3.94 inches
Centimeter	cm	0.01 (1/100)	0.394 inches
Millimeter	mm	0.001 (1/1000)	0.0394 inches (very short)

For example, to convert 50°F to Celsius, you would subtract 32 from 50, resulting in 18. Then, you would multiply 18 by 5/9, to arrive at the answer 50°F = 10°C.

Converting from Celsius to Fahrenheit:

$$F = \frac{9}{5}C + 32$$

For example, to convert 50°C to Fahrenheit, you would multiply 50 by 9/5, resulting in 90. Then, you would add 32 to 90, to arrive at the answer 50°C = 122°F.

TABLE 5-2
Common U.S. Measurements

Volume

Unit	Abbreviation	Amount	Metric Equivalent
Teaspoon	tsp	$\frac{1}{6}$ ounce	4.93 ml
		$\frac{1}{3}$ tablespoon	
Tablespoon	tbsp	$\frac{1}{2}$ ounce	14.8 ml
		3 teaspoons	
Ounce	oz	$\frac{1}{16}$ pint	29.57 ml
		2 tablespoons	
Cup	cup	8 ounces	237 ml
		$\frac{1}{2}$ pint	
Pint	pt	16 ounces	473 ml
(Note: a pint of liquid, by volume,		2 cups	
is also a pound, by weight)		$\frac{1}{2}$ quart	
Quart	qt	32 ounces	0.946 l
		4 cups	
		$\frac{1}{4}$ gallon	
Gallon	gal	128 ounces	3.784 l
		4 quarts	

Weight

Unit	Abbreviation	Amount	Metric Equivalent
Ounce	oz	$\frac{1}{16}$ of a pound	28.35 g
Pound	lb	16 ounces	0.454 kg

Length

Unit	Abbreviation	Amount	Metric Equivalent
Inch	in	$\frac{1}{12}$ of a foot	2.54 cm
Foot	ft	12 inches	30.48 cm
		$\frac{1}{3}$ of a yard	
Yard	yd	3 feet	0.914 m

 ## Zero Fahrenheit

Although most people don't realize it, Daniel Gabriel Fahrenheit based his scale on the temperature of ice mixed with salt (like the mixture you would use in an ice-cream freezer). If the blend is created perfectly, it equals 0°F.

Converting Recipes to Larger or Smaller Amounts

You will often have to make a recipe for an amount different from your establishment's printed standardized recipe. If a recipe is for 25 portions, you might be asked to prepare it for 40 portions. You would have to use more of each ingredient, but how much more? To demonstrate how to do this type of conversion, let's convert the "Whipped Potatoes" recipe shown in Figure 5-1.

To convert the amounts, you need a **conversion factor**, using the formula

$$\frac{new\ yield}{old\ yield} = conversion\ factor$$

The old yield of the Whipped Potatoes recipe was 25 portions and we need 40, so our formula would be:

$$\frac{40}{25} = 1.6$$

We now multiply each ingredient by 1.6:

- Potatoes: 9 pounds × 1.6 = 14.4 pounds
- Butter: 8 ounces × 1.6 = 12.8 ounces
- Cream: 1 cup × 1.6 = 1.6 cups
- Milk would remain "as necessary."
- Salt: 2 tbsp × 1.6 = 3.2 tbsp
- White pepper: 1 tsp × 1.6 = 1.6 tsp
- Nutmeg: $^1/_2$ tsp × 1.6 = 0.8 tsp

You get the idea. Naturally, the process of conversion can get much more complicated than this example, especially if you are converting complex recipes to very large amounts. Of course, there is computer software available to perform this task, but you should know how to do it in case your computer isn't handy.

Developing Menus

"An inherent liking for good food, a lack of prejudice, a flair for planning based on creativity and intelligence, and the ability to merchandise food attractively are traits that aid the menu planner."

—Payne-Palacio and Theis, Introduction to Foodservice

Menu has two related meanings in the foodservice industry:

1. The foods you choose to offer at your establishment
2. The printed list of your foods you show to your customers (Fig. 5-4)

FIGURE 5-4   Printed menus are your guests' first impression of the food. Menus should be attractive, clean, and easy to read.

Selecting the Foods to Offer on Your Menu

To decide what selection of foods to offer to your guests, you must ask yourself several questions, which are detailed in the next section. You should also consider how well you vary color, shape, texture, and flavor, and how efficiently your menu utilizes ingredients. You must also consider the nutritional balance of your menu as well as alternative diets.

Questions to Ask

Several questions must be answered when you are deciding what selections to offer to your customers:

- *What do my customers want?* You must determine not only the tastes of your typical customers, but such things as how much money they are willing to spend, the ethnic and cultural mix of your area, the nutritional requirements of your customers, and the age groups you will serve.

- *What meals will I serve?* Are you going to serve breakfast, lunch, and dinner, or just one or two of these meals?

- *What type of menu will I have?* There are many types of menus, among them: the **static menu**, a menu that is the same every day; the **cycle menu**, a menu that changes every day for a certain number of days, then repeats; the **selective menu**, which offers choices in every item category; the **à la carte menu**, which prices items separately; the **table d'hôte** (TAHB-luh-DOHT) **menu**, which offers a full meal at a set price.

- *What ingredients are available in my area?* In some areas, the ingredients for, say, a Thai menu may not be readily available from the local suppliers.

- *What style of service will I offer?* There are various styles of service. For example, the customers may serve themselves cafeteria style, or they might go to a counter to order, or they may be served at the table. In addition, some food may be prepared at the table or everything may be prepared in the kitchen.

- *What type of equipment will I have?* You must determine if you have the proper equipment to handle the type and quantity of food you want to serve.

- *What personnel will I require?* You must have a sufficient number of employees with proper training to perform the required tasks for your menu.

Include Variety in Your Menu

You can make your menu offerings and platings appealing by using a variety of factors in your food, including color, texture, shape, temperature, height, and flavor. **Color** is one element you can use to generate eye appeal. Obviously, some cuisines, like Creole or Mexican, have an advantage in this area because they inherently contain more colorful tropical ingredients than do, say, the foods of Eastern Europe. Always try to add more color to your offerings. Use multicolored vegetables, for example, to lend interest to a soup. Or, add sun-dried tomatoes or chives to your butter to make it more tempting.

Try also to pay attention to food **textures** in your menu. Texture not only lends interest visually, but in the mouth as well. Indonesian cooks are masters of texture, having identified several they try to include in every *rijstaffel* banquet. Among these are not only obvious ones like crispy and chewy, but also wet, coarse, spongy, hard, and slimy (as in noodles). (Uh-uh. Watch the foodism!)

Shapes are not so obvious, but think how interesting a pizza looks (Fig. 5-5) topped with a variety of shapes: round slices of pepperoni, straight shreds of cheese, cubes of pineapple, and loops of bell pepper.

Temperature is another aspect of variety you should utilize, especially in salads, soups and desserts.

Height is often used to create a sense of drama. To achieve this, foods such as mashed potatoes or cooked spinach are used as a **socle** (SAH-kul), an item placed beneath another food to elevate the presentation on the plate.

Flavor is, of course, the biggie. Your menu should include the entire range of sweet, sour, salty, bitter, and savory, with inventive combinations of all. An innovative example of flavor fusion is served in Modena, Italy: vanilla ice cream drizzled with aged balsamic vinegar. *Molto squisito* (very delicious)!

FIGURE 5-5 A variety of textures, shapes, and colors lend visual interest to a pizza.

Use Ingredients Efficiently

Select menu items that use the same ingredients or that use different parts of the same ingredient. For instance, if you are buying whole chickens and fabricating them (cutting them up) in your kitchen, use all the scraps to make chicken stock. Also, if you're using the breasts and legs in entrees, make certain to serve the wings as an appetizer. Or, if you use a lot of egg yolks in sauces, use the whites in a meringue on a dessert.

In addition, make sure that you have menu items that use leftovers. If you commonly have scraps of roast beef left over, use them in a beef stew the next day or in French dip sandwiches.

Consider Nutritional Elements and the "Balanced" Diet

"Our duty is to be cooks, not doctors."

—Paul Bocuse, French chef

Although Chef Bocuse's sardonic comment regarding low-fat cooking may seem somewhat blunt, it does make a valid point: Restaurants are in business to create foods people *like* to eat, not what they *should* eat. To make the most profit, restaurants are pressured to serve people what they crave most—mountains of sugar, fat, and cholesterol—without worrying about health considerations.

In today's world, though, it is not realistic, at least from a public relations standpoint, to omit "healthy" items from your menu or to offer only gigantic portions. You are expected to give your customers the options to select low-fat, sugar-free, low-cholesterol items, and to offer them a variety of portion sizes.

To design a balanced menu, the foodservice professional should be knowledgeable about the various elements that comprise a healthy diet, and should offer a sensible variety of foods to customers. There are various sources available to help you learn about good nutrition. A conscientious chef may use government guidelines as a source for information about healthy diets. For example, the interactive USDA food pyramid (available at mypyramid.gov) was released in 2005 (Fig. 5-6). It's based on such sources as the Mediterranean food pyramid (discussed later), the DASH diet (dietary approaches to stop hypertension), and other sensible plans. The USDA food pyramid allows users to tailor a color-coded plan to their needs.

The on-line USDA pyramid makes the following basic recommendations:

- Grains—Make half your grains whole; eat at least 3 ounces of whole-grain breads, crackers, pasta, cereals, or rice every day.

- Veggies—Eat more dark-green veggies, more orange veggies, and more dried peas and beans.

- Fruits—Eat a variety of fruit; go easy on fruit juices.

- Oils—Get most of your fats from fish, nuts, and vegetable oils; limit solid fats like butter, stick margarine, lard, and shortening.

- Milk—Choose fat-free or low-fat milk and milk products.

- Meats and beans—Choose lean meats and poultry, baked, broiled, or grilled; vary protein choices with more fish, beans, peas, nuts, and seeds.

In addition, the pyramid recommends 30 minutes per day of physical activity for adults, and 60 minutes for children and teens.

FIGURE 5-6 The 2005 USDA food pyramid is an on-line tool for personalizing nutrition requirements.

As we said, these relatively new USDA recommendations are based largely on established healthy eating patterns from other cultures. One of the better examples is the Mediterranean food pyramid (Fig. 5-7).

This pyramid reflects the eating patterns in Crete, Greece, and southern Italy. The people in these areas have historically had fewer health problems and a higher life expectancy than other areas. Note some of the significant features:

- Olive oil, in a category by itself, is recommended for daily consumption because it is a **monounsaturated** fat that has a beneficial effect on cholesterol. (Canola oil is another monounsaturated fat.)

- At the base of the pyramid is Daily Physical Activity, something only recently added to the U.S. guidelines.

- Animal products are deemphasized; they are mostly marked for once-a-week consumption.

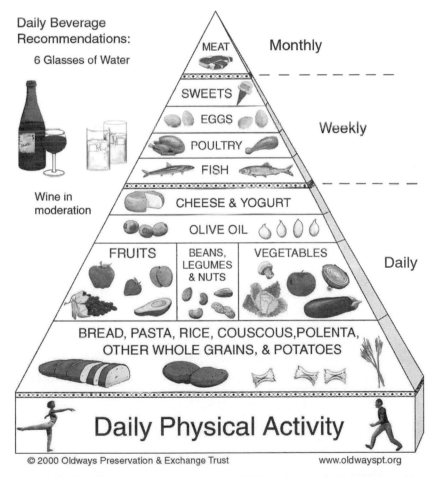

FIGURE 5-7 The Mediterranean food pyramid is based on healthy eating patterns in southern Europe.

- At the point of the pyramid, marked for once-a-month consumption, red meat is shown as the least necessary item.

- Nuts and beans are included with fruits and vegetables in the "daily" area, making them the primary source of protein.

- Beverages (water and wine), omitted from the USDA guidelines, are included.

By the way, this pyramid strongly resembles the food pyramid from Asia, another region that stresses fruits and vegetables over animal products.

Consider Alternative Diets When Designing Your Menu

Another factor that complicates the issue of designing a menu that satisfies everyone involves the large variety of alternative eating patterns and diets that people follow. For example, **vegetarians** chiefly eat plant products and limit their intake of animal products, a practice certainly popular in many cultures of the world. They fall into four categories: **ovolacto vegetarians**, who allow eggs and dairy products; **pesco vegetarians**, who eat fish in addition to plant products; **lacto vegetarians**, who allow dairy products; **vegans** (VEE-guns), who strictly adhere to a plants-only regimen. It is a good practice to feature items on your menu in each of these categories, or at least be ready to adapt existing menu items.

Kosher diets are those that follow the strict rules of Jewish food preparation. See the Web site listed at the end of this chapter for more information.

The Robert De Niro Diet

My favorite diet is one that I invented: "The Robert De Niro Diet." I named it in honor of an answer De Niro gave in response to the question "How did you gain and lose 60 pounds when you played Jake LaMotta in *The Raging Bull*?"

De Niro responded, "Well, when I want to gain weight, I eat more, and when I want to lose weight, I eat less." Gee! Could it be that simple?

Other diets that may affect your menu decisions include the vast array of commercial diets that captivate the public from time to time. The most persistent of these include

- The Pritikin® Diet—low fat, high veggie

- The Scarsdale Diet—low carb, low fat, lean protein

- The Atkins® Diet—low carb, high protein, high fat

- The Jenny Craig® Diet—low calorie

- Weight Watchers®—low fat, low calorie, high fiber

You get the idea. Every commercial diet has a different notion of "balanced." Just keep in mind that if a diet becomes extremely popular, it might be a good idea to adapt or add menu items to fit its requirements.

The Bottom Line

So, with so many factors involved in deciding what to offer and serve your customers, what do you do? How do you decide? Essentially, it's best to follow a few simple guidelines regarding your offerings:

- Make sure your food has lots of flavor.
- Use fresh foods.
- Make efficient use of ingredients.
- Maintain quality.
- Offer a variety of foods from every food group.
- Offer a variety of portion sizes.
- Be willing to alter a menu item to meet specific needs.
- Make sure your staff is well informed about your menu and ingredients, and sympathetic regarding various dietary needs, especially allergies.

Heavyweight Cooks

Cooks have the toughest time in our society maintaining a healthy weight, because, despite the fact that they usually get a more than average amount of exercise on the job, they take in too many calories. They are continually tempted to eat and are required to taste their foods as part of their jobs. Here are a few suggestions to try to avoid becoming a heavyweight cook:

- Just taste the food enough to maintain quality.
- Don't gobble habitually as you are walking around the kitchen.
- Avoid the temptation of pigging out on leftovers at "family meal" at the end of the day. You've been eating for hours; what do you need with another meal?
- Drink lots of water during working hours to make yourself feel full.
- If you go to a bar to socialize after work, avoid the heavy consumption of bar food and beverages just before you go to bed.
- Cut back on calories and get plenty of exercise on your days off.

Designing the Printed Menu

Printed menus are your written communication with your customers. Menus are your food's first impression to your guests. Often, prospective customers will read your menu on the door outside your establishment, or on the Internet, to decide whether to visit your restaurant.

Many chefs do not understand the importance of the written menu. They often feel that they only need to know how to cook the food, not to spell it or describe it. They might say that customers won't notice the inaccuracies on the menu anyway. This is a very short-sighted attitude, because the very people who *will* become annoyed by the typos, inconsistencies, errors, and design flaws are the people who can affect the popularity of your restaurant (for example, food critics, other chefs, and gourmets).

Menus don't have to be fancy and expensive. Some of the most effective menus are the simplest: items written on a whiteboard on a wall, listed on a letter board, or copies on typing paper. Just make sure you take the time to make certain your menu is correct, clear, and that it says what you want it to say.

A Menu as Entertainment

At a recent meeting of a chef's organization I attended, part of the evening's entertainment was provided by passing around an elegant menu from one of the most famous restaurants in southern California—with the typos circled. Most people in the room were astonished, and somewhat amused, that such an expensive and upscale restaurant couldn't bother to check the spelling of "escarole" (a type of green), "granité" (GRAN-uh-TAY, a dessert), or "dacquoise" (dak-WAH, a pastry). It made us wonder, naturally, if they gave the same attention to their cooking and sanitation as they did to their menu.

Design Considerations

When designing your printed menu, there are certain points to keep in mind:

- Allow plenty of space to make it easy to read. Don't cram all the text together.

- Group things together logically, usually in the order in which they are consumed (for example, appetizers, salads, soups, entrees, desserts).

- Use a typeface that is large, dark, and easy to read. Exotic typefaces in pale colors are often hard to make out in the dim light of a dining room.

- Make sure the foods are described clearly and accurately. In some areas, there are criminal fraud penalties for describing, for example, margarine as "butter," milk as "cream," choice beef as "prime," or a 14-ounce steak as "one pound."

- Mention information like "spicy" and note ingredients from the common allergens list in Chapter 2.

- If you are not good at grammar, spelling, and punctuation, have your menu edited by someone who is. But, you, as a chef or hospitality professional, should always be adding to your mental library of how to spell and define various foods. There are excellent reference works listed in the Suggested Readings Section in Chapter 1. Get them and use them.

- After the menu is in use, do not allow the copies to become stained and tattered. Replace them as needed.

Determining the Selling Price of Your Menu Items

Now you've got your menu items selected and the printed menu designed, but there's one more thing, isn't there? Right! What selling price do you put on your menu items? To determine what price to put on your selections, you need two numbers: food cost and food cost percentage. The **food cost** is the amount you pay to the supplier for your ingredients. **Food cost percentage** is determined by you, or your management, during the budgeting process. It's the percentage of the menu price that the chef is allowed to spend on food.

The formula (yes, more math!) for determining the menu price of an item is

$$\frac{food\ cost}{food\ cost\ percentage} = menu\ price$$

For the following *very simple* example, we'll assume that the food cost percentage has been set at 30%. Let's say you want to determine the menu price of an 8-ounce New York steak dinner. You know that the supplier charges you $5.52 per pound for the steak. You know that 1 pound equals 16 ounces. Therefore, an 8-ounce steak weighs one-half pound. One half of $5.52 is $2.76, the food cost of the 8-ounce steak. You then add in the food cost of the potato and vegetable served with the steak. Let's say these total 84 cents. You now know your food cost for the steak dinner is $3.60 (2.76 + 0.84). You would use the following formula to find the menu price:

$$\frac{\$3.60\ (food\ cost)}{30\%\ (food\ cost\ percentage)} = \$12.00\ (menu\ price)$$

And, yes, to answer your natural question, there are computer programs that perform this math in the "outside world," but you should know how the calculation is performed before you begin to rely on a computer.

Summary and Conclusion

Recipes serve several functions in the foodservice establishment, including documentation of your HACCP system, providing information for ordering supplies, and training of new employees. It is important that you, as a chef or a hospitality manager, know how to write clear recipes. Recipes for a particular establishment are called *standardized recipes*.

To develop effective menus, it is important that you understand your customers, nutrition, various alternative diets, and how to design printed menus that are clear, honest, and logical.

 ## Selected Terms for Review

AP weight

Celsius

EP weight

Fahrenheit

Food cost

Food cost percentage

Kosher

Menu

Menu price

Metric measurement

Portion control

Recipe

Standardized recipe

U.S. measurement

Vegetarian

Review Questions

1. Which of the following is not a component of a standardized recipe?

   a. Portion size

   b. Ingredients

   c. Expiration date of ingredients

   d. Directions

2. True or false? In a bakery, flour is measured by cups, as in "5 level cups of flour."

3. Metric measurements are based on the number _____.

4. Convert the following metric measurements:

   1 liter = _____ deciliters

   2.5 kilograms = _____ centigrams

   11,545 milligrams = _____ kilograms

   2387 centimeters = _____ meters

5. Convert the following U.S. measurements

   $4^3/_4$ pounds = _____ ounces

   76 ounces = _____ pounds

   $3^1/_4$ gallons = _____ cups

   27.33 tablespoons = _____ teaspoons

   112 tablespoons = _____ pints

6. How many pounds are in half a kilogram? How many liters are in 2 gallons?

7. Rewrite the following recipe instruction more clearly: "It is a good idea that the batter should be stirred gently after the frozen blueberries are added."

8. Your chef tells you to freeze a batch of ice cream to a temperature of −40°. You ask, "Celsius or Fahrenheit?" The chef responds that it doesn't matter. Why not?

9. What type of menu is the same every day?

10. Name three food characteristics you can alter to add variety to your menu.

11. What item is listed at the top of the Mediterranean food pyramid (as the least necessary item in the diet)? How are such items handled in the USDA guidelines?

12. What type of fat is beneficial to your health and should be consumed regularly? Name two examples.

13. What type of vegetarian would eat cheddar cheese, but not a cheddar cheese omelet? What type of vegetarian would eat seared tuna? What type would reject a potato salad that included hard-boiled eggs or salad shrimp or sour cream?

14. Kosher diets are related to the _____ faith.

15. Which is not a characteristic of a well-designed menu?

    a. Foods are described accurately

    b. The typeface is very fancy

    c. The typeface is dark and easy to read

    d. The foods are arranged in a logical order

16. True or false? Because Dover sole is so scarce, it's OK if you serve flounder and call it Dover sole on the menu. It's practically the same thing.

17. What conversion factor would you use if you were converting a recipe for 50 portions to 75 portions? What would you use to convert 75 portions to 50 portions?

18. Calculate the menu price of a dinner including a 6-ounce salmon fillet that you purchased from the vendor at $4.16 per pound (already cleaned and trimmed), using a food cost percentage of 25%. To the salmon's food cost for each dinner, add a food cost for rice and vegetables of 69 cents.

Suggested Readings/Web Sites to Visit

Drummond, K. E., Brefere, L. M. (2004). *Nutrition for Foodservice and Culinary Professionals.* Hoboken, NJ: John Wiley & Sons.

Liebman, B. DASH: A Diet for All Diseases. *Nutrition Action Health Letter.* Available at www.cspinet.org/nah/dash.htm

Luban, Rabbi Y. How Do I Know It's Kosher? *OU Gateway to the Jewish Internet.* Available at www.ou.org/kosher/primer.html

Mediterranean Diet Pyramid. *Oldways Preservation and Exchange Trust.* Available at www. oldwayspt.org/pyramids/med/p_med.html

United States Department of Agriculture. *My Food Pyramid.* Available at mypyramid.gov

Willett, W. C. Food Pyramids: What should you really eat? *Nutrition Source, Harvard School of Public Health.* Available at www.hsph.harvard.edu/nutritionsource/pyramids.html

The World of Stocks, Sauces, and Soups

Learning Objectives

By the end of the chapter, you should be able to

1. Define a stock, name the major ingredients in a stock, and name the ratio of the three major ingredients

2. Describe a mirepoix and the ratios of its three ingredients

3. Describe a sachet and a bouquet garni

4. Describe the general procedures for making a brown stock, a chicken stock, a Japanese fish stock, and a vegetable stock

5. Define a sauce

6. Define a roux and describe how to make one

7. Name the five classic French mother sauces, and name small sauces made from each mother sauce

8. Define emulsification and name the mother sauce made using emulsification

9. Describe soy-based sauces, fish-based sauces, herb-based sauces, and pepper sauces

10. Define the two main types of soup

11. Describe consommé and the materials used to clarify it

12. Describe vegetable soups and noodle soups, and give examples

13. Describe cream soups, pureed soups, and the process for making each

14. Describe other examples of thickened soups

Chapter Outline

Stocks

> Brown Stock
>
> Chicken Stock and Fish Stock
>
> Japanese Fish Stock
>
> Vegetable Stock
>
> Bases

Sauces

> Classic French Sauces
>
> > Roux and Other Thickeners
> >
> > Butter, Clarified Butter, and Emulsification
> >
> > The Mother Sauces
> >
> > The Small Sauces
>
> World Sauces
>
> > Soy-Based Sauces
> >
> > Fish-Based Sauces
> >
> > Herb-Based Sauces
> >
> > Pepper Sauces
> >
> > Peanut Sauce
> >
> > Mayonnaise-Based Sauces

Soups

> Soup Toppings
>
> Unthickened Soups
>
> > Consommé
> >
> > Vegetable Soups
> >
> > Noodle Soups
>
> Thick Soups
>
> > Cream Soups
> >
> > Pureed Soups
> >
> > Other Thick Soups

Summary and Conclusion

Selected Terms for Review

Review Questions

Suggested Readings/Web Sites to Visit

Cooking foods in hot water is one of the oldest culinary techniques. Early humans learned that they could make their scarce food supply feed more people if they simply threw whatever bits of food they had into a container, covered them with water, and boiled the mixture to allow the food to flavor the water. The resulting broth became the major part of the dish.

Today, of course, this technique has evolved into the art form performed in the classical kitchen by the saucier. But, far beyond the classical kitchen, the creation of great soups and sauces has become a high art form in every corner of the planet. In this chapter, you'll not only learn something about the classic sauces and soups of Europe, but we'll also touch upon Asian, African, and New World examples of this craft.

Stocks

Stocks are the basis of most classic European sauces and soups. Even though most restaurants do not make their own stocks today (because it is considered to be too time-consuming), stock making is an important skill to acquire, because it teaches the aspiring chef the technique of extracting maximum flavor from a few basic ingredients.

This section discusses basics of stock making. Although there are many different types of stock around the world, we'll touch on five of the most important: brown stock, chicken stock, fish stock, Japanese fish stock, and vegetable stock.

A **stock** is a clear liquid created by extracting flavor and gelatin from beef bones, fish bones, poultry bones, or vegetables, plus other ingredients, in water. Three of the most common flavoring items added to stocks are

1. **Mirepoix** (MEER-pwah)—the most important ingredient after bones and water, a mixture of 50% chopped onions, 25% chopped carrots, and 25% chopped celery (Fig. 6-1), by weight

2. A **sachet** (sa-SHAY)—a combination of herbs and spices (for example, parsley stems, peppercorns, thyme, cloves, and bay leaves) tied in a cheesecloth for easy removal from the liquid (Fig. 6-2)

3. A **bouquet garni** (boo-KAY gar-NEE)—may be used instead of a sachet, a bundle of herbs (for example, leeks, thyme, parsley stems, and bay leaves) with a string tied around it, again, for easy removal (Fig. 6-3)

FIGURE 6-1   Mirepoix normally has twice the amount of onions as carrots and celery.

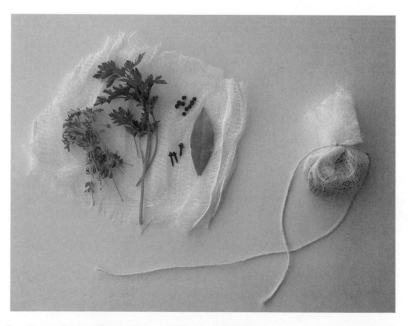

FIGURE 6-2   A sachet allows the cook to add flavor to a soup or stock without leaving fragments in the liquid.

FIGURE 6-3   A bouquet garni is tied with string but is not wrapped in cloth.

Mirepoix

Mirepoix is named after the French Duke de Mirepoix, whose cooks invented the blend in the 18th century. Mirepoix is used to flavor many soups and sauces in French and Italian cuisine.

The ratio, by weight, of the three basic ingredients in a stock is illustrated in Table 6.1. You normally don't add salt to a basic stock. Salt is added when preparing a soup or sauce.

Brown Stock

Stock made from roasted beef or veal bones is called *brown stock* or *veal stock*. A brown stock normally includes some sort of tomato product, like tomato puree, usually half the amount, by weight, of the mirepoix. For example, if you have 1 pound of mirepoix, you'd include 8 ounces of tomato puree. The acid in the tomatoes helps to dissolve the tissues

TABLE 6-1
Ratio of Basic Ingredients in a Stock

Ingredient	Parts	Example
Water	10	20 pints (pounds)
Bones	5	10 pounds
Mirepoix	1	2 pounds

in the bones—chiefly, gelatin. Gelatin gives bone-based stocks their sumptuous, velvety quality.

The sachet used in brown stock normally consists of bay leaves, fresh thyme, peppercorns, fresh parsley stems, cloves, and whole, peeled garlic cloves. However, keep in mind that the flavors in the sachet should not overwhelm the flavor of the stock. For 10 quarts of stock, a sachet the size of a golf ball is enough.

The general procedure for making a brown stock is as follows:

1. Cut the bones into 4-inch lengths and place them in a roasting pan.

2. Place the pan in an oven heated to 400°F (200°C). Bake for 30 minutes.

3. Add the mirepoix. Continue to bake until the bones and mirepoix are very brown.

4. Place the bones and mirepoix in a stockpot with the required amount of *cold* water (see Table 6-1).

5. Add water or red wine to the roasting pan and stir to **deglaze** (dissolve) the browned particles and drippings. Pour the liquid from the roasting pan into the stockpot.

6. Add the tomato paste and the sachet.

7. Simmer for 6 to 8 hours. Skim the scum that rises to the surface. Add water as necessary to keep the bones covered.

8. Strain the stock through a china cap lined with cheesecloth.

9. Chill the stock in ice, venting it according to the guidelines you learned in Chapter 2.

10. Cover, label (with product name and date), and refrigerate.

Chicken Stock and Fish Stock

Chicken stock, made from unroasted chicken bones and trimmings, is one of the most popular stocks in soup making. Fish stock, made from fish bones and trimmings, is essential for making **bisques** (bisks), which we'll discuss later. The sachet used in these stocks normally consists of bay leaves, thyme, peppercorns, fresh parsley stems, and cloves.

The general procedure for making a chicken or fish stock is as follows:

1. Place the bones and mirepoix into a stockpot with the required amount of *cold* water (see Table 6-1).

2. Add the sachet.

3. Simmer according to these guidelines: For chicken stock, simmer for 3 to 4 hours. For fish stock, simmer for 30 to 45 minutes.

4. Skim the scum that rises to the surface. Add water as necessary to keep the bones covered.

5. Strain the stock through a china cap lined with cheesecloth.

6. Chill the stock in ice, venting it according to the guidelines you learned in Chapter 2.

7. Cover, label (with product name and date), and refrigerate.

Japanese Fish Stock

Japanese fish stock, called *dashi*, gives a distinctive flavor to Japanese **miso** (MEE-so) soups. The ingredients are water, dried bonito tuna flakes called *katsuobushi* (KAHT-soo-oh-boo-shee), and kelp (a type of seaweed) called *kombu*. The ingredients are used in the following ratios, by weight: 1 part kombu, 1.5 parts bonito flakes, 80 parts water.

To make dashi, follow these steps:

1. Wipe the kombu with a damp paper towel.

2. Cut the kombu into strips and soak it in the correct amount of cold water for one hour.

3. Heat the soaking water with the kombu until it begins to simmer, but not boil. Remove the kombu.

4. Add the bonito flakes and bring to a boil. Remove the pan from heat.

5. After the bonito has sunk to the bottom of the stock, strain the stock.

6. Cover, label (with product name and date), and refrigerate.

Vegetable Stock

As we mentioned in Chapter 5, there are many vegetarians in the world. Vegetable stocks are important ingredients to have on hand for creating soups and sauces for this significant segment of the population.

Generally, to make a vegetable stock, you might want to experiment with different ingredients. Here are some guidelines:

- Use ingredients with fairly mild flavors (Fig. 6-4), like carrots, celery, onions, leeks, bell peppers, tomatoes, mushrooms, parsley, and thyme. Also, try adding mild, firm fruits, like apples or pears.

FIGURE 6-4   Select ingredients with fairly mild flavors for vegetable stock.

- Start out with equal amounts of each ingredient, but if you decide you want a particular flavor to dominate, like onions, use more.

- Caramelize the ingredients in a little oil before simmering them to intensify the flavor, if you like.

- Avoid strong ingredients, like Brussels sprouts or jalapeños.

- Avoid starches; they make the stock cloudy.

- Avoid vegetables with dark colors, like beets and dark leafy greens.

- Start with just enough water to cover the vegetables. After the stock is done and strained, you can dilute it as necessary. Besides, the vegetables will give off additional fluid as they cook.

- Simmer for about 45 minutes, but don't overcook. The flavors will fade.

Bases

Many chefs today have decided that it is too time-consuming to make stocks in-house. As a result, many kitchens today use **bases**, which are commercially available concentrated pastes that make an acceptable, and much handier, substitute for the real thing. Bases come in a wide variety of flavors, including not only beef, chicken, and vegetable, but also such flavors as clam, roasted turkey, garlic, and ham. There is also a concentrated substitute for dashi called *dashi-no-moto*.

Buying a Good Base

There are many really bad-tasting bases on the market. The major consideration when purchasing a high-quality base is to make certain that the first ingredient listed on the label is the same as the flavor of the base. For example, chicken should be the first ingredient listed for chicken base.

Sauces

"Of all culinary operations, sauce making surely seems one of the quirkiest."

—*Harold McGee*, On Food and Cooking

The word *sauce* refers to a wide variety of foods around the world. In general, the word refers to any liquid or semiliquid used as a dressing for food.

Originally, sauces were considered to be simply an alternative means of adding salt to your food. As we said in Chapter 4, the word *sauce* comes from the word *salt*. However, today the word is used to refer to many different types of cuisine, from stand-alone foods like applesauce and cranberry sauce to entire one-pot meals like Cajun sauce *piquante* (pee-KAHNT) to simple, thin liquids used as ingredients, like soy sauce, pepper sauce, and fish sauce. This section provides a rapid tour and description of sauces as they are made and/or used around the world.

Classic French Sauces

In classic French cuisine, **sauces** are specifics, thickened liquids created by a cook to enhance the juiciness, appearance, flavor, aroma, and richness of a food. In the early 20th century, Escoffier declared five sauces to be the **mother** or **leading sauces**, each of them having numerous spin-offs called **small sauces**. Regardless of whether you ever use French sauces in your professional cooking, there are many techniques associated with making them that you can apply to foods of any culture.

Roux and Other Thickeners

Before we talk about the French sauces, let's talk about thickeners, especially roux. **Roux** (roo) is a mixture of equal parts (by weight) of flour and fat, cooked by various methods to varying shades of white or brown. It is used for thickening, coloring, and flavoring three of the five mother sauces.

Cajun Roux

Vast quantities of roux, in shades ranging from blonde to dark-chocolate, are used in Louisiana Cajun cooking, especially to prepare the classic gumbos, étouffées, and sauce piquantes. Roux is so prevalent in the culture that there is a popular joke, "You know you're a Cajun if your angel food cake recipe starts 'First, you make a roux.'"

To thicken, roux uses gelatinization, the swelling of a starch (in this case, the flour) when it comes into contact with a liquid. The fat in the roux surrounds the particles of flour and prevents it from forming lumps. The fat may be butter, margarine, animal fat (for example, lard), or vegetable oil. The darker the roux, the less it thickens, because, as it cooks, the flour in the roux loses its ability to absorb liquid (Fig. 6-5). By the way, roux is available as a **convenience product**—that is, a commercially prepared, labor-saving item.

Other starch thickeners include **beurre manié** (burr mahn-YAY), a paste made from raw flour and butter; **cornstarch**, a flour made of corn endosperm, which produces a clear, glossy sauce but breaks down if heated over time; and **arrowroot**, which produces a very clear, shiny sauce but is more expensive than flour or cornstarch.

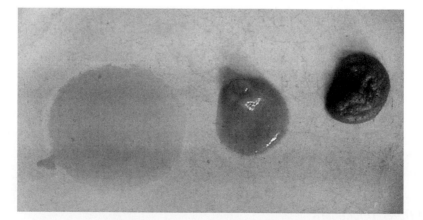

FIGURE 6-5   Various shades of roux. (Left) A white roux after a couple of minutes of cooking and stirring, thin and pale. (Center) A medium-brown roux after several minutes of cooking, thicker and darker. (Right) A very dark, very thick chocolate-brown roux after many minutes on the heat.

Made from the cassava root, **cassava flour**, also called **manioc** (MAN-ee-ahk), **yuca**, or **tapioca**, is a popular thickener in South America and Africa. Cassava has a tendency to form strands when mixed with water.

Reduction—that is, simmering a liquid until its water evaporates and it thickens—is also an effective, commonly used means for creating sauces.

A **liaison** (lee-AY-zahn) is a mixture of egg yolks and cream used as a thickener in sauces. To prevent curdling when adding a liaison to a hot sauce, you must first mix a little of the hot liquid into the egg mixture. This technique is called *tempering*.

Butter, Clarified Butter, and Emulsification

Melted whole butter may be used as a sauce on its own or may be swirled into a mixture of white wine and shallots to make **beurre blanc** (burr BLAHNK), a creamy butter sauce.

An ingredient crucial to classic sauce making is **clarified butter**—that is, butter that has been melted to allow the solids to sink to the bottom and the liquid to evaporate. The clear fat that rises to the top is clarified butter (Fig. 6-6). Many restaurants have a pan of

FIGURE 6-6 Clarifying butter isn't difficult. For this photo, we simply "nuked" a stick of butter for half a minute in a microwave-safe glass, skimmed the foam, then allowed the solids to settle for a few minutes.

melted butter on low heat at all times, so that the cooks can dip out the clarified butter when it is needed.

In Indian cooking, there is a widely used type of clarified butter called *ghee* (gee, with a hard "g"). Ghee is slightly browned, with a nuttier flavor than standard clarified butter.

Clarified butter has a much higher smoke point than whole butter, making it much more desirable for sauces and sautéing. Clarified butter is used in making Hollandaise and Béarnaise, sauces that are thickened by combining egg yolks with clarified butter to make a uniform mixture. This process is called *emulsification*, which is the act of forcing two unmixable liquids (for example, a fat and water) to mix. The product of emulsification is called an *emulsion*.

The Mother Sauces

The following is a list of the five classic sauces declared by Escoffier to be the mother sauces, the foundation of the multitude of French sauces.

1. **Brown sauce**—also called **espagnole** (ESS-pan-YOL, Spanish), made from brown stock thickened with a brown roux

2. **Béchamel** (BESH-um-EL) **sauce**—made from milk thickened with a white roux

3. **Velouté** (vel-oo-TAY) **sauce**—made from chicken or fish stock thickened with a blonde (light brown) roux; *velouté* comes from the word *velvet*.

4. **Tomato sauce**—made from various stocks thickened with tomatoes and/or tomato products and sometimes roux

5. **Hollandaise sauce**—which means "sauce from Holland," made from clarified butter thickened with egg yolks (Fig. 6-7)

Recipes for the mother sauces may be found on the *Culinary Creation* CD-ROM.

The Small Sauces

Small sauces are made by adding ingredients to the mother sauces. There are literally dozens of small sauces. Table 6-2 lists a few of the most common small sauces and the chief ingredients used to make them. Recipes for these small sauces may be found on the *Culinary Creation* CD-ROM accompanying this book.

World Sauces

As stated earlier, sauces come in all colors, textures, flavors, and aromas. This section touches on some of the more popular sauces used in the culinary arts around the world, including sauces based on soy, fermented fish, herbs, peppers, peanuts, and mayonnaise.

Soy-Based Sauces

Although most soy-based sauces are not made in the kitchen, but instead purchased from a vendor, it is a good idea to know what they are so that you can add them to your mental

FIGURE 6-7 Hollandaise sauce is a popular topping for steamed asparagus.

TABLE 6-2

Small Sauces and Their Chief Ingredients

Sauce Name	Added Ingredients
Brown (espagnole) sauce: small sauces	
Bordelaise (BOR-duh-LAYZ)	Red wine, shallots
Diable (dee-AHB-luh)	White wine, shallots, cayenne
Bercy (bair-SEE)	White wine, shallots
Béchamel sauce: small sauces	
Mornay	Parmesan cheese and stock
Mustard	Dijon mustard
Soubise (soo-BEESE)	Onions
Velouté sauce: small sauces	
Supreme	Cream
Aurora	Tomato puree
Hungarian	White wine, onions, paprika
Tomato sauce: small sauces	
Creole	Onion, celery, bell pepper, garlic
Spanish	Mushrooms, onion, bell pepper, garlic
Hollandaise sauce: small sauces	
Béarnaise	Tarragon
Mousseline	Whipped cream

list of potential ingredients. The soybean has been cultivated in China since 1000 BCE. Today, it is a huge source of protein and oil the world over. One of the ancient products of soybeans is **soy sauce**, the distinctive, dark, salty liquid that is certainly the most recognizable Asian condiment. Soy sauce is made by fermenting soybeans in brine for up to a year. It is used as an ingredient in many Asian dishes, as well as a condiment and a basting sauce. Soy sauce especially exploits the *umami* taste bud mentioned in Chapter 1.

Variations on basic soy sauce include **tamari**, a Japanese version that is thicker, darker, and more mellow than traditional soy sauce; **hoisin** (HOY-sin) **sauce**, a thick, sweet Chinese sauce made from garlic, soybeans, chiles, and spices; and **ketjap manis**, sweet soy sauce from Indonesia.

Fish-Based Sauces

Fish sauce made from fermented, salted fish (uh-uh, watch that foodism!), usually anchovies, has been a very popular seasoning ingredient since ancient times in both Europe and Asia. It probably evolved as a by-product of the fish-curing industry about 3000 years ago. The Romans had various versions of fish sauce that they called *liquamen* and *garum*. The recipes of the Roman gourmet Apicius in the first century AD included fish sauce as a standard ingredient. One of the most popular brands of garum was Umbricius Scaurus, sold in gourmet shops throughout the Roman Empire.

After the fall of Rome in about 500 AD, the culinary community shunned fish sauce because it was considered to be a reminder of the extravagance of the Roman aristocracy. As a result, it faded from use in Europe, but it didn't die out completely. As a matter of fact, the British used a fish sauce they called *ketchup* (from the Malay word for fish sauce) up until the American colonists adopted the word for their tomato condiment in the 18th century. Currently, the chief use of fish sauce in Europe is as an ingredient in Worcestershire (WISH-ter-sher) sauce, a British condiment adapted from Indian cuisine.

Despite its decline in Europe, fish sauce has remained popular in southeast Asia throughout the centuries. Today it is used in nearly every savory recipe in Thailand, where it is called *nam pla*, and in the *pho* (soups) of Vietnam, where it goes by the name **nuoc mam** (NOOK-mahm). Vietnamese cooks also make a citrus/pepper sauce called *nuoc cham* that's based on fish sauce. See the *Culinary Creation* CD-ROM for a recipe for nuoc cham. Fish sauce is also very popular in the Philippines, where it's called *patis*.

As an ingredient, fish sauce is more a seasoning, enhancing existing favors, than a flavoring. It's hard to believe when you smell it (it smells very fishy), but it lends almost no fish flavor when added to dishes, only richness.

Another popular Asian seasoning based on seafood is **oyster sauce**, a reduction of ground oysters with soy sauce and brine.

Again, as with soy-based sauces, fish sauces are purchased from vendors, not made in the kitchen. As we mentioned in Chapter 2, be certain to alert customers to the presence of fish sauce in nonseafood dishes, because of potential allergic reactions.

Herb-Based Sauces

Another type of sauce that seems to have arisen independently in many areas of the world is the herb-based sauce, made from fresh, pulverized, aromatic leaves. In Italy, a very popular version of herb sauce is **pesto**. Basic pesto is made from basil, olive oil, garlic, cheese, and pine nuts, and is served uncooked over hot pasta. It is also used as a pizza topping and as a dip for bread. (By the way, did you notice how the ingredients of pesto are all found in the "Daily" section of the Mediterranean food pyramid in Chapter 5?)

South and Central Americans have developed **chimichurri**, a sauce similar to pesto except it uses parsley instead of basil. Indian cuisine features **mint chutney**, an herb sauce made from mint, cilantro, and lemon juice. Recipes for these herb-based sauces are included on the *Culinary Creation* CD-ROM.

Pepper Sauces

Even though pepper sauces originated in the Americas before Columbus, their popularity has grown in many cultures on many continents. Every society seems to have developed its own version of this spicy concoction. Here are some examples.

The Scoville Scale and a Word about Sensible Heat

The heat of peppers is measured on the Scoville scale. On this scale, the bell pepper is 0, the jalapeño (hah-lah-PAYN-yo) is 5000, and the habañero (ah-bahn-YARE-oh, also known as Scotch bonnet) hits a blistering 100,000! Levels of heat at that level (the same as in the can of pepper spray used as a defensive weapon) are not to be taken lightly. Keep in mind that when you use hot peppers in a dish, hotter isn't always better. There is a certain level of heat that enhances flavor and excites the palate without killing the customer's taste buds with the first bite. It's a better idea to allow diners to add heat to their own taste with pepper sauces used as condiments.

In Thailand, **sriracha** (sree-RAH-juh), is a ketchuplike pepper sauce in a squirt bottle. Many people prefer it because its heat is tempered with sweetness and mellowness.

In Indonesia, there is an array of complex pepper sauces called **sambals** that range from mild and sweet to very hot. **Sambal oeleck**, a moderately hot variety containing whole pepper seeds, is the most widely used around the world.

In the United States, Tabasco® brand pepper sauce, a deceptively simple blend of fermented peppers, vinegar, and salt, was developed almost 140 years ago in Louisiana by

E. A. McIlhenny. To this day, Tabasco provides the benchmark standard for numerous American-style hot sauces.

Of course, in Mexico, where chile peppers originated, cooks create dozens of **salsas** (sauces) and **mole**, using peppers of every color, variety, and level of heat. Sauces made from the Mexican **chipotle** (chih-POHT-lay) pepper, a smoked jalapeño, are currently gaining popularity worldwide.

Peanut Sauce

Peanut sauce is everyone's favorite southeast Asian treat. It's used chiefly as a sauce for **satay** dishes (seasoned grilled meats on skewers), and it also provides a delicious dip for spring rolls. Classic peanut sauce is a blend of coconut milk, fish sauce, peanut butter, and brown sugar. Recipes for peanut sauce and satay are provided on the *Culinary Creation* CD-ROM.

Mayonnaise-Based Sauces

Mayonnaise is an emulsion of egg yolks, vinegar or lemon juice, oil, and seasonings. It's normally used as a spread for sandwiches, but it also provides the basis for delicious sauces.

Mayonnaise Is Not the Villain

There is a popular belief that if you leave mayonnaise out in the sun, it will spoil rapidly and make you sick. This is not true if you are using commercially produced mayonnaise; it contains a high enough acid content to prevent the growth of bacteria. However, you should be cautious with homemade mayo produced in your own kitchen that may not contain enough acid to prevent spoilage. Also, you should keep mayonnaise-based salads chilled, not because the mayo is dangerous, but because other ingredients like potatoes and chicken are subject to bacterial growth.

Perhaps the greatest mayonnaise-based sauce is also one of the simplest. **Aioli** (ay-OH-lee), a blend of fresh garlic and mayonnaise, is used in Spain and in the south of France. The name is simply a combination of the French words for garlic and oil. Aioli is used as a dip for toasted bread, and as a sauce for seafood, meats, and potatoes in France. It's also becoming increasingly popular worldwide as a dip for French fries.

Tartar sauce is a familiar mayonnaise product, made with pickles, onions, and capers. Tartar sauce is popular as a fish topping in many cultures. Recipes for mayonnaise and mayonnaise-based sauces are available on the *Culinary Creation* CD-ROM.

Soups

> "It is impossible to think of any good meal, no matter how plain or elegant, without soup."
>
> —*M. F. K. Fisher, culinary writer*

No food item is more closely linked to a nation's heart and soul than its soups. From the gumbo of New Orleans to the borscht of Russia, soups are a source of pride and identity. Why? Because soups are derived from the history and ingredients unique to each region. Soups are basic comfort foods: filling, flavorful, eye appealing, nutritious, and diverse. Almost every ethnicity has spawned an array of soups closely identified with its character.

From a commercial standpoint, soups are especially useful because they provide a profitable means for using leftovers of all shapes and sizes. The soup of the day at lunch one day is often made from the leftover chicken, fish, beef, pasta, or potatoes from the night before.

This section describes the two basic types of soup—unthickened and thick—and gives examples from around the world in each category. Recipes for the various soups discussed are included on the *Culinary Creation* CD-ROM.

Soup Toppings

Before we discuss the specific types of soup, let's talk about a very important part of the presentation: the toppings. Everyone ordering a soup in a foodservice establishment expects that there will be tasty food items to put on it, whether the soup is part of a self-service buffet or served at the table in a five-star restaurant. These items are called *toppings* or *garnishes*, and they come in several varieties.

Creamy toppings, such as cream, yogurt, or sour cream, may be drizzled or spooned onto the soup just before service. Depending on the consistency of the soup, a toothpick or knife blade may be swirled through it to make an attractive design (Fig. 6-8).

Crispy toppings lend a contrasting crunch to the liquid of the soup. Crispy toppings may include croutons (toasted bread cubes or slices), crackers, nuts, bacon, or corn chips. **Fresh chopped herbs** such as parsley, cilantro, or basil are a pleasant, attractive addition. **Shredded cheese** is another popular option, especially if the bowl of soup is placed under a grill to brown the cheese after it is added.

Unthickened Soups

Unthickened soups are often referred to as "clear" soups, but this is somewhat of a misnomer, because not all unthickened soups are clear. Obviously, ingredients like milk or coconut milk are going to turn the liquid cloudy or even opaque. No matter what you call them, unthickened soups tend to be less substantial than thick soups, but they can be just as satisfying and certainly equally as complex and delicious.

FIGURE 6-8   Cream or sour cream may be swirled attractively on top of a thick soup.

Consommé

Although most people think of it as simply a broth with a fancy French name, **consommé** (kon-suh-MAY), the ultimate clear soup, is magical. Do not confuse classic consommé with the stuff in the can. Real consommé is intensely flavored and velvety in the mouth, making it one of the great soups of the world. But, making consommé is a challenge of the chef's skills.

Consommé is produced by coagulation (discussed in Chapter 4), a process that renders a soup so clear as to be almost invisible. The coagulation is achieved by a protein structure that floats on top of a stock, gathering up all the impurities. The structure is called a *raft*, and the materials used to build it are called the *clear meat*. The clear meat, made of ground meat, egg whites, flavorings, and an acid, is simmered in the stock and removed after the process is complete. The consommé is then strained and prepared for service.

Vegetable Soups

Most unthickened soups fall into the category of vegetable soup. **Vegetable soup** is any soup made from a stock or broth, usually chicken or meat stock, with added vegetables and meat or chicken. **Vegetarian vegetable soup** is made from vegetable stock and vegetables only.

Basic, classic vegetable soup is made with onions, carrots, celery, and kohlrabi or turnips. All the vegetables are diced small to ensure even cooking and an attractive presentation.

Mexican cooks create a hearty, unthickened vegetable soup called **posole** (po-SOL-ay) that contains bits of pork, chiles, and **hominy** (large corn kernels that have been treated to remove the outer hull).

Noodle Soups

Noodle soups are very satisfying unthickened soups that are usually made with a stock, a meat or poultry, and some type of pasta or egg noodle. American-style chicken noodle soup is a popular example of this type of soup. Containing egg noodles and chicken stock, it probably evolved from the soups of the German Amish in Pennsylvania.

Another family of noodle soups, called *pho* (as we said in Chapter 1, pronounced like "foot" without the "t") are relished by the Vietnamese. These normally contain rice noodles in a rich beef stock. The most popular pho is called *pho tai*. It contains slices of rare steak, added at the last minute before serving. Tripe (beef stomach lining) and meatballs are other common ingredients in pho. Many U.S. veterans of the Vietnam War acquired an appreciation for the complex, rich flavor of pho.

The most unusual feature of Vietnamese soups is the platter of fresh ingredients that are served with the soup as garnishes. A fairly large quantity of herbs, sliced peppers, bean sprouts, and lime slices are provided to add as you eat your soup. These provide a unique, refreshing piquancy.

Thick Soups

Soups may be thickened by various means, in addition to the methods listed under "Roux and Other Thickeners" in the "Sauces" section. Thickening may be accomplished by adding cream or coconut milk, adding pastes such as tomato paste, or by pureeing the soup.

Cream Soups

Cream soups are normally made with velouté or béchamel sauce. Normally, to make a cream soup, a main ingredient such as mushrooms, tomatoes, or broccoli is **sweated** (softened over medium heat without browning), then cooked in the sauce until tender. The mixture is then passed through a sieve or a food mill. Additional liquid is added to get the right consistency (the consistency of heavy cream), then the soup is seasoned to taste with salt and pepper.

If cream soups are overheated, they will **curdle**—that is, the cream will separate into liquid and solids. To prevent this, don't add cold cream to a hot soup, and don't boil the soup after adding the cream.

Although **bisque** is a word that can be used to mean any cream soup, it is often used to refer to cream soups with seafood, such as lobster or crawfish. These are normally more complex than other cream soups.

A **chowder**, such as New England clam chowder, is simply a cream soup that is traditionally left chunky and not passed through a food mill.

Pureed Soups

Pureed soups are made by cooking a vegetable in a stock until tender, then blending the mixture in a food processor until smooth, then seasoning it. Typical pureed soups include bean and carrot.

Other Thick Soups

Other great examples of thick soups on the *Culinary Creation* CD-ROM include the following:

- Cajun chicken and *andouille* (ahn-DOO-ee, a spicy sausage) **gumbo**, made with smoked pork sausage and a very dark roux (Fig. 6-9)

- Thai **kao soi** (kow-soy), a chicken and noodle soup with Thai red curry paste and coconut milk

- African **peanut soup**, a savory, rich soup thickened with peanut butter

- **White gazpacho** (gass-PAH-cho), a cold soup made from almonds, grapes, and olive oil and thickened with bread. This soup from Spain is a product of the Moorish influence of 1000 years ago.

FIGURE 6-9   This chicken-and-sausage gumbo is a hearty meal on its own.

Summary and Conclusion

Stocks, sauces, and soups—each involves the manipulation of liquids to produce a memorable culinary creation. They are interrelated items that utilize many of the same ingredients and culinary reactions, including mirepoix, sachets, bouquet garni, gelatinization, emulsification, and coagulation.

It's important that the aspiring chef understand the principles involved in preparing the major stocks, the five classic mother sauces, and the major types of soup, because the techniques used in preparing them are used in cooking similar dishes in every cuisine. This knowledge also provides the foundation skills useful in preparing foods in many of the upcoming chapters.

 ## Selected Terms for Review

Clarified butter

Clear meat

Emulsification

Fish sauce

Liaison

Mayonnaise

Mirepoix

Miso

Mother sauce

Pesto

Pho

Reduction

Roux

Sachet

Salsa

Sauce

Small sauce

Stock

Tempering

Thick soups

 ## Review Questions

1. Which of the following is not a major ingredient in a stock?

   a. Bones

   b. Mirepoix

   c. Brandy

   d. Water

2. What is the ratio of the three major ingredients in a stock?

3. The three ingredients in a mirepoix are _____, _____, and _____.

4. True or false? A sachet is enclosed in a cheesecloth bag.

5. Put in correct order the following steps to make brown stock:

   _____ Deglaze the pan.

   _____ Add the tomato product.

   _____ Strain the stock.

   _____ Skim the scum.

   _____ Cut the bones into 4-inch lengths.

   _____ Brown the bones.

6. True or false? Dashi stock is used to make miso soups.

7. Define a roux.

8. The five classic mother sauces are _____, _____, _____, _____, and _____.

9. Which of the following is not a small sauce?

   a. Béarnaise

   b. Worcestershire

   c. Diable

   d. Mousseline

10. Give two alternate names for fish sauce.

11. What are the two main categories of soup?

12. What is the name of the major protein reaction that clarifies a stock to make consommé?

13. What cream soup chiefly uses seafood? What cream soup is left chunky?

14. True or false? White gazpacho was created by the Mayan civilization of Mexico.

Suggested Readings/Web Sites to Visit

Association for Dressings and Sauces. *Mayonnaise: The Misunderstood Dressing.* Available at www.dressings-sauces.org/pdf/mayoo.pdf

de Castro, T. Iberian peninsula. *Web site of Teresa de Castro.* Available at www.geocities.com/tdcastros/Historyserver/papers/IberianPeninsula.htm

Mayhew, D., ed. (2000). *The Soup Bible.* London: Anness.

McGee, H. (1990). Beurre Blanc: Butter's Undoing. In *The Curious Cook* (pp. 89–99). New York: Macmillan.

Tallyrand. *Tallyrand's Culinary Fare.* Available at www.geocities.com/NapaValley/6454/

Finger Foods: Appetizers and Sandwiches

Learning Objectives

By the end of the chapter, you should be able to

1. Define an appetizer

2. Describe canapés

3. Name the three components of a canapé and give examples of each

4. Describe crudités, and provide some items that can be used as crudités and some dips that might be used with them

5. Define tapas and dim sum and provide some examples

6. Define sandwiches

7. Relate the history of the sandwich

8. Describe the functions performed by bread on a sandwich

9. Name some types of bread

10. Describe various varieties of fillings for a sandwich

11. Discuss condiments and spreads, and give some examples

12. Describe how to set up a sandwich station

Chapter Outline

Appetizers

    Canapés

        Use Your Imagination

        Presentation of Canapés

Appetizers are an important category of food that are especially crucial for banquet work. Preparing a variety of thousands of attractive finger foods is a challenge for any kitchen staff. This chapter discusses the basic types of appetizers and also describes alternatives from around the world.

Sandwiches, once a simple convenience food, have become a major venue for creativity in foodservice. Nancy Silverton, owner of the popular, upscale Campanile restaurant in Los Angeles, reports that when she decided to feature a sandwich night on Thursdays, to her surprise it quickly became the busiest night of the week. This chapter deals with the basics of the structure and components of these two related items, and introduces the student to appetizer and sandwich variations around the world.

Appetizers

An **appetizer** or **hors d'oeuvre** (or-DERV; literally, "outside the main work") is a finger food served before a meal that can be eaten in one or two bites. (The term *appetizer* also may apply to the first course of a meal, but it is not used in that sense in this book.)

Appetizers are intended to excite and amuse diners, but not to fill them up (something that's overlooked by many restaurants and customers today). As a matter of fact, the

FIGURE 7-1   Canapé bases may include bagel chips, crackers, or toast points.

French call appetizers *amusé bouche* (AH-mew-ZAY BOOSH), meaning "amuse the mouth," in recognition of the role they play in the meal.

There are various types of appetizers. Two categories we'll discuss are *canapés* (KAN-uh-PAYZ) and *crudités* (KRU-di-TAYZ). We'll also touch on two important categories of appetizers: Spanish tapas and Cantonese dim sum.

Canapés

A **canapé** (KAN-uh-PAY) is an open-faced sandwich to be eaten in one or two bites. It consists of bread topped with a garnish and a spread. The chef's own creativity is the only limiting factor in how a canapé may be built.

Their component parts of a canapé are a foundation or **base** (for example, a slice of toast, a cracker, a triangle of pita bread, or a circle of puff pastry; Fig. 7-1), a **spread** like a dip or a flavored whipped cheese or butter (more on spreads in the "Sandwich" section), and a **garnish** that can be, literally, anything edible, like ham, cheese, caviar, salad shrimp, or fresh herbs.

Examples of typical canapés include

- Smoked salmon spread on toast rounds with caper garnish

- Caviar butter on pâte à choux (see Chapter 14 and recipe on *Culinary Creation* CD-ROM) with lobster garnish

- Olive tapenade on rye toast with prosciutto garnish

FIGURE 7-2   The California roll is a popular canapé.

Use Your Imagination

Turn your imagination loose when making canapés. For example, serve **bruschetta** (broo-SKEH-tuh), pleasingly crunchy Italian appetizers, using toasted garlic bread as the base. Or, offer Vietnamese salad rolls, *goi cuon*, as canapés, where rice paper is the base, peanut sauce the spread, and shrimp, greens, and herbs the garnish. However, in this case the base is wrapped around the spread and the garnish, then the resulting roll is sliced into bite-size circles. A drop of sriracha hot sauce on top of each slice adds zest and color.

California rolls (a style of sushi with cooked crab) are popular canapés, in which *nori* (NOR-ee, crispy dried seaweed) is the base, seasoned sushi rice is the spread, and crab meat and avocado are the garnish (Fig. 7-2). A slice of pickled ginger is often placed as an additional garnish on top of the roll to add visual and flavor interest.

Presentation of Canapés

Here's the difficult part about canapés: To be effective, they have to be attractive and they have to be identical, as nearly as possible. They also have to be fresh. This presents a challenge when you are preparing 5000 items for a banquet, doesn't it? To create mass quantities of canapés successfully, you really must have your mise en place in order and your workers trained, so that your canapés don't look like random piles of food on crackers.

Crudités and Dips

Crudités are *very fresh* raw vegetables, cut into bite-size pieces, served as appetizers. They are usually served with dips. The vegetables used commonly include carrots, broccoli, cauliflower, cucumbers, bell peppers, celery, cherry tomatoes, and *jicama* (HEE-kah-mah), a sweet root vegetable from Latin America.

Dips used for crudités may be mayonnaise based (for example, aioli or remoulade), sour cream based (for example, roasted garlic dip), cream cheese based, tomato based (for example, salsa), or herb based (for example, pesto or chimichurri). Other international options include

- Italian *bagna cauda* (BAN-yuh KOW-duh), made from olive oil, butter, garlic, and anchovies

- Mexican *guacamole* (WAHK-uh-MO-lay), made from flavored, mashed avocados

- From the Middle East, *babaghanoush* (bah-bah-gah-NOOSH), made from pureed eggplant, and *hummus* (HUM-us), made from pureed chickpeas

Appetizers from Other Traditions

In addition to canapés and crudités, appetizers can take many other forms. The chefs of two cultures in particular have proved themselves to be masters of creating appetizers: Spain and China.

Tapas

The word *tapas* (TAH-puss) is used for an entire range of foods served as appetizers in the tapas bars of Spain. The name *tapas* comes from the way these delicacies were originally served, on plates covering the tops of customers' glasses of sherry (some say to keep flies out of the wine). The Spanish word *tapar* means "to cover," so they called the appetizers "tapas."

Today, there are hundreds of varieties of tapas. Here are a few that might give you some ideas for appetizers of your own. (Recipes for these are on the *Culinary Creation* CD-ROM.)

- Spanish *manchego* cheese slices topped with sliced *membrillo* (mem-BREE-yo, a firm quince jelly)

- Almond meatballs

- Chorizo (not the Mexican kind, but a Spanish hard sausage like pepperoni) canapés with anchovy garnish

- Sausage with figs

- Aioli and toasted bread

Dim Sum

About a thousand years ago, Chinese (specifically, Cantonese) chefs began the tradition of creating delicate, attractive little snacks called *dim sum*, meaning "touching your heart." Usually served at noontime, dim sum, some experts believe, may have been the origination of the modern brunch.

FIGURE 7-3   **Won tons may be filled with meat, seafood, veggies, or even cream cheese.**

Dim sum include a variety of filled dumplings and steamed dishes, including steamed barbecue pork buns, *won tons* (square noodles with various fillings; Fig. 7-3), *shu mai* (shoo-MY, steamed dumplings), and deep-fried mini egg rolls.

Aspiring chefs can benefit by studying the methods and ingredients used in creating dim sum, not only to learn about the flavors and textures, but also to learn the techniques used in their preparation and presentation.

Sandwiches

Today, sandwiches are becoming an increasingly important item in the culinary repertoire. Not only is it important to know how to prepare the various types of European and American sandwiches, but it is also important to learn about the various world variations on the sandwich.

A Brief History of the Sandwich

Most of us have heard the story that, in the 1700s, Lord Montagu, the fourth Earl of Sandwich, while competing in a marathon session of gambling in the BeefSteak Club in

London, did not want to put down his cards to eat with a knife and fork. So, he told the servers to bring him salt beef between slices of bread that he could eat with one hand. Others at the table asked for "the same as Sandwich." The name stuck. That food item became ever after known, in English anyway, as the sandwich. Although this popular story may tell us how the sandwich got its name, it certainly doesn't explain how or when the sandwich was invented.

People had been eating meat, cheese, and other foods enclosed in some type of bread for thousands of years before Lord Montagu's fateful card game. We may define a **sandwich** as

- Two or more pieces of bread with a filling between
- A filling wrapped in a piece of bread
- A single piece of bread covered with food

Therefore, food wrapped in flatbreads—like pitas in the Middle East, tortillas in the Americas, naan in India, injera in Ethiopia, crepes in France, and pancakes in China—certainly all qualify as forms of sandwiches that have been around for millennia. We know that, at least 2000 years ago, Jews ate foods between two pieces of *matzoh* (MOT-zuh, a crisp flatbread) during Passover.

In the Europe of the Middle Ages, blocks of hard bread called *trenchers* were used as edible plates for food, forerunners of the open-face sandwich. Later, during the reigns of Henry VIII and Queen Elizabeth I, the phrases *bread and meat* and *bread and cheese* often appeared in the plays and literature of the time. Most food historians feel these were early references to sandwiches.

Today, the sandwich is easily the number one food configuration in the world. Think about it: Hamburgers, subs, hot dogs, pita wraps, and tacos all qualify as types of sandwiches. And what about the pizza? Isn't a pizza just a big, hot, open-face sandwich?

Let's look at the components of the sandwich and then look at some of the sandwich variations from around the globe.

The Sandwich's Exterior

As we said, the exterior of the sandwich is usually some sort of bread. If it is of high quality, it should perform several functions:

- Bread provides the diner's first visual impression. Hopefully, it enhances the appearance of the sandwich.
- It adds flavor and texture to the sandwich.
- Bread provides structure; it supports the sandwich.

FIGURE 7-4   The croissant makes an exotic, flavorful sandwich exterior.

- It provides a surface that can be comfortably held with the hands and it insulates against hot interior items.
- Bread adds volume and it provides nutrition.

There are many different types of breads that can be used: French bread, Italian bread, rye bread, pita bread and other flatbreads, rolls, English muffins, *focaccia* (foh-CAH-chuh, a seasoned Italian bread), *ciabatta* (CHEE-uh-BAH-tuh, a wide crispy Italian bread), *brioche* (bree-OSH, a rich egg bread), *challah* (HAH-luh, a rich, braided Jewish bread), *croissants* (kwah-SAHNTS, buttery, flaky crescent rolls; Fig. 7-4), and bagels.

A very common type of bread used for making sandwiches in the commercial kitchen is called the *pullman loaf*, a long, rectangular bread with even sides and square corners that resembles generic white bread from a grocery store, but is firmer and more regularly shaped.

Freshness and Staling

The best practice is to use breads the same day they are baked. Bread starts to become stale as soon as it comes out of the oven. Staling involves two different processes: loss of moisture and a chemical change in the starch. To prevent moisture loss, keep standard breads tightly wrapped when not in use. (Exception: Don't wrap crusty French-style breads that are being held at room temperature for one day or less; their crust becomes chewy. Leave them out in the air.)

To slow the starch change, store bread for short periods of time (one day or less) at room temperature, or, for longer periods, in the freezer, tightly wrapped. Do not refrigerate bread; bread stales fastest in the refrigerator.

Today, **artisan breads** are becoming increasingly popular for sandwiches. These breads usually have an intricate, weblike interior, and a crusty, artistic exterior. Most important, artisan breads have a great deal of flavor.

The Sandwich's Interior

The interior of the sandwich can contain a wide variety of hot or cold items, including meats, poultry, fish, cheese, eggs, and fruits and vegetables. Also used inside are various spreads and condiments.

Sandwich Fillings

Possible sandwich fillings include the following examples

- Meats—beef, including hamburger, roast beef, corned beef, and barbecued beef; pork, including breaded pork tenderloin, pork sausage, "pulled" pork (shredded pork from the southern United States), salami, ham, and bacon; lamb, including roast lamb, ground lamb, and **gyros**, a Greek lamb loaf

- Poultry—chicken, including ground chicken, sliced chicken breast, creamed chicken (open face), or chicken salad; turkey, including sliced turkey breast, ground turkey, or turkey luncheon meats

- Fish—lobster (as in the New England lobster roll), fried catfish, tuna (fresh or canned), tuna salad, or smoked salmon

- Cheeses—cream cheese and cream cheese spreads, Swiss, cheddar, American, provolone, or mozzarella

- Eggs—in egg salad or fried

- Fruits and vegetables—tomatoes, shredded cabbage, coleslaw, mushrooms, onions, various types of lettuce, dates, cranberries, olives, or bean sprouts

Condiments and Spreads

It's difficult to define condiments and spreads precisely. Some condiments are also spreads, and some spreads are also condiments. A **condiment** is any flavoring, cooked or prepared, that is added to the sandwich. In general, condiments are added by the diner after the item is served. Condiments include not only ketchup, mustard, salsa, pepper sauce, olive oil, horseradish, and relish, but also flavorings like celery salt or lemon pepper. A condiment need not be liquid or semiliquid.

Salsa versus Ketchup

Many of you have heard the factoid that, during the 1990s, salsa became the number one condiment in the United States. Well, that's not really true. It is true that people started spending more money on salsa than ketchup, but that's because salsa is more expensive. In terms of quantity, people in the United States still eat five to ten times more ketchup than salsa.

Spreads, on the other hand, are flavorings that are spreadable with a knife. Spreads add interesting flavors and textures to the sandwich. If they have a high fat content, like butter or mayonnaise, spreads also protect the bread from becoming soggy. Spreads are normally added by the cook as part of the construction of the sandwich. Some of the most commonly used spreads in the United States are mayonnaise, salad dressing, butter, margarine, pickle relish, peanut butter, and various jams and jellies.

Internationally, there are interesting options available (some of them mentioned in the Appetizers section of this chapter, or in the Sauces section of Chapter 6), including hazelnut spread, hummus, babaghanoush, olive tapenade, basil pesto, chimichurri, and Indian chutneys.

Yeast Spreads

There are two unusual spreads that are wildly popular in their native countries, but are considered to be acquired tastes elsewhere: Marmite®, from England, and Vegemite® from Australia. These are yeast by-products that resemble very thick, black molasses. There is a raging controversy between the two nations over which product is best. It's quite entertaining to visit the Web sites of each product, listed at the end of this chapter. The Marmite site is especially fun; it allows you to choose between paths for Marmite lovers and Marmite haters.

In addition, it's fun to experiment with the sambals from Indonesia, chutneys from India, and **wasabe** (wah-SAH-bee), green horseradish paste from Japan.

Setting up the Sandwich Station

Preparing sandwiches in the commercial environment takes as much organizational skill and knowledge as any other food category. The following guidelines fall into the two categories that have been stressed earlier: mise en place and sanitation.

Sandwich Mise En Place

For maximum efficiency, you must understand the importance of having everything in place and ready to go before attempting to assemble your sandwiches (Fig. 7-5).

- Make sure all the fillings, condiments, breads, and spreads are at hand and ready to use. Make certain that meats, cheeses, tomatoes, and onions are sliced; lettuce is washed; and spreads are mixed.

- Place all the ingredients where they will be easily accessible.

- Divide items into portions beforehand, when possible.

- Have all your utensils at hand (knives, spatulas, forks). Make certain that your cutting board is clean and secure.

- Make certain that all grills and broilers are heated, and refrigerators are cold.

FIGURE 7-5 In an ideal sandwich mise en place, everything should be within easy reach.

Sanitation

Because sandwiches require such a wide variety of ingredients of different temperatures, it's easy for contamination to occur. Follow these guidelines to ensure that you keep a sanitary workstation:

- Because almost all sandwiches are RTE items, wear gloves while preparing them. Change your gloves often. It doesn't do any good to wear gloves if you continue to handle foods after your gloves become contaminated.

- Remember the FDZ; make certain your cold ingredients are kept cold, and your hot ingredients are kept hot.

- Don't allow cross-contamination. Don't pile meats, fish, and poultry on the same cutting board with bread and vegetables. Make certain you clean the cutting board with sanitizer after preparing a potentially hazardous food item before you move on to the next item.

- Don't wipe your hands on your apron. Change your apron if it becomes soiled.

Classic Sandwiches

The following are examples of classic sandwiches from around the world. The recipes for these are included on the *Culinary Creation* CD-ROM. Some of them are grilled in a **panini machine**, an Italian two-sided sandwich grill like a waffle iron that is becoming very popular in trendy sandwich establishments. **Panini** is actually the plural of *panino*, the Italian word for "sandwich," but it is commonly used to mean one sandwich.

- New Orleans muffuletta—from the French Quarter; salami, ham, provolone, and olive salad on a large French loaf, drenched in olive oil

- The Italian panini—prosciutto and mozzarella in a ciabatta grilled in a panini machine

- The Cuban sandwich—a favorite in Little Cuba in Miami; ham, roast pork, pickle, Swiss cheese on French-style bread, grilled in a panini machine

- The classic burger—grilled hamburger with lettuce, onion, and tomato on a hamburger roll (Fig. 7-6)

- The portobello burger—vegetarian hamburger made with a teriyaki-marinated portobello mushroom cap

- The Peacemaker po' boy—From the Deep South in the United States, fried oysters, remoulade slaw, tomatoes, and hot sauce on a crunchy French roll

- The New England lobster roll—lobster chunks with mayonnaise on a hot dog roll

FIGURE 7-6 **The hamburger is easily the most popular sandwich in the United States.**

- The naanini—turkey wrapped in naan (Indian flatbread), with lettuce, tomato, and mint chutney
- The Gyros sandwich—Gyros slices in pita bread with feta cheese, tomatoes, and yogurt dressing

Summary and Conclusion

In this chapter you learned about two of the most important items in the culinary repertoire: appetizers and sandwiches. Easily dismissed as simple finger foods, they actually represent some of the most popular and creatively challenging food categories.

We looked at two of the most important categories of appetizers—canapés and crudites—and also looked at alternative selections from a variety of countries, especially Spain and China.

We discussed the structure of the sandwich and described the importance of organization and sanitation during the sandwich-making process.

Selected Terms for Review

Artisan breads

Canapés

Condiment

Crudités

Dim sum

Gyros

Hors d'oeuvre

Panini

Pullman loaf

Sandwich

Spreads

Staling

Tapas

Trencher

Wasabe

Review Questions

1. Define appetizer.

2. Name the components of a canapé and give examples of each.

3. True or false? Canapés are easy to prepare because any unskilled kitchen worker can be recruited to make them.

4. Which of the following is not an example of a crudité?

    a. Broccoli florets

    b. Baby carrots

    c. Buffalo wings

    d. Sliced bell peppers

5. True or false? Tapas are so named because the customers tap the table when they want to order more tapas.

6. Dim sum come from _____. The name means "_____ the _____."

7. True or false? Although the sandwich was named for the Earl of Sandwich, he didn't invent it.

8. Name four functions the bread performs on a sandwich.

9. The _____ loaf—a long, even, rectangular bread—is commonly used in commercial kitchens.

10. Which of the following is not a method to slow the staling process?

    a. Wrap breads tightly.

    b. Refrigerate breads.

    c. Freeze breads.

11. Name three items that can be used as sandwich fillings.

12. Name two functions performed by spreads.

13. Name four things that should be done as part of the mise en place at a sandwich station.

14. True or false? Don't waste gloves. You should only use one pair of disposable gloves per shift at a sandwich station.

15. The sandwich grilling machine that resembles a waffle iron is called a _____ machine.

Suggested Readings/Web Sites to Visit

Binns, B. L. (2001). *Williams-Sonoma Hors D'oeuvre*. New York: Simon & Schuster.

Borghese, A. (1978). *The Great Sandwich Book*. New York: Rawson Associates.

Casas, P. (1985). *Tapas: The Little Dishes of Spain*. New York: Alfred A. Knopf.

Hong Kong Dim Sum Dishes. *Global Gourmet*. Available at www.globalgourmet.com/destinations/hongkong/hkdishes.html

La Place, V. (1994). *Panini, Bruscetta, Crostini: Sandwiches Italian Style*. New York: Hearst.

Love it or Hate It? Marmite: www.marmite.com

Silverton, N. (2002). *Nancy Silverton's Sandwich Book*. New York: Alfred A. Knopf.

Stradley, L. (2004). History and Legends of Sandwiches. *What's Cooking America?* Available at whatscookingamerica.net/History/SandwichHistory.htm

Sunset editors (1991). *Sunset Appetizers*. Menlo Park, CA: Sunset.

Vegemite: www.vegemite.com.au

Creating Salads

Learning Objectives

By the end of the chapter, you should be able to

1. Define salads

2. Define dressings

3. Discuss the history of the salad

4. Name the four parts of a salad

5. List the categories of salad ingredients

6. Name regional salad ingredients from around the world

7. List and describe the major greens most commonly used in salads

8. Describe various types of salads

9. Define vinaigrettes, and name the oils and vinegars that may be used in a vinaigrette

10. Distinguish between temporary emulsions and permanent emulsions

11. Describe creamy dressings and Asian dressings

12. Describe the guidelines to follow when creating a salad

Chapter Outline

Definition and History of Salads

Salad Elements

    Parts of a Salad

    Categories of Salad Ingredients

    Regional Salad Ingredients

    Universal Greens

        Lettuces

So, what's the big deal about salads? You grab your tray, you grab your plate, and you're off! You sling some spinach, toss some tuna, grab garbanzos (who needs tongs?), collect the cheese, pile on peppers, toss on tomatoes, mound on masses of mystery macaroni mix, hide the whole thing under a river of ranch, then bedeck it with a bevy of bacon bits and a cluster of croutons. Finished! What was so hard about that?

Not a pretty picture.

Creating salads is an ancient art form, performed in the classic kitchen, as we said in Chapter 1, by the pantry chef, also called the *garde manger*. To make even the most basic tossed salad, some thought must be given to its ingredients and its assembly.

There are an infinite number of salad variations around the world, limited only by the imagination of the chef. This chapter introduces the student to the endless potential in the realm of salads.

Definition and History of Salads

"Salad freshens without enfeebling and fortifies without irritating."

—*Jean-Anthelme Brillat–Savarin, 18th century food writer*

Salads are dishes that are usually served cold, made of green leafy vegetables, sometimes combined with other vegetables and fruits, meats, poultry, seafood, eggs, or nuts, with dressing. That last part is important. Traditionally, salad has a **dressing**—that is, a liquid or thickened liquid usually consisting of a fat, other liquids such as vinegar, and seasonings and flavorings. Naturally, as with so many food items, there are exceptions to these definitions, but they are a start.

As with so many categories of food, salad can be traced back to the beginning of written history. It appears from hieroglyphics that Egyptians enjoyed eating mixed greens as early as 2500 BCE. The Greeks advanced the art of salad making, mixing various greens with oil, vinegar, salt, and herbs. The Romans called such a dish *herba salata*, meaning "salted greens," giving us our modern word *salad*.

Salads were popular in England in the 1400s. In the 18th century, King Louis XIV of France was fond of salad dressed with violets. Salads were also popular in the early United States. Thomas Jefferson reportedly enjoyed salads of lettuce, sorrel, endive, and watercress.

Strangely, in the mid 20th century, fresh greens became unpopular in the United States. After World War II, people were convinced by marketers that convenience was a priority and that fresh greens were old-fashioned. They began to eat "modern" canned and frozen vegetables. In addition, the gelatin salad became a culinary staple of the 1950s.

However, things have changed today. Salads made of fresh greens and zesty dressings are more popular than ever the world over, from the salad Niçoise (nee-SWAHZ, greens with tuna and olives) of France, to the *selata* of Ethiopia, to the *tabbouleh* (tuh-BOO-lay, parsley and olive oil with bulghur wheat) of Lebanon, and the lime-and-ginger-dressed *nam sod* of Thailand (Fig. 8-1).

Salad Elements

"You don't have to cook fancy or complicated masterpieces, just good food from fresh ingredients."

—Julia Child

The components of the basic salad are simple: chopped lettuce with dressing. Beyond that, the possibilities multiply with each added category of ingredient. The characteristics of each element enhance the others: cold, crispy, salty, sweet, crunchy, creamy, fragrant, tangy, bitter. The combinations are endless.

Parts of a Salad

When a salad is created in a foodservice establishment, the elements are assembled in four basic structural parts: the **base**, usually dressed green leaves; the **body**, the main part of the salad; the **garnish**, any interesting item to increase visual impact; and the **dressing**.

FIGURE 8-1   Thai nam sod is a delicious, low-fat salad made with ground pork or poultry served warm on cold lettuce.

Categories of Salad Ingredients

The following is a list of the general categories of salad ingredients, with a few examples of each:

- Greens (cabbage, lettuce)
- Herbs (basil, cilantro, mint, parsley)
- Vegetables (onions, celery, carrots, tomatoes, mushrooms)
- Starches (potatoes, rice, pasta)
- Fruits and nuts (apples, raisins, peaches, bananas, apricots, peanuts, walnuts)
- Cheese (Parmesan, mozzarella, cheddar)
- Hard-boiled eggs (sliced or chopped)
- Meats (rare roast beef, diced ham, crispy bacon)
- Poultry (shredded chicken or diced turkey)
- Seafood (tuna, crab, shrimp, lobster)

Regional Salad Ingredients

Let's now take a tour of the salad world and look at some examples of the specific ingredients you may find in various regions. Naturally, any of the ingredients mentioned might be found in restaurants in any nation. This list is intended to give you an idea of the character of salads in various areas.

Eastern Asia

- **Bamboo shoots**—crisp cream-colored baby stalks of the bamboo plant
- **Black sesame seeds**—dark toasted seeds used as a garnish in Japan
- **Bok choy**—from southern China, a member of the cabbage family with long white stalks and somewhat heavy dark green leaves; the baby version is often preferred for salads
- **Banana blossoms**—the flowers of the banana plant, tender and somewhat bitter
- **Durian**—large, spiky fruit; notorious for its objectionable odor; sweet flavor, custardy texture
- **Green papaya**—Unripened flesh of the papaya, a large pear-shaped tropical fruit; delicate, distinctive flavor
- **Kim chee**—spicy pickled cabbage of Korea
- **Mango**—large, sweet, pine-scented fruit; used in mangoes with sticky rice, a Thai dessert salad
- **Noodles**—made from wheat flour, rice flour, or buckwheat; used in Filipino **pancit** (PAHN-seet, noodle) salad
- **Rice**—used hot or cold in salads, including basmati rice, sticky rice, and jasmine rice
- **Tofu**—soybean curd, very mild in flavor, used for appearance, texture, and protein
- **Water chestnuts**—white, crunchy, juicy tubers of southeast Asia

Europe

- **Arugula** (uh-ROO-guh-luh)—peppery, aromatic green; usually associated with Italian salads
- **Basil**—herb with several varieties; most varieties have large, soft, shiny green leaves; flavor like licorice or cloves; especially used in Italian salads
- **Beets**—dark-red edible root; popular in salads in Eastern Europe
- **Capers**—pickled buds of a Mediterranean shrub; often used as a garnish for salads
- **Celeriac** (suh-LEH-ree-ak)—root of a type of celery plant; grated and used in salads, especially in Germany; also called *celery root*
- **Feta** (FEH-tuh) **cheese**—a white, crumbly, salty sheep's milk cheese; used in salads, especially in Greece

- **Fresh mozzarella**—a variety of mozzarella cheese that is packed in water, with a soft, moist texture and a very delicate flavor; plays a key role in Italy's *insalata Caprese* (kah-PRAY-zay), a simple salad of tomato, basil, mozzarella, and olive oil

- **Olives**—olives used in salads in Mediterranean Europe range from the fruity, pale **kalamata** olives, oval and about an inch long, to small, wrinkly **oil-cured** olives, black and very rich

- **Parmigiano–Reggiano** (PAR-muh-JAH-noh rej-ee-AH-noh)—hard, spicy cheese that's often grated on salads

- **Truffles**—underground fungus of France and Italy, white or black, strong earthy flavor, very expensive

The Cheese King

Parmigiano–Reggiano is named for the two towns in the region where it's produced in northern Italy: Parma and Reggio. Some, especially one well-known TV chef, believe its versatility and popularity earn it the title "King of Cheeses."

Do not confuse Parmigiano–Reggiano with the generic "Parmesan" cheese made elsewhere. The real thing from Italy is vastly superior and more complex than the processed domestic stuff you get in supermarkets.

United States and Canada

- **Collard greens**—variety of cabbage that grows atop long stems

- **Dandelion greens**—normally considered a weed; smaller leaves are tender and tangy

- **Fiddlehead fern**—attractive, tightly coiled fronds, similar to the neck of a violin; tastes somewhat like asparagus; found in the northern United States and Canada

- **Poke**—a wild green, not grown commercially; also called *pokeweed* and *poke salat*

- **Gelatin**—clear, jellylike extract of animal bones and hides; with sugar and fruit flavoring added, very popular for dessert salads in the United States; used for molded savory **aspic salads** in some cuisines

Latin America and the Caribbean

- **Chayote** (chy-YO-tay)—pear-shaped, bland, pale green fruit, somewhat like a squash, with a single; large seed; called *mirliton* in the southern United States and *chuchu* in Brazil

- **Callaloo**—spinach-style green of the Caribbean
- **Cilantro**—lacy, green-leafed herb; tangy, fresh flavor; used in South American and Mexican cuisines
- **Avocado**—pear-shaped, dark-green savory fruit with rich, pale-green flesh
- **Hearts of palm**—the tender core of the stem of the cabbage palm tree; pale, cream color, delicate flavor
- **Ackee**—fruit of African origin; resembles a cherry, bright red with white flesh
- **Ugli** (UHG-lee)—large citrus fruit, believed to be a cross between a grapefruit and a tangerine

Africa and the Middle East

- **Peanuts**—legume often used whole, chopped, or grated as a garnish for salads
- **Bulghur**—cracked wheat, cooked, dried, and ground into granules
- **Couscous** (KOOS-koos)—tiny granular pasta
- **Garbanzos**—beige seed the size of a large pea, nutty flavor, also called *chickpea*
- **Mint**—a refreshing, surprising green to include in salads; in the Middle East, mint is added to tabbouleh (Fig. 8-2).

FIGURE 8-2 Made with bulgur wheat, parsley, mint, tomatoes, and olive oil, tabbouleh is standard fare in Middle Eastern restaurants.

The Truth about Peanuts

Originally thought to have come from Africa, the modern peanut is actually native to South America. (There are some accounts that 100,000-year-old fossilized peanuts have been found in China, but the jury is still out on that.) In the 1500s, Portuguese explorers took the peanut from the New World to Africa, where it quickly became very popular. From there, it was taken to the United States during the slave era and planted in the South, where they called it the *goober*, from the African Kimbundu word *nguba*. Today, the peanut is beloved from Thailand to Texas, from Indonesia to Indiana.

Universal Greens

The following greens, although originally found in perhaps one region of the world, may now be found universally in salads worldwide.

Lettuces

Lettuces are the most popular ingredients for salads. They add interesting textures and are nearly universally accepted by diners.

- **Iceberg**—the number one salad ingredient; mild flavor; provides a pleasingly cool, crisp quality
- **Boston**—delicate, buttery lettuce; small head
- **Bibb**—smaller, more delicate than Boston lettuce
- **Romaine**—rather dark green lettuce with a loose, long head and coarse texture; essential ingredient for Caesar salad (Fig. 8-3)
- **Mesclun** (MESS-kloon)—mixture of baby lettuces added to a salad for eye appeal (Note: Many people mispronounce this MESS-kuh-lin, but that's an illegal drug.)

Cabbages

Cabbages are sweeter and stronger flavored than lettuces, and are used especially in classic coleslaw and in Asian salads (Fig. 8-4).

- **Green**—large, compact head; pale-green color
- **Red**—large, compact head; dark-red to purple color
- **Chinese** or **napa**—cabbage with a long, narrow, pale-green head

FIGURE 8-3   Caesar salad is classically made with romaine lettuce.

Bitter Greens

Except for spinach, bitter greens are not normally used alone as an entire salad, but rather are used to add spiciness, texture, and color as part of a medley of greens. Most bitter greens are members of the endive family:

- **Belgian endive**—small, long, pale yellowish head
- **Escarole**—endive with thick, wide, rather chewy leaves
- **Chicory** (CHIK-uh-ree)—endive with curly, firm leaves
- **Friseé** (frih-ZAY)—a tender, pale-yellow version of chicory with delicate leaves
- **Radicchio** (rah-DEE-kee-oh)—endive with red leaves and white ribs
- **Spinach**—mildly bitter vegetable with dark-green leaves and narrow stems

Varieties of Salads

Salads are very versatile. They can be served as a first course, as a main dish, as a side dish, or, even as a dessert. In this section, we'll look at some typical salads in each of these categories. We'll also have a look at salads that use cooked ingredients.

FIGURE 8-4   Multicolored cabbage lends visual interest to Asian salads.

First-Course Salads

If you open a meal with a salad, you want it to excite diners' palates without ruining their appetites. You want to ensure that your salads are not too filling, but still satisfying and interesting. To do this, you need to exploit three elements that will whet their hunger: flavor, texture, and appearance.

The flavor of a first-course salad should be zesty. Two European cheeses serve this purpose nicely. Both Parmigiano–Reggiano, used in Caesar salad, and feta, a standard ingredient in Greek salads, are sharp and tangy, and are perfect to begin the meal on the right note. In addition, a small amount of meat, such as ham or prosciutto, or seafood, such as shrimp or crab, add an interesting savory flavor.

A first-course salad should include a variety of textures. As we said in Chapter 5, textures are important visually as well as on the tongue.

There needs to be a crispy element in a first-course salad, hopefully provided by the greens. **Croutons** (toasted, seasoned bread cubes) also fill this niche. There might also be something smooth, like olives, and something moist, like orange sections, kiwi fruit, or

FIGURE 8-5   Salad bars are a popular way to offer a first-course salad.

tomatoes. A meaty texture is also appealing, but don't overdo the meat. You don't want the salad to be too filling. To add a meat-type texture, you don't really even need meat. Sautéed mushrooms, for example, have a rather meaty "mouth feel."

Appearance, of course, is crucial in a first course. It sets the tone for the whole meal. It's your food's first impression to the customer. Make the ingredients colorful and arrange them artistically. (This is true when serving any type of salad.)

Of course, today, the first-course salad is often delivered in the form of a salad bar (Fig. 8-5). In such circumstances, the pantry chef has little control over the plated appearance or quantity of the food, because the customers serve themselves. But, the chef does have certain responsibilities with regard to the salad bar itself:

- Offer a varied selection of clearly labeled salad ingredients and dressings.

- Make certain the ingredients are well stocked, and kept fresh and attractive throughout the hours of service.

- Ensure that the salad bar is kept clean and tidy, and that any spills are cleaned up immediately.

- Keep potentially hazardous foods out of the FDZ throughout service.

- Use plates and serving utensils that will help control portion size.

- Keep foods protected (with sneeze guards, for example) according to applicable health codes.

Main-Dish Salads

Most one-dish meals are in the form of something cooked in a pot or wok, such as New England boiled dinner, French cassoulet, or Chinese kung pao chicken. However, a main-dish salad is another way to provide a satisfying one-dish meal, with the advantage of it being healthier and lighter.

Salads can actually be more exciting than the normal starch–veggie–meat entrée. They can allow a more artistic use of ingredients and color, as well as a greater variety of flavors and textures.

Above all, the main-dish salad brings one thing to mind: protein. Customers (except for the vegans) rarely expect to eat a main-course salad that is all greens, fruits, and vegetables. The expectation is that there will be, on such a salad, a significant portion of something like broiled chicken breast, sliced beef, or grilled salmon.

The international array of potential components available today offers an exciting opportunity for the chef to exercise creativity in the creation of "the big salad."

Side-Dish Salads

Using a salad as a side dish simply requires common sense on the part of the chef. Obviously, the salad should not dominate the entrée plate with regard to flavor or appearance. It should not be too heavy. Keep it simple and let it harmonize with the other components of the meal, as you would any other side dish.

Coleslaw and potato salad are undoubtedly the most common side salads used in the United States, but small, tossed "dinner" salads are often seen. Fruit salads should be avoided as side dishes; they are too sweet to be served with most entrées.

Cooked Salads

Cooked salads are salads that contain cooked ingredients, such as chicken or potatoes. These ingredients are normally served chilled, but sometimes are served warm, as in German potato salad and Thai nam sod.

A main concern with regard to cooked salads is avoiding contamination. The cooked ingredients and the finished salad must be kept out of the FDZ until service.

A common type of cooked salad is the **bound salad**—that is, a salad in which all the component ingredients are bound with a heavy dressing such as mayonnaise, so that it holds together when it is scooped onto the plate. Tuna, egg, chicken, ham, and potato salads are examples of bound salads in the United States. *Salade à la Russe* is a famous bound salad of various vegetables that was created by a French chef working in Czarist Russia in the 1880s. See recipe on the *Culinary Creation* CD-ROM.

Tokyo's Mayo Clinics?

Mayonnaise is very popular in Japan. There are actually mayonnaise restaurants in Tokyo where every food item, including pizza, uses the dressing prominently. Japanese mayonnaise tends to be creamier than the Western version.

Dessert Salads

Dessert salads tend to be sweeter and to utilize more fruit than salads served during other parts of the meal. Dessert salads also often contain sweet gelatin and nuts, and may be topped with sweetened whipped cream.

In Italy, fruit dessert salads are often dressed with balsamic vinegar. This is a surprisingly effective way to enhance the flavors of fruits like melons or strawberries.

One very satisfying dessert salad comes from Thailand: hot, sweet sticky rice with cold mango, topped with sweet coconut sauce. The contrast between the hot rice and the cold mango is similar to eating a hot fudge sundae.

Dressings

A good dressing must harmonize with and highlight the flavors of your salad, without dominating. The two basic types of dressing are vinaigrette and creamy.

Vinaigrette Dressings

Vinaigrette (VIN-uh-GRET) **dressings**, also called *vinegar-and-oil dressings*, are mixtures of vinegar, oil, and other flavorings and seasonings. The normal ratio of oil to vinegar in a vinaigrette is 3:1, but this may vary according to taste.

Vinaigrettes are **temporary emulsions**. This means that the oil and vinegar do not form a permanent mixture, like mayonnaise, but separate after a short period of time. However, the dressing is applied to the salad before the ingredients separate.

The oil used may have a relatively bland flavor or a stronger flavor, depending on the type of salad. **Bland oils** include canola, corn, soybean, and cottonseed. **Strong-flavored oils** include **olive oil**, a greenish, fruity oil that should only be used when its distinctive flavor is applicable and desirable, not for general purposes; and **toasted sesame** (SESS-uh-mee) **oil**, an aromatic Asian oil with a very strong, toasted, nutty flavor that should be used only as a flavoring in very small amounts, mixed with other oils.

Infused oils may also be used. These are oils to which flavorings such as basil, rosemary, or truffle have been added to provide an enhanced flavor.

Balsamic Vinegar

Balsamic vinegar is produced in Modena, Italy. It begins its life as red Trebbiano grape juice, but it is allowed to ripen and evaporate in barrels of oak, ash, cherry, chestnut, and mulberry wood for up to a hundred years. As it ages, balsamic vinegar becomes more intense, sweet, and syrupy. The best vinegars, designated ABTM (*Aceto Balsamico Tradizionale di Modena*), are sold in a distinctive bottle (Fig. 8-6) modeled by the designer of the Ferrari automobile. The oldest vinegars can sell for hundreds of dollars per ounce.

Less expensive, younger balsamics are more often used in the foodservice industry. These may be intensified and thickened to approximate the expensive stuff by reducing them in a pan to about half the original volume. (Of course, by reducing the volume, you increase the cost.)

FIGURE 8-6   ABTM balsamic vinegar is packaged in this distinctive "Ferrari" bottle.

Vinegar is an acetic acid solution made by fermenting fruit or grains. The vinegar used in a vinaigrette may be **white**, with the most neutral flavor; **cider**, with a mild apple flavor; **white or red wine**, with mild wine overtones; **balsamic vinegar**; or **infused vinegars** that have added ingredients like herbs or fruit to enhance their flavor. Lemon juice may be substituted for part or all of the vinegar to instill a citrusy flavor.

Basically, vinaigrettes are prepared by simply combining the ingredients and beating or shaking them together vigorously until a fairly uniform mixture is achieved. Examples of vinaigrettes include basic French dressing, Italian dressing, and herb vinaigrette.

Creamy Dressings

Creamy dressings are normally based on mayonnaise, but may also be based on, or combined with, yogurt, whipped cream, or sour cream. The same oils and vinegars may be used in creamy dressings as described with vinaigrettes. Most creamy dressings are permanent emulsions. It is fairly simple to turn a vinaigrette into a permanent emulsion by adding a raw egg yolk to the mixture to keep the oil and vinegar from separating.

Pasteurized Eggs

Salmonella **is found inside a very few eggs, about 1 in 20,000. Furthermore,** *Salmonella* **bacteria are killed in the stomachs of healthy people who have normal amounts of stomach acid. However, those with less stomach acid—the very young and the elderly—are at risk from salmonella in raw eggs. Therefore, for absolute safety, when serving foods containing raw eggs, use pasteurized eggs—that is, eggs that have been heated briefly to kill bacteria, but not cooked. Pasteurized eggs are available from food suppliers.**

Examples of creamy dressings include ranch, thousand island, Caesar, and bleu cheese. See the recipes for dressings on the *Culinary Creation* CD-ROM for more information.

Asian Dressings

Asian salad dressings tend to rely on flavor, rather than fat, for richness. Typical liquids used in these dressings are soy sauce, fish sauce, rice wine vinegar, and citrus juice (lime, lemon, orange). For flavorings, grated fresh ginger, pepper flakes, cilantro, mint, basil, or garlic are often used. Although they hold their own with any dressings, Asian dressings are especially at home in the low-fat, low-calorie section of your menu.

Salad Guidelines

Use the following *general* guidelines when creating salads.

- Store greens in a refrigerator in a container with holes to allow for air circulation. Make sure the greens are well chilled and crisp before service.

- Use greens that are fresh, bright, crisp, attractive, and free of rust. Just one spot of rust on a lettuce leaf can mar a salad's appeal. Sort the greens if necessary to eliminate unattractive greens.

- Make sure the greens are washed and well drained. There are commercial-grade salad spinners that are very good at ensuring the washed greens are moisture free.

- To enhance their flavor, toast nuts and seeds in a 325°F (165°C) oven before adding them to a salad.

- Bring cheeses to room temperature before adding them to a salad.

- Wash fruits and vegetables before use.

- If using fruits or vegetables that brown on exposure to air, rinse them in water with acid (citrus juice or vinegar) added. Such items include apples, avocados, eggplant, peaches, pears, and potatoes.

- Cut items neatly into bite-size pieces.

- Use cold plates (for cold salads).

- When plating, try to make the salad or garnish stand high above the plate. This adds drama to the presentation.

- Add the dressing only when the salad is ready to be served; otherwise, the greens will become limp.

Summary and Conclusion

Although they are usually not a focal point of a meal in most modern Western dining rooms, salads are an ancient art form that date back many millennia. Furthermore, each region of the world has its favorite salad ingredients. It is important that the modern chef be acquainted with the various ingredients available.

A versatile element, the salad may be served as any course, from appetizer, to main dish, to dessert. Furthermore, it may include ingredients from any of the foods groups. The chef should take care to create salads only with the freshest ingredients and to make them attractive and colorful.

Selected Terms for Review

Arugula
Avocado
Balsamic vinegar
Bok choy
Bound salad
Cilantro
Crouton
Dressing
Endive
Feta
Garbanzo
Iceberg lettuce
Mesclun
Parmigiano–Reggiano
Pasteurized
Radicchio
Salad
Tofu
Truffle
Vinaigrette

Review Questions

1. What is a salad? What is a dressing? Why might it be difficult to define the two terms precisely?

2. Which of the following is not one of the four parts of a salad?

   a. Garnish

   b. Base

   c. Spread

   d. Body

3. Name four categories of salad ingredients.

4. Match the ingredients in the first column with the area of the world where they are most commonly used as a salad ingredient.

    ____a. Bok choy   1. United States and Canada

    ____b. Truffles   2. Eastern Asia

    ____c. Tofu   3. South America and the Caribbean

    ____d. Cilantro   4. Africa and the Middle East

    ____e. Garbanzos

    ____f. Couscous

5. You want to make a mixed salad of escarole, Belgian endive, and chicory, only. Would that combination probably make a desirable salad? Why or why not?

6. The two most common side salads in the United States are _____ and _____.

7. Which of the following is not a chef's responsibility with regard to a salad bar?

a. Make sure the salads are plated attractively.

b. Keep foods protected according to local health codes.

c. Ensure the salad bar is tidy.

d. Ensure the salad bar is well stocked with fresh ingredients.

8. True or false? Customers expect that a main-dish salad will have a significant portion of protein.

9. Name two ingredients that might be found in a dessert salad that would not be common in other types of salads.

10. Name two vinegars that may be used to add flavor to a vinaigrette. What ingredient may be used in place of vinegar?

11. Describe the difference between temporary and permanent emulsions. What ingredient may be added to a temporary emulsion to make it permanent?

12. Distinguish between temporary emulsions and permanent emulsions.

13. True or false? Asian-style dressing are very high fat because of their high oil content.

14. Describe the guidelines to follow when creating a salad.

15. True or false? Dressing should be added to all the salads before the restaurant opens, to save time later when it's busy.

16. Describe your own "perfect" salad.

Suggested Readings/Web Sites to Visit

Balsamico di Modena. *Ottavia's Suitcase.* Available at www.ottavia.com/vinegar_consortia.html

Blakemore, K. (1994). *50 Ways with Salads.* New York: Crescent.

Brennan, G. (2001). *Williams-Sonoma Salad.* New York: Simon and Schuster.

History of the Peanut. *Texoma Peanut Inn Web site:* www.texomapeanut.com/inn/peanut%20history.htm

Salads. South America for Visitors: gosouthamerica.about.com/od/salads

Schlesinger, C., Willoughby, J. (1996). *Lettuce in Your Kitchen.* New York: William Morrow.

Schwartz, L. (1992). *Salads.* New York: HarperCollins.

Serbe, D. F., Moore, E., Trimmer, J. Salads and Salad Dressings. *In Mama's Kitchen.* Available at www.inmamaskitchen.com/FOOD_IS_ART_II/food_history_and_facts/salads_and_dressings.html

Creating with Meats

Learning Objectives

By the end of the chapter, you should be able to

1. Discuss the history of meats and meat consumption around the world

2. Define primal cuts and name the primal cuts of each of the four major meat animals

3. Name the major fabricated cuts obtained from each of the primal cuts

4. Discuss the difference between meat inspection and meat-quality grading

5. Name and define the major quality grades of beef, lamb, pork, and veal

6. Name the major components of meat

7. Define muscle and connective tissue

8. Define the different types of fat

9. Discuss aging of meat and why it's necessary

10. Name the lengths of time various types of meat can be stored while refrigerated or frozen

11. Define the IMPS and how it helps the process of purchasing meats in the United States

12. Discuss when to use high temperatures or low temperatures to cook meat

13. Discuss when to use moist heat or dry heat

14. Discuss how to tell when a piece of meat is done to order and discuss carryover

15. Discuss pathogens in meats

16. Define offal and describe some of the more popular types of offal in the foodservice industry

Chapter Outline

Meat: Past and Present

Types and Cuts of Meat

"My favorite animal is steak."

—*Fran Lebowitz, author, humorist*

All the arguments about the benefits of a vegetarian lifestyle aside, people, especially in the Western world, want meat. More often than not, when folks go to a restaurant, they

FIGURE 9-1   Beef tenderloin is a flavorful and very tender cut.

desire animal tissue. Meat's a best seller, number one at the box office. Porterhouse steak, *carne asada*, sweet 'n' sour pork, barbecued ribs, *osso buco*—people love to eat the flesh of red-blooded animals (Fig. 9-1). As a chef, or as the manager of a foodservice establishment, you have to know how to deliver what they want. You must understand not only how to cook the various cuts and types of meats, but how to store them, how to buy them, and how to cut them.

Although most animals have muscle tissue, the term *meat* in foodservice means the muscle tissue of mammals. This chapter introduces the four major types of meat served in the modern foodservice establishment. It discusses the various cuts of meat, the components of meat, and how to store and cook the tender cuts as well as the tough cuts.

Meat: Past and Present

Humans have eaten their fellow mammals as far back as *Homo erectus*, the version of humans that came immediately before *Homo sapiens* (us). Bones have been found around the cooking fires of primitive peoples that lived tens of thousands of years ago. The great cave paintings at Lascaux, France, depict animals that were hunted for food by the early humans of 17,000 years ago. There are not only pictures of deer and boars (pigs), but also beasts that bear a striking resemblance to Texas longhorn cattle. However, as far as can be determined, none of the animals of that era had yet been domesticated—that is, tamed to live with humans.

The sheep was probably the first animal to be domesticated, in the Middle East, about 11,000 years ago. A little while later, the Chinese domesticated the pig from wild boars.

A few thousand years after that, about 8000 years ago, people of Mesopotamia (Iraq) managed to tame cattle, which was not an easy task, because wild cattle are extremely ferocious and powerful. From those beginnings, domesticated food animals spread worldwide.

Pork was by far the favorite meat of the ancients, except for the Hebrews, who forbade its consumption (as they, along with the Muslims, still do). Everyone from the Greeks to the Romans to the Chinese considered pork to be *the* food to be served at a banquet. Our old friend Apicius writes of serving whole roast pigs at Roman banquets, stuffed with small birds, sausages, dates, and eggs.

 ## The Meat of the Subject

A thousand years ago, the English word *meat* was used to mean any food. There were only two categories of consumables: meat and drink. It wasn't until the 1300s that the word *meat* began to be used exclusively for animal products. Even today, though, we still talk about "nut meats" or "coconut meat." This is a holdover from the original meaning of the word ten centuries ago.

In the Middle Ages, before Columbus' voyage to the New World, the world was largely vegetarian, more for reasons of poverty than by choice. Of all the continents, only Europe consumed a significant amount of meat. However, as the centuries passed, even the Europeans had to cut back on meat, because of their growing population and the decrease in grazing land.

The settlers in the American colonies had no such problem, however. When they first arrived, there were as many deer as they could eat, and later they made use of the square miles of open land for pasturing domesticated cattle and sheep. The popularity of meat in the United States has continued to the present day, largely because of the abundance of wide-open spaces for grazing, making possible relatively low prices.

Today, more meat is being produced worldwide than at any time in the history of the world. The United States, China, Brazil, and the nations of the European Economic Union consume more than 60% of the world's beef and more than 80% of the world's pork. The United States leads the pack, downing 130 pounds (54 kg) of beef, pork, veal, and lamb per person in 2004. India, Indonesia, Pakistan, Bangladesh, and Nigeria eat the least meat, less than 11 pounds (5 kg) per person. (Statistics from Iowa State University Department of Economics.) In Asian and African cuisines, meat tends to be used as one ingredient among many in a dish, whereas in the Americas and Europe, meat is often a stand-alone entrée, such as a steak or roast, served with side dishes.

Types and Cuts of Meat

The four major types of meat served in a modern foodservice organization are beef, pork, lamb, and veal. Meat cuts are divided into two general categories: primal cuts and fabricated cuts. **Primal cuts** are the large pieces into which the **carcass**, the whole animal (minus certain parts that we'll discuss under each of the following topics), is divided. **Fabricated cuts** are the smaller pieces the diner consumes (steaks, chops, roasts, and so on).

Meat Inspection and Grading

Meat inspection is the examination of meat for wholesomeness, ensuring it's free of diseases and able to be consumed by humans. In the United States, this inspection is performed and the meat is stamped by the United States Department of Agriculture (USDA; Fig. 9-2). In the United States and in the major meat-producing nations, meat inspection is required by law. Furthermore, in this era of economically emerging nations, work is being done on establishing international standards for meat inspection.

Meat inspection does not determine the quality of the meat (flavor, tenderness, and so on). These factors are determined by **meat-quality grading**, again, performed in the United States by the USDA. Graded meat is stamped with the proper stamp (Fig. 9-3).

FIGURE 9-2 USDA meat inspection stamps.

FIGURE 9-3 USDA meat grade stamps.

Meat grading is not required. The criteria for the various meat grades are discussed in the following sections.

Beef

"Beef is the soul of cooking."

—*Chef Marie-Antoine Carême, 1784–1833*

A **beef carcass** is the whole animal without the head, feet, skin, and entrails. The carcass is cut down the spine into two **sides** of beef. These are then cut between the 12th and 13th ribs into the **forequarter** and **hindquarter**. These are then cut into primal cuts (Fig. 9-4).

Beef Words

There is a popular legend that the sirloin got its name because King Henry VIII became so enthusiastic at one meal about the excellent meat that he took out his sword and knighted it, dubbing it "Sir Loin." It's a funny story, but it isn't true. The word *sirloin* actually comes from a French word meaning "over loin."

The word *steak* comes from a Scandinavian word, *steikja*, meaning "to cook on a stick," referring to the fact that chunks of meat were often impaled on a wooden stick and cooked over an open fire.

Beef Fabricated Cuts

Table 9-1 lists the major fabricated cuts that are created from the beef primal cuts.

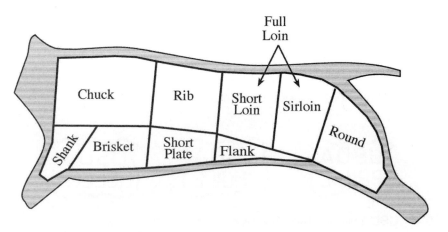

FIGURE 9-4   Beef primal cuts.

TABLE 9-1

Beef Fabricated Cuts

Primal Cut	Typical Fabricated Cuts
Chuck	• Clod (a subprimal cut, further cut into steaks and roasts)
	• Flatiron (top blade chuck steak)
	• Ground chuck
	• Stew meat
	• Cube steak
	• Chuck short ribs
Rib	• Standing rib roast (prime rib)
	• Ribeye roast
	• Rib steak
	• Ribeye steak
	• Short ribs
Short Loin	• T-bone steak
	• Porterhouse steak
	• Short tenderloin
	• Strip loin (New York strip)
Sirloin	• Top sirloin
	• Bottom sirloin
	• Tri-tip
Round	• Sirloin tip (knuckle)
	• Bottom round
	• Top round
	• Rump
	• Eye of round
Flank	• Flank steak
	• London broil
	• Stew meat
Short Plate	• Short ribs
	• Stew meat
	• Ground beef
Brisket	• Boneless brisket
	• Corned beef brisket
Shank	• Stew meat
	• Ground beef

Beef-Quality Grades

The USDA grades of beef quality are

- **USDA Prime**—highest quality, most tender, juicy, flavorful; also most expensive
- **USDA Choice**—most popular quality, very tender, juicy, flavorful
- **USDA Select**—very lean quality, tender, not as juicy or flavorful
- **USDA Standard, Commercial, Utility, Cutter, Canner**—quality only suitable for canning and processed foods; not normally used in foodservice

Pork

> "I place the fatted pig upon the coals. I pray what better food need man?"
>
> —*Aeschylus, Greek playwright, 525–456* BCE

A **pork carcass** is the whole animal without the head and entrails. Unlike beef, however, the skin and feet are left on the carcass. Also unlike beef, the carcass is not cut into sides but it's left whole, then cut into primal cuts (Fig. 9-5).

Pork Fabricated Cuts

Table 9-2 lists the major pork fabricated cuts that are created from the primal cuts.

Pork-Quality Grades

Pork is produced from young animals and is more uniformly tender than beef. As a result, pork is not graded for quality in the United States.

Lamb

Lamb is the meat of a sheep slaughtered before it is one year old. A **lamb carcass** is, like beef, the whole animal without the head, feet, skin, and entrails. The lamb carcass is not

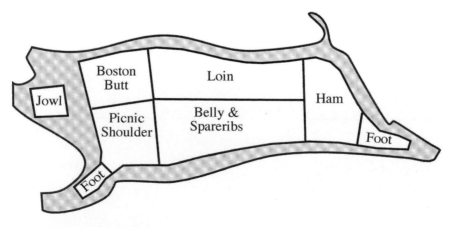

FIGURE 9-5   Pork primal cuts.

TABLE 9-2

Pork Fabricated Cuts

Primal Cut	Typical Fabricated Cuts
Boston butt	• Daisy ham
	• Shoulder roast
	• Butt steak
	• Ground pork
Loin	• Chops
	• Canadian bacon
	• Loin roast
	• Country-style ribs
Ham	• Ham steaks
	• Smoked ham
	• Fresh ham
Foot	• Pig's feet
Belly	• Bacon
Spareribs	• Spareribs
Picnic shoulder	• Fresh picnic ham
	• Smoked picnic ham
	• Hocks
	• Ground pork
Jowl	• Smoked Jowl

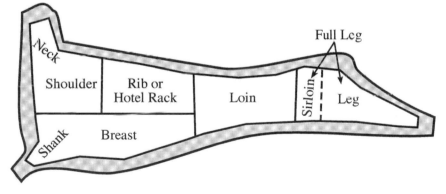

FIGURE 9-6   Lamb primal cuts.

cut into sides, however. Instead, the carcass is cut between the 12th and 13th ribs (or after the 13th rib, depending on the customer's wishes) into the **foresaddle** and **hindsaddle**. These are then cut into primal cuts (Fig. 9-6).

Lamb Fabricated Cuts

Table 9-3 lists the major fabricated cuts that are created from the lamb primal cuts.

TABLE 9-3

Lamb Fabricated Cuts

Primal Cut	Typical Fabricated Cuts
Shoulder	• Shoulder roast
	• Shoulder chops
	• Ground lamb used in gyros (Fig. 9-7)
Rib or hotel rack	• Rib roast
	• Crown rack
	• Rib chops
Loin	• Loin roast
	• Loin chops
Leg	• Sirloin chops
	• Shank
	• Leg roast
	• Leg chops
Breast and shank	• Breast
	• Stew meat
	• Ground lamb
	• Riblets

Lamb-Quality Grades

The USDA grades of lamb quality are

- **USDA Prime**—highest quality, most tender, juicy, flavorful; also most expensive

- **USDA Choice**—most popular quality, very tender, juicy, flavorful

- **USDA Good**—very lean quality, tender, not as juicy or flavorful

- **USDA Utility, Cull**—quality only suitable for canning and processed foods; not normally used in foodservice

Veal

Veal is the meat of cattle slaughtered at an age younger than 3 months. The meat is, of course, very pink and tender as a result. A **veal carcass** is handled in a similar way to a lamb carcass. Like beef, the veal carcass is the whole animal without the head, feet, skin, and entrails. However, the carcass is not cut into sides. Instead, the carcass is cut between the 12th and 13th ribs into the **foresaddle** and **hindsaddle**. These are then cut into primal cuts, which are the same as for lamb (Fig. 9-6).

Veal Fabricated Cuts

Table 9-4 lists the major fabricated cuts that are created from the veal primal cuts.

FIGURE 9-7 **Gyros is a popular Greek lamb loaf cooked on a vertical rotisserie.**

Veal-Quality Grades

The USDA grades of veal quality are

- **USDA Prime**—highest quality, most tender, juicy, flavorful; also most expensive
- **USDA Choice**—most popular quality, very tender, juicy, flavorful
- **USDA Good**—very lean quality, tender, not as juicy or flavorful
- **USDA Standard, Utility, Cull**—quality only suitable for canning and processed foods; not normally used in foodservice

TABLE 9-4
Veal Fabricated Cuts

Primal Cut	Typical Fabricated Cuts
Shoulder	• Shoulder roast
	• Shoulder clod steak
	• Shoulder chops
	• Ground veal
Rib or hotel rack	• Rib roast
	• Rib chops
Loin	• Loin roast (saddle)
	• Loin chops
Leg	• Sirloin chops
	• Shank
	• Leg roast
	• Scaloppine (SKAL-oh-PEE-nee)
	• Shank (*osso buco*)
Breast and shank	• Breast
	• Ground veal
	• Shank (*osso buco*)

Goat Meat

With the emerging popularity of Caribbean cuisine in the United States, goat meat is being used increasingly in foodservice establishments for such dishes as Jamaican curried goat, an especially rich, succulent dish. Goat is the major source of animal protein consumed in North Africa and the Middle East.

Components of Meat

Meat is made up of essentially three building blocks: water (about 75%), protein (18–20%), and fat (3–5%). These building blocks combine to form the tissues in meat: muscle, connective tissue, and types of fat. Nutritionally, meat supplies vitamins B_6 and B_{12}, niacin, iron, phosphorus, and zinc.

Muscle and Connective Tissues

Protein is the main building block of two types of tissue: muscle fiber and connective tissue. **Muscle fiber** is made up of long, thin cells that are organized in bundles. When muscles exercise, these bundles stretch and contract.

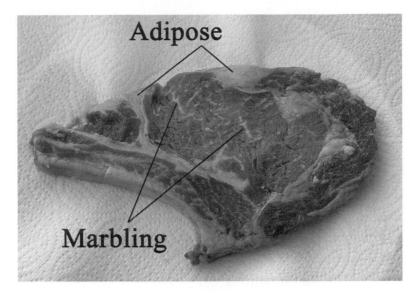

FIGURE 9-8   This ribeye steak shows examples of both adipose fat and marbling.

The more exercise a muscle gets, the tougher the piece of meat. For example, back muscles in the loin that get almost no exercise are very tender, whereas leg muscles that exercise constantly are tougher. The reason for this toughness, as we learned in Chapter 4, is another protein, **connective tissue** (collagen and elastin). Muscles that are exercised develop more connective tissues and are therefore, tougher. **Collagen** can be tenderized by long, slow cooking, whereas **elastin** must be trimmed physically.

Fat

Fat is formed in two main types in meats (Fig. 9-8). The first type is called *deposit fat* or *adipose* (ADD-ih-pohss) *tissue*. This is the fat that surrounds muscle tissue—the type of fat that you see around the edge of a steak or a pork chop. This fat can be trimmed to suit specific needs.

The second type of fat is actually distributed within muscle tissue. You can see it as white streaks in the red of the raw meat. This is called *marbling*. Marbling is a desirable component in meat, because it adds juiciness, tenderness, and flavor when the meat is cooked. The main reason the top grade of USDA Prime is assigned to a piece of beef is because of the large amount of marbling in the meat.

Historically, fat could account for as much as 20% or 30% of the weight of a piece of meat. Today, beef and pork are leaner versions of the meat people ate 50 years ago. In response to public demand for less fat, producers have actually changed their livestock feeding and management programs. Today's ranchers fatten their livestock for shorter periods of time before sale. They've even changed the genetic makeup of their breeding stock to produce consistently leaner carcasses. Also, most visible fat is trimmed off at the processing plant. Because of these changes, today's fresh pork and beef products have considerably less fat than they did just a decade ago.

 ## A Brief on Beef

The beef of Japan is recognized as the finest (and most expensive) in the world. This high-quality beef was developed by sheer luck as a result of historical quirks. Until the middle of the 19th century, a Buddhist edict banned raising cattle for food. As a result, no beef cattle were imported and Japanese cattle were isolated from other cattle of the world. In that isolation, without outside influence, one breed, the Japanese Black or wagyu (meaning "Japanese cattle") developed extraordinarily tender beef with so much marbling that it is called *shimofuri* or "fallen frost." The most famous wagyu beef is Kobe (KOH-bay).

You may have heard that wagyu cattle are fed beer and massaged. This is true. However, these factors do not directly affect the quality of the beef. The alcohol and massaging relax the cattle, because they are forced to stand still for long periods of time, to prevent the overdevelopment of connective tissues.

Aging Meats

Like cheese and wine, meat can improve with age. Because meat stiffens for a while after it is freshly slaughtered (this is called *rigor mortis*), it must be allowed to soften for 2 to 4 days before it becomes edible. The softening is caused by the very enzymes in the cells that were used to absorb protein when the animal was alive.

After the initial softening, some meats, especially beef and lamb, benefit from further **aging**, allowing the meats' natural enzymes to tenderize and flavor the meat further under controlled conditions. In beef, true "beef flavor" develops after about 11 days.

Aging can be done either **dry** (that is, storing meats unwrapped in controlled conditions) or **wet** (sealed in Cryovac® vacuum packaging). Keep in mind that *aging should only be attempted by professionals trained in the technique.* Aging meat doesn't mean just letting it rot.

Storing Meat

Meat can become inedible if it is improperly exposed to light, heat, enzymes, or pathogens. Storing meats under refrigeration does two things: (1) it slows the growth of bacteria and

TABLE 9-5
USDA Meat Storage Guidelines

Product	Refrigerated (40°F, 4°C)	Frozen (0°F, −18°C)
Bacon	1 week	1 month
Chops	3–5 days	4–6 months
Ground meats	1–2 days	3–4 months
Ham, fully cooked, whole	7 days	1–2 months
Roasts	3–5 days	4–12 months
Sausage, hard (for example, pepperoni)	2–3 weeks	1–2 months
Sausage, raw	1–2 days	1–2 months
Smoked sausage links	7 days	1–2 months
Steaks	3–5 days	6–12 months

(2) it retards the action of the meat's enzymes. In Chapter 2, we looked at the guidelines for safely storing foods as refrigerated or frozen. Table 9-5 provides the meat storage guidelines of the USDA.

Buying Meats

In the United States, there is a standardized method by which foodservice organizations may purchase cuts of meat. The **Institutional Meat Purchase Specifications (IMPS)**, also called the National Association of Meat Purveyors Specifications (NAMPS), provide a detailed, standard list by which specific meat cuts may be ordered precisely by number (for example, 405, pork shoulder, picnic). Go to www.ams.usda.gov/lsg/stand/imps.htm for a complete set of the IMPS documents.

In addition to the number and the product name, the IMPS also provides a complete list of what you, as the purchaser, should specify when ordering meat. These include the USDA grade; the state of refrigeration (frozen or refrigerated); fat limitations (surface fat thickness); portion cut weight, thickness, and shape; weight range; netting and tying; and packaging.

When deciding which cut of meat to order, make sure you take into consideration the meat fabricating capabilities of your staff and the amount of space you have to store large cuts of meat. It may be more economical for you to pay a higher price per pound for meat that has already been cut into the required portions.

When meat is delivered, make sure you cross-check it with the order form to make sure the delivery is accurate. Also, check to make certain the interior of the truck is at the proper temperature. If meat is delivered in Cryovac or similar packaging, don't open it until you are ready to use it.

Cooking Meats

See the *Culinary Creation* CD-ROM for recipes related to this topic. When cooking meats, there are three basic questions you must ask yourself:

1. Should I cook it at low temperature or high temperature?

2. Should I use moist heat or dry heat?

3. Is it done yet?

Low Temperature or High Temperature?

There are times when lower temperatures are beneficial, and times when higher temperatures are preferred. In most cases, meat cooked at lower temperatures is juicier and more tender than meat cooked at high temperatures. For example, a beef rib roast cooked slowly in the oven at a temperature of 300°F (150°C) will shrink less and retain more moisture than a roast cooked at 400°F (204°C). This is because the proteins in the roast cooked at the higher temperature will coagulate more intensely and force out more water, toughening the meat and making it drier.

Searing: The Myth That Refuses to Die

You've heard it a thousand times: "Searing meat seals in the juices." Wrong! This is a myth that seemingly will never go away. Despite the fact that eminent food scientists like Harold McGee have proved beyond any doubt that seared meat loses *more* moisture than unseared meat, many cooks and chefs still repeat the tired urban legend that searing makes meat juicier. It doesn't. Searing is good for several things, however. When performed properly, it adds flavor, color, texture, and aroma to meat, and provides bits of residue, called *fond*, that are used to flavor sauces. Just don't expect searing to make meat juicier.

However, there are exceptions to the low-heat rule. If a cook wants to **sear**, or quickly form a brown crust on the outside of a tender cut of meat (such as a steak or a chop) while leaving it rare to medium on the inside, then high temperatures are appropriate. Searing may be achieved by sautéing, broiling, or grilling.

High heat is also used for cooking meats in Asian cooking, for which the meat is cut into small bite-sized piece and stir-fried briefly over very high heat in a wok, just long enough to cook the meat without toughening it.

The ultimate high-heat cooking is Cajun **blackening**, for which a meat, poultry, or seafood item is coated in oil, crusted with seasoning and flavoring, then cooked on a dry, red-hot cast-iron skillet until it's literally blackened.

Moist Heat or Dry Heat?

As we discussed in Chapter 4, moist heat refers to cooking with water. As we learned, the types of moist heat include pressure steaming, steaming, boiling, simmering, poaching, braising, and stewing.

The tougher cuts of meat—that is, meats with more connective tissue and less fat—fare better when cooked with moist heat, because the collagen dissolves and the meat becomes more tender. The cuts of meat that benefit most from moist-heat cooking include

- The beef round, chuck, flank, brisket, plate, and shank

- The lamb and veal breast, shoulder, and shank

- The pork shoulder picnic

There is an exception to this list. London broil is a thick cut from the beef flank that is normally cooked very rare with dry heat, and is sliced very thin to minimize its chewiness.

The Tastiest Beef

Although it doesn't seem logical, and nobody knows exactly why, cuts of beef that have the most beef flavor also tend to be the toughest. Therefore, it's worth the effort for you to take the time to slow cook those less trendy cuts if you want to maximize flavor.

Again, as we learned in Chapter 4, dry-heat cooking involves cooking without water, with or without fat. Sautéing, pan frying, and deep frying all are dry-heat methods involving fat. Dry-heat cooking without fat falls into the categories of baking, roasting, grilling, griddling, and broiling. The most tender cuts of meat with the least connective tissue and the highest fat content come from the ribs and loins. These benefit most from dry-heat cooking.

Fat can be used to enhance lean meats, as well as poultry and fish, before cooking by two processes: *barding* and *larding*. **Barding** involves wrapping the piece of meat in a fatty substance (for example, bacon). **Larding** involves inserting fat inside the meat.

Is It Done Yet?

You can understand the various cuts of meat from every part of every animal, and have a full knowledge of how to season and flavor the meat, but all those things mean nothing if you don't know when meat is done the way your customer orders it. That's the most difficult part of cooking meat.

Moist-heat cooking is easy, because meats cooked with water are almost always cooked well done (except in cases like Vietnamese *pho tai*, for which the beef in the soup is served medium rare). It's hard to overcook tougher meats because you *want* the tissues to break down.

In general, pork and veal almost always tend to be cooked toward the well-done level, or at least medium well, so cooking them isn't quite such a challenge. However, when you want to cook beef and lamb to a precise degree of doneness, you have to know what you are doing. Taking the temperature of meat, preferably with a digital instant-read thermometer inserted at the thickest part, is the most precise way to check its doneness.

Keep in mind that meats, especially larger cuts like rib roasts, should be removed from the heat about 5°F or 10°F (2°–5°C) below where you want the temperature to be when you serve the meat. This is due to **carryover**—that is, an increase in temperature that occurs from the residual heat in the meat after it is removed from the heat source. In other words, the meat keeps cooking for a little while. If you take it out of the oven rare, it will be medium rare by the time you serve it.

To what temperature should you cook meat to achieve the desired doneness? Table 9-6 shows the USDA's somewhat cautious temperature doneness guidelines compared with the "real" temperatures to which meat is cooked in a commercial kitchen. You will find that the USDA temperatures produce a higher degree of doneness than the descriptions shown, often resulting in customer dissatisfaction.

TABLE 9-6

Real-World Doneness Temperatures Compared with USDA Guidelines (Beef and Lamb)

Doneness Level	Description	Real-World Temp (after carryover)	USDA Recommended Temp
Very rare	Very large, raw, cool center	125°F (52°C)	None
Rare	Large, raw, cool center	130°F (54°C)	140°F (60°C)
Medium rare	Bright-red center, a little warm	135°F (57°C)	150°F (66°C)
Medium	Rosy pink, warm center	140°F (60°C)	160°F (71°C)
Medium well	Very little pink	150°F (66°C)	170°F (77°C)
Well done	No pink	160°F (71°C)	170°F (77°C)

Pathogens

As noted in Chapter 2, trichinosis is a parasite that embeds itself in the host's muscle. Historically, this parasite was rather common in pork, and for that reason pork has always been cooked well done. However, trichinosis isn't the threat it once was. It has completely disappeared from Canadian pork and is very uncommon in pork in the United States. Besides, trichinosis is killed at 137°F (58°C), in the medium-rare range, so if you cook pork to the temperature recommended in Chapter 2, 150°F (66°C), a little pink, you will ensure that any potential worms are killed without drying out the meat.

Now, let's talk about other food-borne pathogens in meats. The inside of a solid piece of meat is virtually pathogen free, Why? Remember FAT TOM. Pathogens have no air inside the meat. So, the only bacteria on a whole piece of meat, like a steak or a roast, would be found on the few square inches of outside surface. These will be killed as soon as the outside of the meat reaches 140°F (60°C), in other words, almost immediately in a hot pan or oven. So, whether you cook the inside of the steak or roast to rare or well done, the bacteria on the outside are going to be exposed to a fatal temperature.

Ground meats are another matter. As soon as meat is ground, its surface area is increased to hundreds of square inches. Every strand of meat that comes out of the grinder is exposed to the air and the bacteria in the air. The clock begins to tick and the bacteria begin to grow. Did you ever notice that the inside of a chunk of raw hamburger is sometimes gray? That's graphic evidence of bacteria at work.

Therefore, you should be more careful with ground meat. The safest bet is always to cook ground meat until the center of the meat is outside the FDZ—that is, more than 140°F (60°C)—for a length of time before serving it. For example, exposure to a temperature of 150°F (66°C) for one minute will kill pathogens and leave the meat slightly pink and still juicy.

Offal

Before we leave this chapter, let's talk about **offal**. (It's supposed to be pronounced "AW-ful," but many chefs say "OH-ful.") These are edible parts of the animal that don't come with the carcass, such as the liver, kidney, stomach, tongue, intestine, **sweetbreads**, veal thymus gland, and heart. These are also sometimes called *variety meats*.

Although it can be argued that consumption of variety meats was originally an act of desperation by poor people who had nothing else to eat, today variety meats are considered in many cultures to be delicacies. For example, in the southern United States, chitterlings or **chitlins**, a portion of the pig's intestine, are breaded and deep fried and served with hot sauce as a delicious snack. In Florence, Italy, *trippa* (TREE-puh, **tripe** or beef stomach; Fig. 9-9) is a popular sandwich filling. In southeast Asia, tendon (connective tissue) is a common ingredient in soups. In Brazil, beef tongue is smoked and braised to

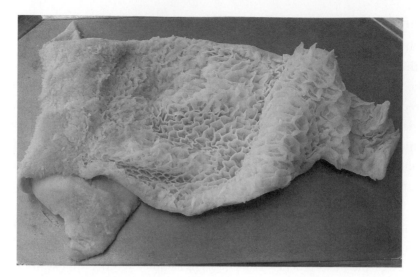

FIGURE 9-9 **Honeycomb tripe is the lining of a cow's second stomach.**

a point where it becomes one of the most succulent and delectable meats imaginable. Sweetbreads are among the more tender, delicious entrees served in fine restaurants around the world. Also, calves brains are often served with browned butter in France.

You'll find recipes for selected variety meats on the *Culinary Creation* CD-ROM. Try them, and keep an open mind. Watch that foodism!

Summary and Conclusion

Meats are the most popular items in a restaurant. As a chef, you must understand how to deliver meats to your customers that are properly purchased, stored, and cooked.

In this chapter you learned not only about the composition and structure of various types of meat, but also about primal cuts and their various fabricated cuts. You also learned about USDA grading and inspection, and about the history of meat consumption and how meats are served in various cultures around the world.

Selected Terms for Review

Adipose tissue
Aging
Carryover

Connective tissue

Fabricated cut

Fond

Marbling

Meat

Meat inspection

Meat quality grading

Primal cut

Variety meats

 ## Review Questions

1. Would the term *meat* normally be used in the foodservice industry to describe a lobster tail? Why or why not?

2. Which meat animal was last to be domesticated? Why?

3. Match the primal cut on the left with the associated fabricated cut on the right.

   ____a. Round   1. Rib chops

   ____b. Chuck   2. Daisy ham

   ____c. Hotel rack   3. Canadian bacon

   ____d. Boston butt   4. Sirloin tip

   ____e. Belly   5. Bacon

   ____f. Pork loin   6. Shoulder clod

4. True or false? The maximum age of a lamb is two years old.

5. Name the top three USDA grades for beef, lamb, veal, and pork, and define each.

6. What's the difference between a pork carcass and all other carcasses?

7. Which of the following is not a building block of meat?

   a. Water

   b. Calcium

   c. Protein

   d. Fat

8. Name the two types of connective tissue. What is the main difference between the two?

9. What type of fat surrounds muscle? What type of fat is found within muscle? Which type is desirable? Why?

10. True or false? Today's pork and beef are much leaner on average than the products of 50 years ago.

11. The Japanese cattle that are considered to produce the best beef in the world are the _____. The most famous beef from these cattle is _____ beef.

12. When meat is aged, the natural _____ are allowed to tenderize the muscle tissue.

13. Storing meat under refrigeration does two things to prevent the meat from spoiling. Name them.

14. Which of the following is not something a purchaser needs to specify when ordering meat?

    a. Degree of doneness

    b. USDA grade

    c. State of refrigeration

    d. Weight range

15. Name a cooking technique that you might use to sear meat at high temperatures.

16. The cuts of meat that benefit from moist heat cooking include

    a. Round

    b. Brisket

    c. Shank

    d. Chuck

    e. All the above

17. The most tender cuts of meat with the least connective tissue and the highest fat content come from the _____ and _____.

18. True or false? The USDA temperatures indicating degree of doneness tend to run lower than real-world temperatures.

19. Explain why pathogens tend to thrive on ground meats rather than solid pieces of meat.

20. Define offal. Name three popular types of offal.

Suggested Readings/Web Sites to Visit

Aidells, B., Kelly, D. (1998). *The Complete Meat Cookbook*. New York: Houghton Mifflin.

Appleby, P. A Global Stampede to the Meat Counter. *The Oven Newsletter*. Available at www.ivu.org/oxveg/Publications/Oven/Articles_General/wi_meat.html

China Cooperating on Food Safety. *Meat News*. Available at www.meatnews.com/index.cFm?Fuseaction=Article&artNum=6201

Epley, R. *Aging Beef*. University of Minnesota Extension Service. Available at www.extension.umn.edu/distribution/nutrition/DJ5968.html

Inspection and Grading: What's the Difference? *Food Safety and Inspection Service, USDA*. Available at www.fsis.usda.gov/Fact_Sheets/Inspection_&_Grading/index.asp

Institutional Meat Purchase Specifications. Agriculture Marketing Service Livestock and Seed Program: www.ams.usda.gov/lsg/stand/imps.htm

McGee, H. (1990). The Searing Truth. In *The Curious Cook* (pp. 13–21). New York: Macmillan.

Schlesinger, C., Willoughby, J. (2000). *How to Cook Meat*. New York: William Morrow.

Creating with Poultry

Learning Objectives

By the end of the chapter, you should be able to

1. Discuss the history of poultry

2. Discuss poultry inspection and grading

3. Name the four major kinds of poultry and the classifications of each

4. Discuss the components of poultry flesh, and the difference between "white meat" and "dark meat"

5. Name the USDA-recommended storage times for poultry

6. Truss a bird and fabricate a whole bird

7. Determine the doneness of poultry

8. Know how to use the various types of dry-heat and moist-heat cooking with regard to poultry

Chapter Outline

Poultry: Past and Present

Types of Poultry

    Poultry Inspection and Grading

    Chickens

    Turkeys

    Ducks

    Geese

    Other Kinds of Poultry

Components of Poultry

Buying Poultry

"Poultry is to the cook what canvas is to the painter."

—Jean Anthelme Brillat–Savarin

So, even 200 years ago, during the lifetime of our friend Brillat–Savarin, it was recognized that poultry, especially chicken and turkey, is an extremely versatile item. It can be prepared in hundreds of different ways, with dry heat and moist heat, with low temperatures and high temperatures, spicy or plain, and it almost never fails to satisfy the customer.

For the most part, poultry is less expensive than meats, generating a higher profit for the foodservice establishment. Poultry is also perceived as being healthier and more guilt free than meat, so, for that reason, today's health-conscious customer often prefers to order chicken or turkey instead of beef or pork. This chapter discusses the major types and varieties of poultry, as well as its history, components, inspection and grading, cooking techniques, and sanitary issues.

Poultry: Past and Present

Poultry is any domesticated bird used as food. Poultry is popular in virtually every cuisine, from the *yakitori* of Japan to the Peking duck of China, the *tandoori murgh* (tan-DOR-ee merg, roasted chicken) of India, the *doro wat* (chicken stew) of Ethiopia, the *mole poblano* (MOH-lay poh-BLAH-noh) of Mexico, and the Buffalo wings of the United States.

The four major types of poultry are chickens, turkeys, ducks, and geese. Chickens were originally domesticated about 4000 years ago in India and China. Their ancestors were the red fowl of the jungles of southeast Asia. Originally, chickens were more valued for their eggs, because the flesh of early chickens had a tendency to be tough and stringy when cooked. The ancient Greeks discovered, much to the dismay of roosters, that if you castrated a young male chicken, it resulted in more tender chicken flesh when it matured. This operation is still practiced today. The resulting bird is called a *capon* (discussed later).

The Dorking is perhaps the oldest pure breed of chicken. Julius Caesar took it with him from Italy when he invaded England about 2000 years ago. Having very tender and succulent flesh, the Dorking is the ancestor of many of the modern breeds of chicken we know today.

Chickens—Not Always Cheep

Although it's known today for being reasonably priced, chicken has only recently become inexpensive. Until World War II, chickens were affordable only to the most affluent members of society in the United States. When Herbert Hoover said he wanted "a chicken in every pot" during the Depression, that was a significant financial wish for his citizens. After the war, more efficient farming techniques made chicken the economical food it is today.

Turkeys were originally domesticated by the Aztecs from the wild turkeys that roamed the forests of North America for millions of years. In the mid 1500s, the Spanish took some of the birds back to Europe, where they were named *turkeys* by confused Europeans who thought they had come from Turkish territory. Despite the confusion, the birds became very popular in Europe.

The type of turkey consumed in the United States today, the White Holland, actually came back to the Americas after it was developed in Europe. During the past hundred years or so, domestic turkeys have been bred for one trait: to produce larger and larger breasts. It's hard to believe that the gigantic, dull-witted beast that we know today is the descendant of the lean, quick, smart wild turkey that can still be found in the forests of North America—the bird that Benjamin Franklin favored over the bald eagle to be the national symbol of the United States.

Ducks were originally domesticated in China at least 2000 years ago. The major variety of duck produced in that country throughout the centuries was the White Pekin, a large white variety with a bright orange bill (picture Donald without the sailor suit). In 1873, nine of these ducks were taken from China to New York by a sea captain who thought they were small geese. Upon arrival, to make the bird more marketable to North

Americans, the White Pekin was renamed the Long Island duck. Those original nine birds have produced millions of descendants and have became the standard domesticated breed consumed in the United States.

Geese were domesticated in ancient Egypt, China, and India. They have been domesticated in Europe for at least 3500 years. The Romans held them in high regard for their ability to act as watchdogs. In northern Europe, roast goose is still the traditional poultry served at Christmas, although the turkey has become the holiday bird of choice in many countries.

Literary Poultry Upsell

As you may recall, in Dickens' *A Christmas Carol* (set in England), the poverty-stricken Cratchit family plans to settle for an inexpensive goose for Christmas dinner, until a reformed Scrooge bestows a turkey upon them and joins them for a true holiday feast.

As mentioned in Chapter 1, in France, geese are used for the production of *foie gras* (fwah-GRAH, "fat liver"), which is created by force-feeding the bird to enlarge its liver abnormally, until the organ actually acquires the consistency of butter.

Types of Poultry

In this section, we discuss the various **classifications** (subtypes) of each **kind** (type or species) of poultry. We also talk about the inspection and grading of poultry.

Poultry Inspection and Grading

As with meat, **poultry inspection** is examined for wholesomeness, ensuring that the birds are fit for human consumption. In the United States, inspected poultry is stamped as illustrated in Figure 10-1. Poultry inspection is required by law in the United States.

Poultry quality is determined by **poultry-quality grading**, again, performed in the United States by the USDA. Graded poultry is stamped as illustrated in Figure 10-2. Poultry grading is not required by law.

In the USDA system, Grade A, is, of course, the top grade. The quality is determined by such things as the number of defects and the amount of fat and flesh. (For further information, see the *USDA Poultry Grading Manual* listed under "Suggested Readings/

FIGURE 10-1   USDA poultry inspection stamp.

FIGURE 10-2   USDA poultry grade stamp.

Web Sites to Visit" at the end of this chapter.) Grades B and C are normally used in processed foods.

Chickens

The **chicken** is the most common kind of poultry. It has very little fat, and both white and dark muscle tissue (see "Components of Poultry" later in this chapter). There are several classifications of chicken.

The **capon** we discussed briefly in the last section. It's a castrated male that grows quite large, up to 10 pounds (4.5 kg), and is usually slaughtered before 10 months of age. Capons are ideal for dry-heat cooking, especially roasting.

The **broiler–fryer** weighs up to 3.5 pounds (1.6 kg) and is about 2.5 months old. Of course, it is most suited for dry-heat cooking (that is, broiling and frying). The **roaster** is older, up to 5 months old, heavier at 4 to 5 pounds (1.8–2.3 kg), and tastier. Again, it's suited to dry-heat cooking in the oven.

The **Rock Cornish game hen** is small, usually less than 2 pounds (0.9 kg), and is suited for single servings. It's normally roasted or broiled.

The **stewing chicken**, also called a **hen** or **fowl**, is female, more than 10 months old, and heavier, up to 6 pounds (2.7 kg). It's the most flavorful chicken, but requires moist heat (simmering or braising) because of the large amount of connective tissue in the flesh. The older male chicken, called a **cock** or **rooster**, is suitable for soups and stocks.

Turkeys

"Turkey is one of the handsomest gifts the New World made to the Old World."

—*Jean Anthelme Brillat–Savarin*

Turkeys are large birds native to North America. Like chickens, turkeys are low in fat. Although they are prized for their white flesh, turkeys also have a great deal of succulent dark muscle tissue on their legs and thighs. There are just four major classifications of turkeys. **Fryer–roasters** are compact birds weighing 5 to 8 pounds (1.8–3.6 kg) that are becoming more and more popular. They are normally slaughtered at an age of less than 4 months. **Young turkeys** reach an age of 5 to 7 months and a weight of 8 to 22 pounds (3.6–10 kg). **Yearlings** reach an age of 8 to 15 months and a weight of 10 to 30 pounds (4.5–14 kg). **Old (mature) turkeys** are more than 15 months old and weigh 10 to 30 pounds (4.5–14 kg). These birds are suitable for moist-heat cooking only.

The Turkey: Bringer of Agriculture

In the folklore of the Dineh (also called *Navajo*) of the southwestern United States, a huge turkey hen delivered the first corn to humankind and taught people how to grow crops.

Ducks

Ducks may be any of various species of web-footed swimming birds with short necks and legs. Although the Long Island is the major food variety in the United States, the muscovy is also popular. Duck flesh is all dark and it has a higher fat content than chicken or turkey.

There are three major classifications of ducks. **Broiler–fryers** are 2 months old or less, and may weigh up to 4 pounds (1.8 kg). **Roasters** are up to 4 months old and weigh up to 6 pounds (2.7 kg). The **mature** duck is more than 6 months old and weighs up to 10 pounds (4.5 kg).

Confit (kon-FEE) is a popular cooking method for preparing ducks and geese. With this technique, the bird is cooked slowly until tender, then preserved in its own fat, sometimes for many weeks, intensifying its flavor. See the *Culinary Creation* CD-ROM for further information.

Geese

The **goose** is a large, long-necked, web-footed water bird. Like the duck, it has dark flesh and a high fat content. There are really only two classifications of geese.

The **young** goose is less than 6 months old and weighs up to 10 pounds (4.5 kg). The **mature** goose is more than 6 months old and may weigh as much as 16 pounds (7.3 kg). The flesh of the young goose is very rich and buttery. The flesh of the mature goose is very tough and must be cooked with moist heat.

Other Kinds of Poultry

Many other types of poultry are enjoyed around the world. The smallest is the **quail**, which is normally roasted on a spit. The **squab** is a small pigeon. The **pheasant** is a larger, meaty game bird. The domesticated descendant of the pheasant is called the **guinea** (GIN-ee). The flesh of the **ostrich**, the world's largest bird, originally from the African continent, is becoming increasingly popular and available. Ostrich is very much like beef in flavor and appearance, but is much leaner.

Components of Poultry

The components of poultry flesh are the same as meat: water (about 75%), protein (18–20%), and fat (3–5%). As with meat, the protein forms two things: muscle fiber and connective tissue. In poultry, the flesh with little connective tissue is popularly called *white meat* and the flesh with a lot of connective tissue is called *dark meat*. The dark color actually comes from stored oxygen in the muscle cells. The poultry muscle fibers that get little exercise and need less stored oxygen, like those in chicken and turkey breasts, are white meat. Body parts that get a lot of exercise and need lots of stored oxygen, like the legs and thighs, are dark.

In poultry, there is little, if any, marbling. Fat is found directly under the skin and around the internal organs.

Buying Poultry

In addition to the kind and class, described earlier in this chapter, poultry is sold according to its **style**—that is, the amount of processing it has had. In general, there is only one style of poultry sold to foodservice institutions: **ready-to-cook**—that is, dressed and eviscerated, without head and feet. Ready-to-cook birds are sold whole or in parts. When buying poultry, it's also expected that you should specify the state of refrigeration desired—that is, frozen or chilled.

As with meats, make certain you inspect the condition of the product when it arrives at your establishment, including its temperature. Make certain fresh poultry is packed in ice. Also make certain you verify the temperature of the delivery truck to make certain it is less than that of the FDZ.

TABLE 10-1
USDA Poultry Storage Guidelines

Product	Refrigerated (40°F, 4°C)	Frozen (0°F, −18°C)
Chicken, turkey, duck, or goose, whole	1–2 days	1 year
Chicken, turkey, duck, or goose, in pieces	1–2 days	9 months

Storing Poultry

As we said in Chapter 2, nearly all chicken, and much other poultry, carries *Salmonella*. Therefore, it is extremely important that you exercise good personal hygiene and avoid cross-contamination when handling poultry.

Poultry, especially fresh poultry is much more perishable than meat. Fresh poultry should be stored in ice. Table 10-1 shows the recommended storage times for poultry.

Cooking Poultry

See the *Culinary Creation* CD-ROM for recipes for cooking poultry using various techniques. This section covers the various means by which poultry may be cooked. First, though, we'll discuss trussing and how to cut up, or fabricate, poultry.

Trussing

Trussing is a means by which a whole bird may be formed into a compact package for efficient, even roasting. Trussing also makes the finished product more attractive for serving and prevents stuffing from falling out. There are many types of trussing, and each chef has his/her preferred method. See Figure 10-3 for one simple method. Alternatively, the cavities at each end may be sewn with a trussing needle, or secured with toothpicks or skewers.

Fabricating Poultry

Every culture has its preferred method of fabricating poultry—that is, cutting a bird into parts for cooking. Examples of the various methods include

- Cutting into halves
- Cutting into quarters (leg/thigh units and wing/breast units)
- Cutting into eighths (legs, thighs, wings, and breasts [or breasts in two halves with wing still attached])
- Cutting into ten pieces (with the thighs cut in half)

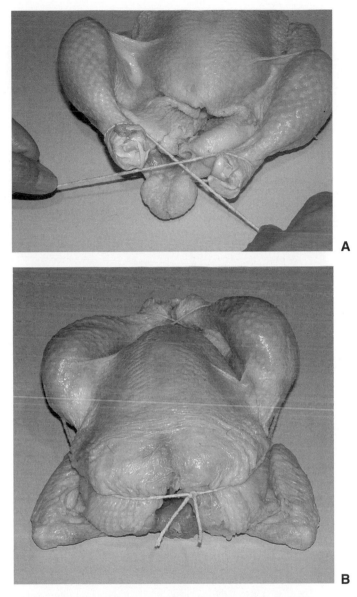

FIGURE 10-3 **(A) To truss poultry, run twine under the tail, then make a figure-eight around the ends of the legs. (B) Then run the twine along the sides and tie the ends securely in front of the opening at the neck cavity. Tuck the wing tips under the body.**

- Boning, partially or completely, and leaving the major pieces of flesh intact or cutting them into bite-size pieces

Figure 10-4 illustrates one method for a cutting a chicken into pieces. The same method may be used for any type of poultry.

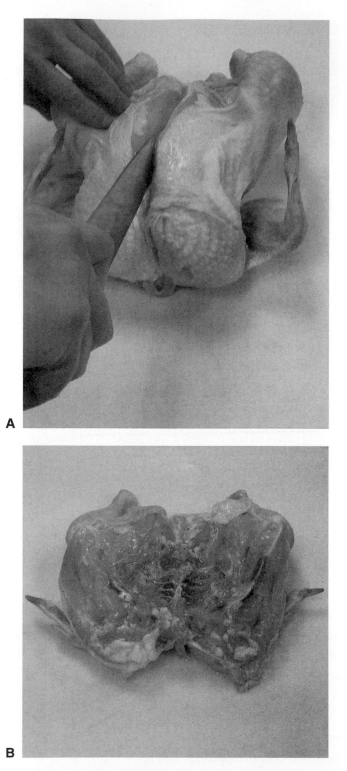

FIGURE 10-4   (A) Cut the chicken lengthwise through the breast. (B) Open up or "butterfly" the chicken and press it flat.

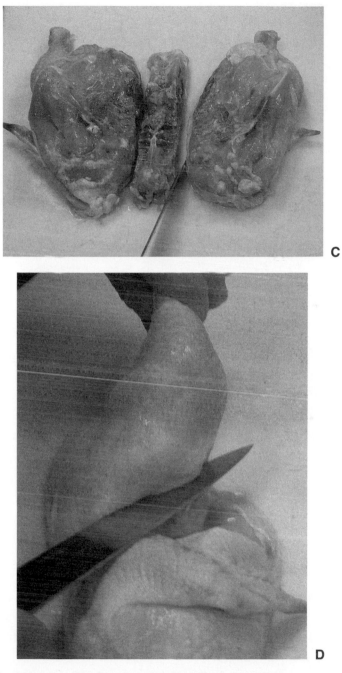

C

D

FIGURE 10-4 *Continued*   (C) Cut lengthwise along one side of the backbone, then the other. Save the backbone for stock. The chicken is now in halves. (D) Turn each half over and cut through the skin behind the thigh.

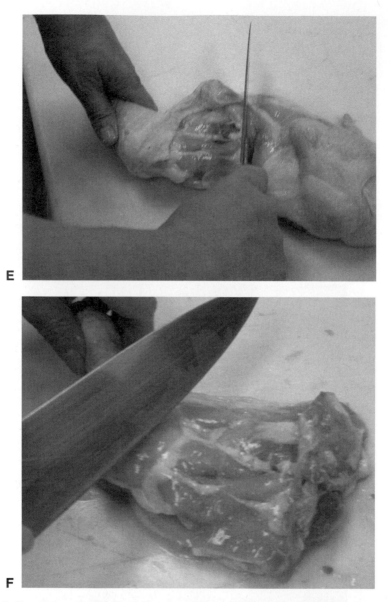

E

F

FIGURE 10-4 *Continued*   (E) Pull the leg back. You'll see the joint between the thigh and the body. Cut through the joint to remove the leg/thigh. You now have four pieces. (F) Find the stripe of fat between the leg and the thigh. Cut through it to separate the leg from the thigh.

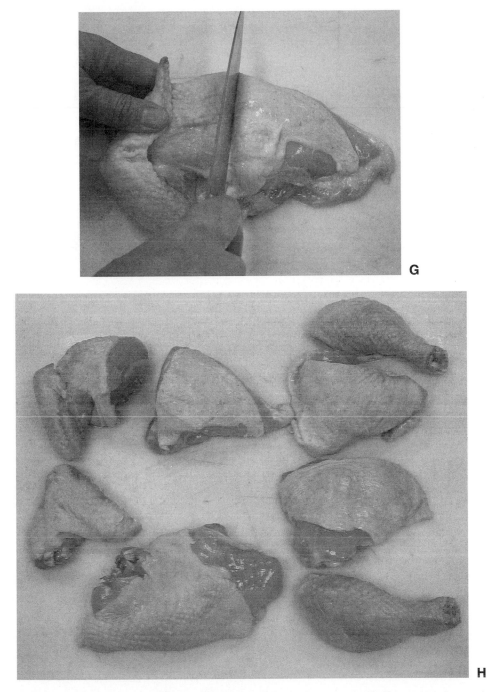

G

H

FIGURE 10-4 *Continued* (G) Cut the breast in half or detach the wing from the breast. Cut off the tip of each wing. (H) Eight pieces of chicken. For illustration purposes, one breast is separated from the wing, the other is cut in half with the wing attached.

Doneness of Poultry

To kill pathogens, poultry is normally cooked well done. Large poultry items like whole turkeys should be cooked to 180°F (82°C), which is determined by taking the temperature with a digital instant-read thermometer at the thickest part of the thigh. Other, smaller poultry items should be cooked until their juices are clear—not pink—and their joints are very flexible.

There are some exceptions to the well-done rule. Some poultry items do not have a reputation for problems with bacteria, including duck breast and squab. These may be cooked to a medium, slightly pink stage.

Dry-Heat Cooking

Dry-heat cooking techniques, including roasting, sautéing, frying, broiling, and grilling, are commonly used for the younger classifications of birds.

Roasting

Larger birds, like turkeys and capons, can be slow roasted at a temperature of 250 to 325°F (120–165°C). This technique results in a juicy, tender bird. High roasting temperatures of 400 to 450°F (200–230°C) can be *carefully* used for smaller birds that cook very quickly, or for ducks and geese that have a protective layer of fat. Medium-size birds should be roasted at about 350°F (177°C) to cook them thoroughly and brown their skin attractively.

Make One of These to Practice Your Boning Skills

Invented in New Orleans to serve on festive occasions, the turducken has become popular in the United States during the past few decades. This creation consists of a boneless chicken filled with stuffing wrapped inside a boneless duck with another layer of stuffing, then wrapped inside a boneless turkey with another layer of stuffing. The entire package is sewn together to look like a whole turkey, then is slow roasted until golden brown. It may then be sliced to reveal the rings of various poultry. See the *Culinary Creation* CD-ROM for the full procedure.

Sautéing and Frying

Like veal and pork, thin-sliced turkey and chicken breast lends itself very well to sautéing. Larger cuts can also be sautéed, then finished in the oven.

Poultry, especially chicken pieces, can be fried either in a pan or in deep fat. Normally, chicken cooked in this manner is breaded according to standard breading procedure or battered. Chicken should be deep fried at a lower temperature—300 to 325°F (149–160°C)—than other foods to ensure the flesh cooks thoroughly before the crust becomes too brown.

There is one very unusual form of deep-fat cooking related to poultry. To prepare duck or goose confit, mentioned earlier in this chapter, pieces of poultry are submerged in oil and cooked slowly at a very low temperature—200°F (93°C)—to keep it as tender as possible. The poultry is then aged under refrigeration in its own fat.

Deep frying has become a popular method for preparing whole turkeys. This process cooks the bird very quickly, making the skin crispy and attractive, and leaving the flesh juicy. A recipe for making confit and for deep frying turkeys is included on the *Culinary Creation* CD-ROM.

Grilling and Broiling

Grilling and broiling smaller pieces of poultry, like chicken pieces, is a fairly simple, straightforward process. Use essentially the same procedures you would use for meats, especially pork. If a piece is too large to cook to internal doneness on the grill or broiler before the outside overcooks, finish cooking it in an oven or by braising.

Often, as when slowly barbecuing poultry on a grill, it is beneficial to season the flesh and skin with various herbs and spices to enhance the flavor of the finished product. In addition, **injecting** the flesh with piquant liquids has become an increasingly popular flavoring technique (Fig. 10-5).

Brining, immersing the poultry in a salty, flavored liquid for a length of time before cooking, usually a few hours, is also a proven technique for improving the juiciness and flavor of a poultry item (or meats or seafood) cooked with dry heat.

Moist-Heat Cooking

Although moist-heat cooking techniques, including simmering, poaching, braising, and stewing, are most suitable for the mature classifications of birds, they can also produce excellent results with younger types.

As you have previously learned, moist heat breaks down the connective tissues in flesh and makes an otherwise tough cut not only edible, but succulent. Whether the product is submerged completely in liquid, as in simmering, poaching, and stewing, or partially submerged, as in braising, long time periods are required to break down the tissues fully.

Summary and Conclusion

Because of its low cost and relatively low fat content, poultry has become a favorite in modern foodservice establishments. It is important for a chef or foodservice manager to

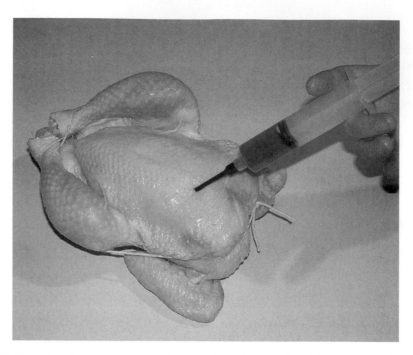

FIGURE 10-5   Injecting marinades is an effective method for adding flavor to poultry.

understand the differences among types of poultry, and the correct means for preparing them.

In this chapter you learned about the history of the four major types of poultry. You also learned about poultry grading and inspection, as well as the various kinds and classifications of poultry. We discussed trussing and fabricating a whole bird, as well as the various methods for cooking poultry and how to determine doneness. Perhaps most important, you learned that poultry, especially chicken, is an extremely hazardous food item and should be handled with extreme care to avoid cross-contamination.

 ## Selected Terms for Review

Brining

Chicken

Classification

Confit

Dark meat

Duck

Goose

Kind

Poultry

Poultry inspection

Poultry-quality grading

Style

Trussing

Turkey

White meat

Review Questions

1. Why is poultry popular in today's foodservice establishments?

2. Define poultry. What are the four major types of poultry used in foodservice?

3. What are the two names for the duck that is most popular in the United States?

4. Define kind in relation to poultry. Define classification.

5. Match the classification in the first column to the kind of poultry in the second column.

    ____a. Yearling   1. Turkey

    ____b. Fowl   2. Chicken

    ____c. Fryer–Roaster   3. Chicken or Duck

    ____d. Capon

    ____e. Broiler–Fryer

    ____f. Roaster

6. Why is the flesh of the wings and breasts of ducks and geese "dark meat," yet chicken and turkey breasts and wings are "white meat"? (Hint: What do ducks and geese do that chickens and turkeys don't?)

7. What is the style of poultry? What is the major style sold to foodservice establishments?

8. How long can you keep fresh poultry under refrigeration?

9. What is trussing? What functions does trussing perform? Name three items that can be used to truss a bird.

10. True or false? If a bird is fully cooked, its juices should be slightly pink.

11. Thin-sliced turkey and chicken breast can be _____, much like veal and pork.

12. Define brining.

Suggested Readings/Web Sites to Visit

Agriculture Marketing Service, USDA. *How to Buy Poultry.* Available at www.ams.usda.gov/howtobuy/poultry.pdf

Agriculture Marketing Service, USDA. *Poultry Grading Manual.* Available at www.ams.usda.gov/poultry/resources/PYGradingManual.pdf

Agriculture Marketing Service, USDA. *Poultry Information.* Available at www.ams.usda.gov/poultry/consumer/

Cook's Illustrated Editors. (1999). *The Cook's Illustrated Complete Book of Poultry.* New York: Clarkson Potter.

Levy, F. (1992). *Faye Levy's International Chicken Cookbook.* New York: Warner Books.

Spier, C. (1993). *Food Essentials: Poultry.* New York: Crescent.

Time-Life Books Editors. (1979). *Poultry.* Alexandria, VA: Time-Life Books.

Creating with Seafood

Learning Objectives

By the end of the chapter, you should be able to

1. Name the most important factor in serving high-quality seafood

2. Name and describe the types of seafood

3. Name and describe examples of each type of seafood

4. Describe how you might determine the freshness of fish

5. Describe how you might determine the freshness of shellfish

6. Name the market forms of seafood

7. Describe how the various types of seafood should be stored

8. Describe how to kill a lobster, shuck an oyster, and fillet a round fish

9. Describe the various ways seafood might be cooked

Chapter Outline

Seafood: Past and Present

Types of Seafood

    Fish

        Flatfish

        Round Fish

        Cartilaginous or Nonbony Fish

    Shellfish

        Univalves

        Bivalves

        Crustaceans

        Cephalopods

"Most seafoods should be simply threatened with heat and then celebrated with joy."

—*Jeff Smith, TV chef*

Freshness. That's the key to great seafood. Above all else, in this chapter you will learn the importance of using only the freshest fish in your culinary creations. You'll learn how to recognize fresh fish and how not to overcook it.

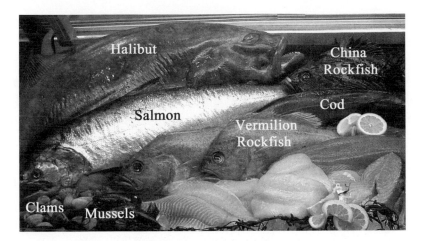

FIGURE 11-1   A wide array of seafood is available to the modern foodservice establishment.

Just a few decades ago, the only seafood available to many people was canned tuna. That was the extent of fish experience for those who lived away from a shoreline. Today, however, as a result of advances in transportation, as well as the increasing availability of Asian (especially Japanese) cuisine, people in all areas of the world are learning to appreciate fine, fresh seafood. As a result, a wider array of seafood dishes is being demanded by discriminating diners. For this reason, the modern chef or hospitality manager must be familiar with not only the various forms of fish and shellfish, but also their preparation (Fig. 11-1).

This chapter makes every effort to categorize fish clearly by their many, sometimes overlapping, distinctions, and to explain how each type of fish may contribute to your culinary repertoire.

Seafood: Past and Present

More than any other food item, seafood has had a major impact on the history of humankind. Why? Because a search for fish is identical to a voyage of exploration. The oceans of early times were not only roads to new sources of seafood, but also gateways to new lands.

In his book, *Cod: A Biography of the Fish That Changed the World*, Mark Kurlansky tells of how the simple codfish altered the course of human events for centuries. Hundreds of years before the voyages of Columbus, the Basques of northern Spain visited the rich fishing grounds off the coast of North America to harvest the vast schools of cod that they found there. They became quite prosperous selling the fish in Europe. However, the

Basques decided to keep their rich finds (and their knowledge of the North American continent) a secret from other Europeans, hoarding the bounty for themselves.

It wasn't until after Columbus' visits to the Caribbean that Columbus' friend and fellow Italian Giovanni Caboto (better known as John Cabot) visited the North Atlantic on behalf of England and discovered the bounty of cod. The seemingly endless stock of fish from the New World eventually became a greater economical treasure for Cabot's British backers than gold or silver, because the fish, in a salted, preserved form, helped feed their empire's worldwide colonies for hundreds of years. Even today, in many areas originally colonized by the British around the world (for example, Jamaica), salt cod is still the fish of choice for the residents. Sadly, cod is much more expensive and scarce now, because it has been overfished.

In other areas of the world, various forms of seafood have shaped the cultures and economies of the local populations. In Russia, of course, the Caspian Sea provides the home for the giant sturgeon that produces Beluga caviar. The Gulf of Mexico has rendered a bountiful harvest for generations of shrimpers in Texas and Louisiana. In northern waters, salmon have provided a livelihood for people from Scandinavia to the Pacific Northwest and Alaska. Perhaps more than any nation, the Japanese have learned to reap the benefits of a vast array of products from the ocean, not only fish and shellfish, but also many forms of edible plant life that live beneath the sea.

Types of Seafood

Seafood is the general name we give to the various sorts of fish and shellfish that we consume, whether they live in the sea or in freshwater. To complicate matters, the word *fish* is a very loose term that refers to a wide variety of animals that happen to live in the water, like cuttlefish (a relative of the squid) and starfish. For our purposes, **fish** are animals that have fins and gills. These are also sometimes referred to as *finfish*. **Shellfish** are animals that have no fins, gills, or spine, but usually have some sort of external shell or internal cuttlebone, except for the octopus. To become familiar with the various terminology, review Figures 11-2 and 11-3. They provide "family trees" of how the various types of seafood may be organized.

Fish

Fish are divided into three groups: flatfish, round fish, and cartilaginous or nonbony fish. They may also be subcategorized as **lean** (fish that are low in body fat) or **oily** (fish that are high in fat). They may be further subcategorized as **freshwater** or **saltwater**.

Flatfish

Flatfish are weird looking but delicious. A flatfish starts out life like most other fish, with one eye on each side of its head, but, as it matures, the eye on one side of the head moves

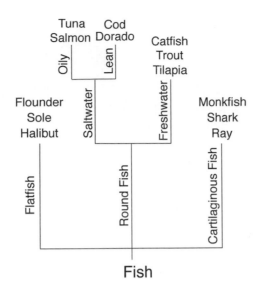

FIGURE 11-2 Family tree of fish.

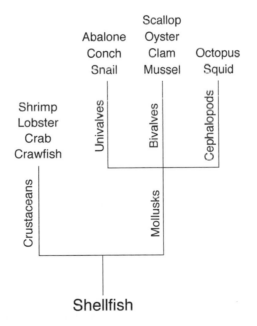

FIGURE 11-3 Family tree of shellfish.

to the other side, so the mature fish has both its eyes on the same side of its head. The flat-fish swims horizontally with its eyes facing upward. When necessary, it hides in the sand on the bottom. The mature flatfish is a very compressed oval. Its topside is dark, and its underside is light, to provide camouflage from either direction. All flatfish are lean fish and all live in saltwater. Examples of common flatfish are Dover sole, flounder, and halibut.

FIGURE 11-4   Yellowtail flounder. Source: *USFDA Fish Encyclopedia*.

Dover sole is smaller and narrower than the flounder, and its flesh is firmer. It may weigh up to 2 pounds (0.9 kg). The Dover sole is one of the most prized food fish in the world.

Flounder (Fig. 11-4) is sometimes misleadingly called *sole* in the marketplace. Its flesh is very delicate and flaky. It may weigh up to 5 pounds (2.3 kg). The flounder is very suitable for poaching or steaming.

Halibut (Fig. 11-5) is a very large flatfish. Its flesh is firm and white, with a delicate flavor. It may weigh up to 200 pounds (90 kg). Halibut is commonly cut into fillets or steaks.

Round Fish

The majority of fish species are **round fish**. Their bodies are thicker than flatfish and their eyes are located symmetrically on either side of the head. Round fish may be either saltwater or freshwater and lean or oily. This section lists examples of some of the common species of round fish.

Catfish (Fig. 11-6) are lean-to-oily freshwater round fish with firm, very flavorful flesh. Catfish have smooth skin with no scales. They may weigh up to 8 pounds (3.6 kg). Catfish are very popular in the southern U.S., usually filleted, breaded, and deep-fat fried.

Cod is a lean, saltwater fish with white, delicately flavored flesh. Various types are called *scrod* (young cod), *haddock*, *hake*, and *pollock*. They may weigh up to 25 pounds (11 kg). Cod are suitable for moist-heat methods. Cod is available preserved with salt, in which case it must be reconstituted with water before use. Cod aficionados insist the salted version tastes better than the fresh. Salt cod is used in the Jamaican national dish **ackee and saltfish**.

Eels (uh-uh, watch the foodism!) are essentially freshwater fish that spawn in the North Atlantic. They have extremely rich, oily, sweet-flavored flesh. The eel isn't popular in the

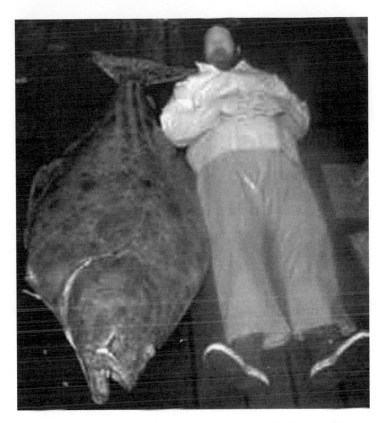

FIGURE 11-5 Halibut get very large. Source: Alaska Fisheries Science Center.

FIGURE 11-6 Channel catfish. Source: *USFDA Fish Encyclopedia*.

United States because of its resemblance to a snake, but it is well loved in many nations of the world because of its exceptional flavor.

Mahi mahi are lean, saltwater fish, also called *dorado, dolphinfish,* or *dolphins*, but, as we said in Chapter 1, not the *mammal* dolphins, like Flipper, but the *fish* dolphins. Mahi mahi have a delicate, sweet flesh, and are suitable for moist- and dry-heat cooking methods. They may weigh up to 40 pounds (18 kg).

Perch are lean freshwater fish with delicate flesh. They may be cooked with moist or dry heat. Perch may weigh up to 5 pounds (2.3 kg).

FIGURE 11-7   Tilapia. Source: *USFDA Fish Encyclopedia*.

Rockfish are members of a family of Pacific lean fish with firm, white flesh and a mild flavor. Two examples are shown in Figure 11-1.

Salmon are somewhat oily with a light-pink to orange-red flesh. The salmon is mostly a saltwater fish, but it spawns in freshwater. There are several species, including chinook (king), coho, Atlantic, and sockeye. Salmon may weigh up to 25 pounds (11.4 kg). They may be grilled, poached, or smoked as **lox**. They are also popular sugar cured as **gravlax**.

Tilapia (Fig. 11-7) are lean, freshwater fish with firm, mild flesh. They may weigh up to 3 pounds (1.4 kg). Tilapia may be cooked with moist or dry heat.

Trout are actually smaller salmon that live mostly in freshwater. They are somewhat oily and have a white to red flesh with a delicate, rich flavor. Some species, like the lake trout, may weigh up to 10 pounds (4.5 kg), but most species are in the 1 to 3-pound (0.5–1.4 kg) range. Trout may be pan fried, grilled, smoked, or poached.

Tuna are oily saltwater fish with firm flesh. The color of fresh tuna ranges from beige to dark red. Tuna may weigh up to several hundred pounds. Canned tuna packed in oil is used in such dishes as salad Niçoise (nee-SWAHZ). Fillets of fresh tuna are often cut into blocks, crusted with spices, and seared rare.

Not Your Average Chicken of the Sea

A small slice of the prized belly (*toro*) of the bluefin tuna sells for $100 US in Tokyo sushi bars.

Cartilaginous or Nonbony Fish

Cartilaginous (KAR-till-A-ji-nuss) or **nonbony fish** have no bones, only cartilage (except for the shark's jaws). Their skin has no scales. Nonbony fish are, therefore, fairly easy to fabricate. Three major nonbony fish are used in foodservice.

Monkfish, a lean saltwater fish, is the ugliest creature in the known universe, but one of the most delicious. Werner Auer, Executive Chef, Houston Hyatt Regency, says "Monkfish is called the poor man's lobster. As long as people never see what it looks like whole, they love it." Monkfish may weigh up to 50 pounds (23 kg). Only the tails are used. Monkfish has a very rich flavor and is normally cooked with moist heat, but it may be prepared using dry heat as well.

Ray, also known as **skate**, are lean saltwater fish with very sweet flesh and are shaped like a stealth bomber. Only the wings are used for food. Although rays can grow to be gigantic, the wings of rays used for culinary purposes seldom weigh more than 4 pounds (1.8 kg). Ray is often sautéd.

Shark is an oily saltwater fish with sweet, firm flesh. *Mako* sharks, the type usually used for foodservice, weigh up to 40 pounds (18 kg). Dry heat is commonly used when cooking shark.

Shellfish

Shellfish may be divided into four groups: crustaceans, univalves, bivalves, and cephalopods. The last three are called, as a group, *mollusks*—that is, animals with very soft bodies that are usually, but not always, enclosed in a shell.

Univalves

Univalves are mollusks with a one-piece shell. **Abalone** (a-buh-LOH-nee) is usually about 6 inches (17.7 cm) in length. The abalone is actually a sea snail. Its flesh is somewhat chewy and mild flavored. Abalone is normally pounded flat, then cooked very quickly, so as not to overcook it, using dry-heat methods.

Conch (konk; Fig. 11-8) is a very popular food in the Caribbean. It has a fairly large, peach-color spiral shell. Conch has a sweet, chewy flesh. It's often cut into pieces, then battered and deep-fried in conch fritters.

Snails, although they sometimes live on land, are really a type of shellfish. Like abalone, their flesh is somewhat chewy. Called *escargot* (ESS-kar-GOH) in French, they are classically served in their shells with garlic butter.

Bivalves

Bivalves are mollusks with a two-piece shell that opens and closes. The most common types are clams, oysters, scallops, and mussels.

Clams normally have fairly smooth, even shells. They come in many sizes and varieties, generally divided into soft shell and hard shell. The largest of the soft-shell clams is the *geoduck* (GOO-ee-duk) from the Pacific Northwest that weighs up to 10 pounds (4.5 kg), with a large 18-inch (50-cm) "tongue" (actually a siphon) protruding from between its shells. Surprisingly tender, these bivalves are often used in Asian dishes. Smaller soft-shell clams are called *longnecks*, because of their siphons. Longnecks are normally steamed. *Hard-shell clams* or *quahogs* (KOH-hogs or KWAH-hogs) come in three sizes:

FIGURE 11-8   Conch is known by its distinctive spiral shell.

littlenecks, the smallest, eaten raw or steamed; *cherrystones*, next in size, eaten raw or steamed; and *chowders*, the largest, also sometimes called quahogs (yes, it's inconsistent!), eaten in soups or fried.

Oysters have very irregular, usually rough shells. They also come in various shapes and sizes. Varieties include *Atlantic oysters*, which are somewhat elongated and have a smooth top shell and vary in size and name according to where they are harvested; *Pacific oysters*, the most common of which is the *Japanese oyster*, which ranges in size from very tiny to very large; and *flat* (also called *Belon*) oysters, originally from Europe, farmed on both coasts of the United States. Oysters are eaten raw, steamed, roasted, fried, and served in soups.

Scallops have the prettiest shell of the bivalves—the one used as the logo for Shell gasoline. Unfortunately for shell collectors, though, scallops are normally sold shucked. Scallops used in foodservice are usually of three types: *bay scallops*, small, about 1/2 ounce (14 g), with a delicate flavor; *calico scallops*, about the same size as bay but of a lower quality; and *sea scallops*, which become quite large—1 to 2 ounces (28–56 g)—but are still quite tender. The main point to remember when cooking scallops is (as with most seafood): *Do not overcook them!* Scallops cook very quickly and toughen very rapidly.

Crustaceans

Crustaceans have segmented bodies with jointed legs and a shell-like covering. Crustaceans include lobsters, crab, shrimp, and crawfish.

Lobsters have a body with ten legs, the front two normally with claws, and a tail. Lobsters are the most prized shellfish. The tail yields the largest portion of meat, but the claws are considered to have the best flavor. The *Maine lobster*, also called the *American lobster*, is the highest quality. The *spiny lobster*, also called the *rock lobster*, found in southern waters, has no claws. Lobsters are categorized by weight: *jumbo*, more than 2.5 pounds (1.1 kg); *large*, 1.5 to 2.5 pounds (0.68–1.1 kg); *quarters*, 1.25 to 1.5 pounds (0.57–0.68 kg); and *chicken*, 1 pound (4.5 kg). Lobster is best when simmered briefly, about five minutes per pound (1/2 kg). Lobster may also be grilled, broiled, or sautéed.

This Proves You Can Get Tired of Anything

Lobster was so abundant in the Americas up until the 20th century that it was considered to be food fit only for farm workers and the poor. It was even used as fish bait. One group of workers went on strike to protest the amount of lobster they were forced to eat. The strike ended when the bosses agreed to serve lobster no more than three times a week.

Crabs don't have a tail, just a body with ten legs. The two front legs normally have claws. Crabs yield much less flesh than lobsters, but the flesh is sweet and succulent. The major varieties include blue, Dungeness (DUN-juh-ness), stone, and king. The *blue crab* is marketed both with a hard shell and as a **soft-shell crab**. The soft-shell crab is harvested immediately after the crab molts (sheds its shell). After it's cleaned, the entire crab is normally breaded and deep-fried. *Dungeness crabs*, a Pacific variety, have very sweet flesh and can weigh up to 4 pounds (1.8 kg). *Stone crab* claws are very popular in the southeastern United States. *King crabs* (Fig. 11-9) can weigh up to 20 pounds (9 kg) and yield the largest chunks of flesh. Crab is normally cooked using moist heat.

Shrimp are the most popular shellfish because of their affordability and versatility. In the United States, they are sold by size according to how many there are to the pound. For example, 11 to 15 jumbo shrimp make a pound, whereas it takes 100 miniature shrimp to make the same weight. Shrimp may be cooked using any means, moist or dry. One especially delicious treatment is the buttery, piquant Creole "bobbakew" shrimp—whole shrimp that aren't really barbecued at all, but are cooked in fat and spices and served over rice with French bread for mopping up the juice.

FIGURE 11-9   Alaskan king crab is prized for its meaty long legs.

 **On Prawns**

Prawn is a very vague, confusing word used to describe various kinds of shellfish. Depending on where you are in the world, a prawn may be (1) a large shrimp, (2) a small lobster, or (3) a freshwater crustacean. If you're purchasing prawns, make sure you and your vendor are talking about the same thing.

Crawfish, also called **crayfish**, are freshwater crustaceans that look like little lobsters. They yield very little flesh, but they are very sweet. Eating them is a sort of labor-

FIGURE 11-10   Deep-fried calamari is often served as a first course in Italian seafood restaurants.

intensive ritual like eating peanuts in the shell. They are normally cooked using moist heat. Shelled crawfish tails are available frozen year-round.

Cephalopods

The word *cephalopod* (SEFF-uh-loh-pod) comes from the two Greek words for "head" (*kephale*) and "foot" (*pod*). They are so named because the mollusks in this category have legs that hang directly beneath their heads. The two major food cephalopods are the octopus and the squid.

The **octopus** has eight legs or tentacles. It's very firm, even chewy. Octopus is very popular in Asian and Mediterranean cuisine.

Squid is a ten-legged cephalopod that is very popular in many cuisines around the world. It may be cut into pieces and cooked in a sauce, or breaded and deep-fried. Squid is called *calamari* in Italian cuisine (Fig. 11-10). Squids squirt a black substance called *ink* to ward of attack. The ink is used to color pasta in Mediterranean cuisine (Fig. 11-11).

Components of Fish

Unlike meat and poultry, the muscle tissue of fish has very little connective tissue, about 3% by weight compared with meat and poultry's 15%. And although muscle in other

FIGURE 11-11   Italian *trecce nere* (TRECH-ay NEHR-ay, "black braid") squid-ink pasta.

animals is composed of long fibers, fish flesh has very short fibers, separated by sheets of very thin connective tissue. This is why most fish is so flaky and delicate after it is cooked. And that's why it overcooks so easily. The tender proteins coagulate and stiffen very quickly.

Now, you're asking, "Why is fish 'white meat' as opposed to 'dark meat?' Didn't you say that muscle that gets lots of exercise is dark? And don't fish swim all the time?"

Yes. You're right. Most fish flesh is very white. This is because fish don't have to contend with gravity. They live in a virtually weightless environment, so, compared with birds, for example, they really don't have to work very hard to get around. Fish like salmon have darker flesh because of the pigments in the things they eat. (Farmed salmon actually have food coloring added to their feed to approximate the color of wild salmon.)

Purchasing and Storing Fish

You've probably noticed that we haven't mentioned inspection and grading anywhere in this chapter so far. That's because, at least in the United States, there is no legally required inspection for fresh seafood. Processors of products like canned tuna may pay for inspection by the U.S. government, but there is no requirement to do so. For this reason, you, as a foodservice professional, must know how to determine whether seafood is fresh when you accept it. You must also know how to store it properly until you prepare it.

Determining Freshness of Seafood

Each type of seafood has specific characteristics that tell the knowledgeable buyer if it is fresh. The most important thing to remember to ensure you are getting fresh seafood is to deal only with reputable vendors. You may be able to get a bargain on shrimp from the van parked in the gas station, but it's worth the extra cost to deal with an honest purveyor who is respected in the industry.

Fish Freshness

You can tell if a fish is fresh by using three of your senses: smell, look, and feel:

- Smell the fish. This is the most important. It should have little or no odor other than a pleasant sea aroma. Reject fish that have a strong odor.

- Look for bright, clear, bulging eyes, not dull, cloudy eyes. Look also for glossy scales and bright-red, not brown, gills.

- Feel to determine if the flesh is firm, not flabby.

Shellfish Freshness

There are basic, commonsense methods for determining freshness of shellfish:

- All shellfish, fresh or frozen, should have a clean smell, with no "off" odors.

- Bivalves purchased fresh (alive) should be tightly closed or should close immediately when tapped.

- Crustaceans purchased fresh should be alive and active until they are cooked. Frozen crustaceans, like shrimp or crawfish, should be solidly frozen and have no odor.

Market Forms of Seafood

Seafood is available in various forms and is normally ordered by foodservice establishments in the form closest to which it is to be served to save labor costs involved in fabrication.

Fish Market Forms

The standard forms for fish include

- **Whole**—intact, the way it was caught
- **Drawn**—gutted
- **Dressed**—gutted; scales, gills, fins, and head removed
- **Fillet** (fill-LAY)—boneless section of flesh, cut from the sides of the fish
- **Steak**—cross-section of the fish, cut in slices through the backbone

Shellfish Market Forms

The standard forms for shellfish include

- Univalves—fresh (alive, in the shell) or frozen (raw or cooked)

- Bivalves—fresh (alive, in the shell), shucked (fresh or frozen), or canned

- Crustaceans—fresh (alive) or frozen (raw or cooked). Shrimp are usually sold **IQF** (individually quick frozen), either **P/D** (peeled and deveined) or **PDC** (peeled, deveined, and cooked), whole frozen shrimp are available in 5-pound (2.3 kg) blocks, rock lobsters are almost always sold as frozen tails only. (Note: **Devein** [dee-VANE] means to remove the digestive tract along the shrimp's back.)

- Cephalopods—fresh or frozen

Seafood Storage

As mentioned at the beginning of the chapter, maintaining the freshness of seafood is crucial. Off flavors not only ruin the taste of the dish, but the odors generated during cooking will smell up the entire restaurant.

Fish Storage

Fresh fish spoil rapidly. Fresh fish should be stored on crushed ice in a drip pan to let the melting water drain out. If crushed ice is not available, the fish should be stored in a refrigerator at 30 to 34°F (−1–+1°C).

Ideally, fresh fish should be consumed within one day. If it cannot be used within one day, it should be frozen or cooked and refrigerated for later use.

They're Lovin' It in There!

Why do fish spoil rapidly, even if chilled? Think about this: The supposed "ideal" storage temperature for fish is 30 to 34°F (−1–+1°C). This, coincidentally enough, is about the same temperature as the seawater in which the fish lived. This means that any bacteria on or in the fish are going to be right at home in that temperature range. They are thriving and feasting on the flesh of the newly killed fish. So, short of freezing or heating, there is no temperature that effectively slows bacterial growth in fish. That's why it should be consumed as quickly as possible to ensure freshness.

Shellfish Storage

Store fresh shellfish as follows: Crustaceans should be kept alive in either special saltwater aquariums, or wrapped in wet seaweed or heavy paper and kept in a cool place.

Unshucked bivalves (that is, still in their shells) should be stored alive in their original containers in a cold, wet place. Shucked bivalves should be kept in their original containers at 30 to 34°F (−1–+1°C). Live or shucked bivalves will keep for up to seven days.

Cooking Seafood

In this section, we briefly review the types of cooking appropriate for the various types of seafood. But first, let's look at three basic techniques that every foodservice professional should know with regard to seafood: how to kill a lobster, how to shuck an oyster, and how to fillet a fish. Recipes related to this section may be found on the *Culinary Creation* CD-ROM.

How to Kill a Lobster

A certain segment of the population feels very strongly that it is necessary to kill a lobster in a so-called "humane" fashion. Now, I'm not an inhumane person, but I have to ask: Why so much concern with lobsters? Why not shrimp or crawfish? Or any other kind of fish or shellfish? Nobody cares about killing *them* humanely. We eat oysters *alive*, for Pete's sake! Don't we care about *their* trauma?

Okay, all whining aside, here are three alternative "humane" methods for killing lobsters:

Method 1: Place the lobster on the table, put the point of your chef's knife against its forehead, then, in one quick motion, thrust the point through its forehead and then bring the knife down to cut the head in half lengthwise.

Method 2: Put the lobster in the freezer for an hour.

Method 3: Put the lobster into a gently steaming pot and cover for ten seconds.

How to Shuck an Oyster

To shuck an oyster, you should wear a heavy glove or put a folded towel in your hand to prevent injury. Then, follow these steps:

1. Hold the oyster securely in one hand, with the flatter shell on top and the rounder shell underneath. Insert the point of an oyster knife at the hinge between the shells.

2. Twist the knife to separate the hinge.

3. Slide the knife along the top shell to cut the muscle along the top.

4. Open the top and slide the knife under the oyster flesh to separate it from the bottom shell.

Filleting a Round Fish

It is sometimes cost-effective to buy fish dressed and fillet them in your own kitchen. Figure 11-12 shows how to fillet a round fish.

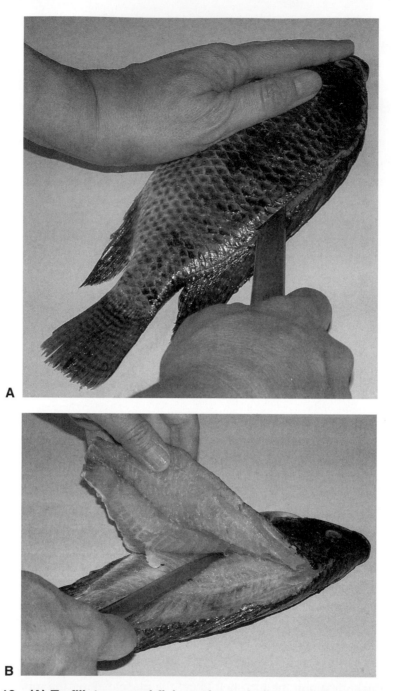

FIGURE 11-12   (A) To fillet a round fish, make a shallow cut along the spine from head to tail. (B) Using the ribs as a guide, work the knife under the fillet until the tail end comes free. Keep working the knife along the ribs from the tail to the head until the entire fillet comes free.

Cooking Seafood

Although we've suggested various cooking techniques in the descriptions of different types of fish earlier in this chapter, in this section we discuss specific techniques as they relate to various seafood recipes around the world. Again, for detailed recipes, see the *Culinary Creation* CD-ROM.

Sautéing

Lean fish especially lend themselves to sautéing. The fish should be lightly coated with flour before cooking and should be handled very gently to avoid breaking.

Oily fish may be sautéed too, but can become too greasy if the cook isn't careful. Oily fish need not be coated with flour before sautéing.

In French cuisine, skate wings are often sautéed and served **à la meunière** (moon-YAIR, "in the style of the miller's wife") with brown butter, lemon juice, and parsley. Brown butter, also called *beurre noisette* (burr nwah-ZET, which means "hazelnut butter," because of its distinctive smell), and its darker version, *beurre noir* (burr NWAHR, black butter), is important in many dishes in French cooking.

Stir-Frying

Small pieces of fish or shellfish are ideal for the high-heat stir-fry method. A popular stir-fried dish in Chinese cuisine is shrimp in oyster sauce, which combines two different categories of the shellfish kingdom: crustaceans and bivalves. In this recipe, the shrimp are quickly stir-fried in oyster sauce, again, so as not to overcook them, in which case they would toughen.

Baking

Drawn or dressed fish are especially suited to baking, but care must be taken with lean varieties to prevent overcooking. In Italy, cooks have discovered the simple joys of baking a lean fish in a hard crust of egg whites and salt. This results in a fish that is very tender and succulent, and no, the fish doesn't become overly salty. The salt is there to insulate the fish during baking. This is really a moist-heat method, because the fish steams in its own juices inside the crust.

Broiling and Grilling

Lean fish may become dry when broiled or grilled. Tuna and salmon are very good candidates for grilling and broiling because the oils in the fish keep them moist.

The native people of the northwestern shore of North America have mastered the art of broiling salmon mounted on a framework next to a fire of alder wood. Because of its high fat content, salmon is the perfect fish for either broiling or grilling, with simple seasonings and flavorings.

Deep-frying

Shellfish and lean fish are suitable for breading (using the standard breading procedure, of course) and deep-frying. In the southern United States, cooks deep-fry nearly everything. Fried catfish fillets are especially good when crusted with some of the local pecans instead of breadcrumbs. The pecans protect the fish while frying, and form an attractive and crispy crust.

In Asia, deep-frying whole fish is an extremely popular preparation method. Fish markets will sell you a live fish from a tank, then immediately dress it, fry it, and wrap it up for you to take home. It doesn't get fresher than that.

In the British Isles, delicate white fish are battered and deep-fried, then served with deep-fried potatoes and malt vinegar as "fish and chips."

Poaching

In poaching, a lean fish is immersed and gently cooked in a warm (160°F [70°C]) liquid that is usually flavored with an acid, fish stock, and/or wine. The classic method for poaching fish is in a French **court bouillon** (kort boo-YAWN), a clear liquid containing mirepoix, acid (vinegar or lemon juice), salt, spices, and herbs. Fillets of flatfish especially lend themselves to this technique.

Stewing

Naturally, fish aren't stewed for as long a period of time as meat or poultry. Normally, other ingredients are cooked first, then the seafood is added to the stew near the end of cooking.

Bouillabaisse (BOO-yuh-base), a famous seafood stew from the south of France, is a melange of tomatoes, olive oil, shellfish, fish, and saffron served with a peppery condiment called *rouille* (roo-ee). The Creole seafood **courtbouillon** (KOO-bee-yawn) from New Orleans, an evolution of the poaching liquid mentioned earlier, is a tomato-y fish stew thickened with roux.

Steaming

Steaming is a method mostly suited to lean fillets of fish. The flesh remains quite tender and flaky, and retains its moisture quite well using this method. The Chinese are especially adept and experienced at steaming fish, having used bamboo steamers for thousands of years. An excellent example of their craft is steamed white fish with ginger. Another steaming method is the technique en papillote discussed in Chapter 4.

Marinating and Curing

Marinating and curing are techniques for "cooking" fish without using heat. The South American specialty, **ceviche** (sev-EE-chay) is white, lean fish that is cold cooked—that is, marinated in acid (usually citrus juice) until the proteins coagulate as though they were cooked.

244

The Swedish treat **gravlax** is salmon "buried" in sugar and salt for a few days until the flesh loses moisture and turns opaque as though cooked. Gravlax actually means "salmon from the grave."

Serving It Raw

As the Japanese can verify, many fish are delicious raw—in **sushi**, seasoned rice with added ingredients, or as **sashimi**, morsels of raw seafood. Two excellent examples are tuna and salmon. Keep in mind that only saltwater fish are suitable for raw consumption. Freshwater fish contain too many parasites.

If you choose to serve raw seafood in your establishment, the precautions you take involve the same common sense you use with any seafood: Make certain that it is absolutely fresh, that it comes from a reliable vendor, and that you exercise strict hygiene and sanitation procedures when preparing it.

Summary and Conclusion

As people look for healthier lifestyles, seafood will become more and more of a major component in the offerings of the foodservice establishments of the 21st century. Many types of seafood, such as catfish, salmon, and tilapia, are farmed, allowing for year-round availability.

This chapter introduced you to the types of fish available, including round fish, flat-fish, and cartilaginous fish, as well as the various varieties of shellfish (namely, mollusks and crustaceans). It described the differences between the muscle tissue of land animals and water animals, and described how those differences affect cooking decisions. Most important of all, you learned about the significance of freshness of seafood, as well as the importance of safe handling and storage. You were also introduced to a variety of ways seafood is prepared in various parts of the world.

Selected Terms for Review

Bivalve
Cartilaginous
Cephalopod
Court bouillon
Crustacean
Dressed fish
Fish

Flatfish

Gravlax

IQF

Mollusk

P/D

PDC

Round fish

Sashimi

Seafood

Shellfish

Sushi

Univalve

Whole fish

Review Questions

1. What is the most important factor in the quality of seafood?

2. Define seafood.

3. What are the two major categories of seafood?

4. The three major categories of fish are _____, _____, and _____.

5. In what movie thriller of the 1970s, did we learn about the unique bone structure of a particular nonbony fish?

6. True or false? Flatfish always look down into the depths of the water.

7. Match the classification in the first column to the kind of seafood in the second column.

____a. Calamari   1. Crustacean

____b. Lobster   2. Cephaolpod

____c. Monkfish   3. Bivalve

____d. Sole   4. Flatfish

____e. Oyster   5. Round fish

____f. Dolphin

____g. Octopus

8. We mentioned the confusion regarding the word *prawn*. In a food reference book or Web site, look up the words *langosta*, *langostino*, *langouste*, and *langoustine*. Explain the differences between the animals and why there might be confusion about their names. (By the way, although some references only have one, you should be able to find two definitions of the word *langoustine*.)

9. What characteristic of a cephalopod give it its name?

10. What type of protein tissue is vary scarce in a fish? How do a fish's muscle fibers differ from those of land animals?

11. True or false? Seafood inspection in the United States is not required by law.

12. Which of the following is not a way to tell if a fish is fresh?

 a. Touch it to see if it is firm.

 b. Smell it to detect "off" odors.

 c. Taste it to see if it has any "off" flavors.

 d. Look at it to see if the eyes are clear and the gills are red.

13. How quickly should you use fresh fish?

14. What are five common market forms of fish?

15. Which is ready to eat, a P/D shrimp or a PDC shirmp?

16. Describe how fresh (unfrozen) fish should be stored.

17. True or false? Live bivalves should be removed from their containers as soon as they are received.

18. Which type of fish should be coated with flour before sautéing?

19. The classic French poaching liquid is called a _____. The Creole fish stew is called a _____.

20. Name two methods by which fish may be "cooked" without heating.

21. True or false? Freshwater fish should never be used to make sashimi.

22. Name the precautions you should take when serving raw fish.

Suggested Readings/Web Sites to Visit

Bluefin tuna data sheet. *Atuna.* Available at www.atuna.com/species/species/datasheet%20bluefin.htm

Brown, E., Boehm, A. (1995). *The Modern Seafood Cook.* New York: Clarkson Potter.

Fish en Papillote. *Chef's Select Parchment Paper.* Available at www.chefsselect.com/htm/jmrecipes/enpapillote.htm

Jenkins, B. (1995). *The Complete Seafood Cookbook.* Boston: Charles E. Tuttle Co.

King, S. (1990). *Fish: The Basics.* New York: Simon & Schuster.

Kurlansky, M. (1997). *Cod: A Biography of the Fish That Changed the World.* New York: Penguin.

Quintana, P. (1994). *Cuisine of the Water Gods.* New York: Simon & Schuster.

Romagnoli, M., Romagnoli, G. F. (1994). *The Romagnolis' Italian Fish Cookbook.* New York: Henry Holt.

U.S. Food and Drug Administration. *Regulatory Fish Encyclopedia.* Available at www.cfsan.fda.gov/~frf/rfe0.html

U.S. Food and Drug Administration. *Seafood HACCP information.* Available at www.cfsan.fda.gov/~comm/haccpsea.html

U.S. Food and Drug Administration. *Seafood information and resources.* Available at vm.cfsan.fda.gov/seafood1.html

U.S. Food and Drug Administration. *Seafood search engine.* Available at www.cfsan.fda.gov/~frf/seaintro.html

Creating with Vegetables

Learning Objectives

By the end of the chapter, you should be able to

1. Define vegetables

2. Describe some of the vegetable specialties one might find on various continents

3. Talk about how cooking affects the texture, color, and nutrients of vegetables

4. Describe the categories of vegetables

5. Give examples of each category of vegetables

6. Describe typical methods for cooking each type of vegetable

7. Describe how the various types of vegetables should be stored

8. Discuss the special issues associated with convenience vegetables

9. Describe types of pasta, both Italian and Asian

10. Discuss the correct method for cooking pasta

Chapter Outline

Vegetables: A World Tour

    Asia

    Central and Southern Africa

    The Mediterranean

    Northern Europe

    The Americas

How Cooking Affects Vegetables

    Effects on Texture

    Pigments

    Nutrients

This chapter is about foods that do not come from animals. **Vegetables** are generally the savory edible parts of plants, including leaves, roots, stalks, and flowers. Vegetables, which can include, fungi (mushrooms) and starchy foods like potatoes, beans, rice, and grains, are becoming increasingly more important in the modern foodservice establishment. As we have previously mentioned, such food items are more often a focal point of the dining experience than they were a few decades ago, when they were relegated to the role of generic side dishes. Today, many more customers are entering restaurants expecting that there will be vegetable entrees prepared and served with the same respect and creativity applied to meats, poultry, or fish.

    As with seafood, freshness is a key to success with vegetables. You must take great care when receiving, storing, and preparing vegetables to ensure they have the most exciting flavors, colors, and textures.

Vegetables: A World Tour

"Throughout the world vegetables are prized for the variety they bring to daily menus. What other food comes to us in as many flavors, shapes, and colors?"

—*Faye Levy, food writer*

Admittedly, vegetables around the world, as well as methods of preparation, do have certain things in common. However, each continent does have noteworthy techniques and styles of handling vegetables (Fig. 12-1). As always, see the *Culinary Creation* CD-ROM for related recipes.

Asia

We have mentioned stir-frying throughout this book as a method of preparation that preserves the texture, color, and flavor of foods. Chinese, Malaysian, Thai, and Indonesian cooks use this method, which involves cutting vegetables like bok choy, snow peas, bean sprouts, mushrooms, and squash into nice bite-size pieces and fast cooking them over high heat. When properly done, the resulting dishes are brightly colored and perfectly textured.

FIGURE 12-1 Produce markets on every continent attract chefs in search of the freshest ingredients.

In Japan, chefs favor a style of deep-frying called *tempura* (tem-POOR-uh), which uses a very light batter, usually based on cornstarch and rice wine. This creates a uniquely delicate, paper-thin crust for vegetables like onions, zucchini, and yams. Another favorite Japanese method is to simmer bite-size vegetables like mushrooms, bamboo shoots, onions, carrots, and noodles tableside in a soy-based sauce, usually with thinly sliced meat. Two examples of this method are **sukiyaki** (skee-YAH-kee) and **shabu shabu** (beef hotpot).

In India, cooks often braise vegetables in spicy sauces. Items like eggplant, potatoes, garbanzo beans, and carrots are stewed with curry spices that may include coriander, turmeric, fenugreek, pepper, cumin, fennel, and nutmeg. They also enjoy fritters called *pakora*, veggies deep-fried in a batter made from chickpea flour.

Central and Southern Africa

In sub-Saharan Africa (south of the Sahara desert), favorite vegetables include yams (the white tropical type), okra, squash, and eggplant. The people of these nations have also enthusiastically adopted two ingredients from the New World—peanuts (often ground as a thickener) and very hot peppers. As mentioned in Chapter 1, Ethiopians enjoy vegetable medleys flavored with their distinctive *berbere* and other spices.

The Mediterranean

In this region, including both the European and African shores, as well as the Middle East, cooks prepare slowly braised vegetables like eggplant with tomatoes, olive oil, onions, and, of course, garlic. The vegetables fade in color, but become very tender. Grilled vegetables, particularly eggplant, zucchini, and peppers, dressed with lemon juice and olive oil, are also a hit. Cooks of this region also prepare **dolma** (from the Arabic "stuffed"), vegetables like eggplant, squash, peppers, and tomatoes, or grape leaves stuffed with a rice-based filling.

Northern Europe

Northern Europeans enjoy root vegetables (like beets and parsnips) and potatoes. Often, vegetables are prepared **au gratin** (oh-grah-TAN)—that is, baked with cream and covered with cheese. Northern European cooks also enjoy preparing items like red cabbage or beets in sugar and vinegar as a sweet-and-sour dish. Dill is a favorite flavoring, as is horseradish.

The Americas

Four of the most popular vegetable items in the Americas are actually native foods: corn, beans, potatoes, and tomatoes. We'll talk more about each of these products later in the chapter.

Corn is eaten in many forms, fresh from the cob, creamed, popped, or as cornmeal, tortillas, or grits. Beans are enjoyed by nearly every culture in every region in the Americas, in one form or another, from New England's Boston baked beans to **frijoles refritos** (free-HOH-layss ray-FREE-tohss, refried beans) in Mexico to *feijoada* in Brazil, where black beans are served with various meats. Of course, potatoes have gone on to become one of the most popular vegetables in the world, as have tomatoes. These western hemisphere staples have traveled around the globe to become two of the most indispensable world ingredients.

How Cooking Affects Vegetables

Cooking vegetables properly has several beneficial effects, including

- Improving taste and smell by releasing aromatic oils
- Eliminating bitterness
- Brightening colors
- Tenderizing

However, on the other side of the coin, overcooking vegetables can have these negative effects:

- Destroying their texture (which, in some dishes in some cultures, is desired, as we'll discuss later)
- Washing out their color
- Eliminating nutrients

Effects on Texture

Texture in vegetables relies on three major components: water, fibers, and starch. Primarily, texture depends on the amount of water in the cells of the plant. The water makes the cells stiff and, as a result, the vegetable crunchy. A crisp stalk of celery, for example, becomes limp if you leave it unwrapped because the moisture in its cells evaporates. Dressed lettuce quickly becomes limp because the water in it is drawn out by the salt and sugar in the dressing.

Second, texture is affected by the fiber in the plant, specifically **cellulose**, a fiber that give the plant structure, and **pectin**, a jelly like substance that acts as the glue holding the cells together. Cellulose doesn't dissolve in heat, but pectin does.

Third, texture is affected by the starch in the vegetable. Obviously, this is more of a factor with vegetables like potatoes, squash, or beans. Starch makes such items very hard and dense. To soften starches, cooks must heat them to a point where they are gelatinized—137 to 150°F (58–68°C). If dried starchy vegetables like beans are involved, they obviously must be heated in water, but potatoes and squash contain enough internal moisture to gelatinize without added water.

In most cases, you have to walk a fine line when cooking vegetables. You don't want them so crunchy that they seem raw, but you do want them to have a little crunch (a little water in their cells) when bitten. The Italians call this slight chewiness **al dente** (al DEN-tay, "to the tooth"). You generally want to cook fresh vegetables as quickly as possible, either by stir-frying, sautéing, or using steam or briskly boiling water, to retain flavor and texture. The correct degree of doneness varies. The best way to ensure doneness is to taste the vegetables as they are nearing completion.

Pigments

Pigments produce the color in vegetables. There are four major pigments in vegetables:

1. **Chlorophyll** (KLOR-oh-fil)—*green*, as in spinach and broccoli. Greens become brighter when heated quickly, because substances between the cells are released and the brighter green is revealed. Greens turn dull if overcooked or cooked in acid. Although it is true that greens are brighter if cooked in alkaline water (that is, with baking soda added), *don't do it*. The cell structure is totally destroyed by baking soda and the veggie becomes mush. (Test this by cooking a broccoli spear in water with soda, then mashing it with a fork.)

2. **Flavones**—*white*, as in potatoes. They turn yellow if cooked in alkaline water or if overcooked.

3. **Anthocyanins** (an-thoh-SI-uh-nins)—*dark red*, as in beets and red onions. These turn blue if cooked in alkaline water or if overcooked.

4. **Carotenoids**—*orange/yellow*, as in carrots and tomatoes (yes, tomatoes!). These remain fairly stable cooked in acid, alkali, or even if overcooked.

From this list, you can deduce that, to retain colors other than green, you should add an acid such as lemon juice or vinegar to the water. For greens, simply heating them without overcooking is the best way to brighten them. If vegetables like broccoli or asparagus must be cooked in advance, blanch and shock them as suggested in Chapter 4, then reheat them at service.

Nutrients

Vitamins are the most important nutritional contributions vegetables make to our diets. However, vitamins may be easily lost as a result of overcooking or enzyme action that starts when plants are chopped and continues until they begin to boil. Chopping releases chemicals in the cells that destroy vitamins.

There is a problem regarding cooking vegetables in water. If you use a lot of water to cook vegetables, there is greater loss of vitamins from high heat. However, if you use less water, the water temperature is greatly reduced when the vegetables are put into the pot, allowing more time for the plant's enzymes to destroy vitamins before the water begins to boil again. The best advice for maintaining the vitamin content of vegetables is to cook them as quickly as possible, in rapidly boiling water or with steam. In other words, minimize the amount of time processing the product.

Description, Basic Preparation, Cooking, and Storage

In this section we examine each of the types of vegetables (as well as pasta, which is handled a lot like a starch vegetable or rice). We discuss how to handle the various types of fresh vegetables, including their storage, cleaning, and cooking. We also discuss handling canned and frozen foods.

There are many ways to categorize vegetables. For our purposes, vegetables fall into ten categories:

1. Leafy
2. Stem
3. "Fruits"
4. Onions
5. Crucifers
6. Roots
7. Mushrooms
8. Potatoes
9. Grains
10. Beans

We'll also discuss convenience vegetables as well as pasta, which is, after all, a starch item similar to rice.

Leafy Vegetables

Leafy vegetables, as the name implies, are those that consist mostly of the leaves of a plant. In Chapter 8, we discussed several types of leafy vegetables used as greens in salads. Two major examples of leafy vegetables used as cooked vegetables are Swiss chard and spinach.

Swiss chard has large, glossy green leaves with red or white ribs and stems. It must be washed thoroughly (but not soaked) before cooking. The ends of the stalks should be trimmed. The leaves may be cooked with the stems, or the stems and leaves may be cooked separately.

Spinach has deep-green leaves with narrow stems. It must also be washed thoroughly (it's very sandy) and any larger stems should be trimmed. Spinach may be cooked very quickly (in a minute or two) in a covered pan with a little water in the bottom.

Leafy vegetables should be stored covered in the refrigerator with some air circulation. They should be used as quickly as possible.

"Smothered" Vegetables

Although the technique violates every principle of cooking vegetables we have discussed, in the southern United States it is very popular to cook leafy greens and/or other vegetables for an hour or longer, usually with a certain amount of pork product, fat, and seasoning, until they have completely broken down. This technique is sometimes called *smothering*. The result is truly delightful (see the Cajun Greens recipe on the *Culinary Creation* CD-ROM), although it's fairly certain that all of the vitamins have been leached out by the end of cooking.

Stem Vegetables

As the name implies, **stem vegetables** are those in which only the aboveground stems are used as food. These include asparagus, fennel, celery, rhubarb, and bamboo shoots.

Asparagus is usually green and has a straight stalk with a fringe of tiny leaves at the tip. **Fennel** has a broad root with pale green stalks and a licorice-like flavor. **Celery** grows in bunches of long, pale-green stalks, and may be eaten raw or cooked. **Rhubarb** has red stalks similar to celery, and large green leaves (which aren't eaten). Rhubarb has a tart flavor and is popular baked in pies. **Bamboo shoots** are the young, cream-colored edible stems of the bamboo plant. They are popular in Asian stir-fry and in Japanese soups.

Stem vegetables must be washed very well before preparation. They should be stored in refrigeration. Stem vegetables are cooked chiefly by simmering or steaming.

"Fruit" Vegetables

"Fruit" vegetables are so named because they are technically fruits (that is, they contain seeds), but they are used culinarily as vegetables. Primary examples are squash, tomatoes, peppers, avocados, and eggplant. Tropical examples include the plantain, a relative of the banana, and the avocado. Olives also fit into the category of "fruit" vegetables.

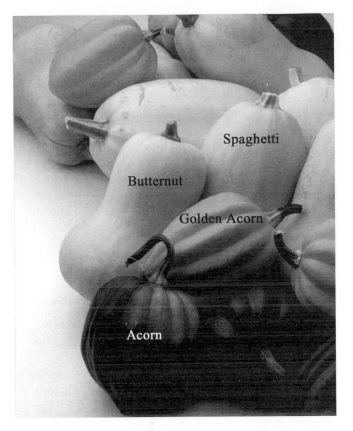

Spaghetti

Butternut

Golden Acorn

Acorn

FIGURE 12-2 Squash come in a wide variety of colors and shapes.

Squash (Fig. 12-2) include summer squash (for example, zucchini) and winter squash (for example, acorn). **Summer squash** are tender and have a mild flavor. To prepare summer squash, wash it well then trim the ends. Summer squash may be sliced, then steamed or sautéed. Store summer squash in the refrigerator. **Winter squash** are denser and have a comparitively strong flavor. Winter squash should be washed, then it may be baked or steamed, and often pureed. Squash should be stored in a cool, dark place, but need not be refrigerated.

Tomatoes come in many varieties, from small cherry tomatoes to large beefsteak tomatoes, and they have a vast number of uses. The **plum** or **Roma** variety is best for cooking, as in sauces and soups. Tomatoes are normally stored in refrigeration to reduce deterioration, although to do so decreases their flavor.

The **tomatillo** (Fig. 12-3), used in Mexican cooking, is a green berry with a husk. It's not a tomato, but a fruit called a *ground cherry* in the United States. It's most often used in stews and salsas.

Peppers range widely in size, shape, color, and levels of heat. The **bell pepper** (Fig. 12-4) or **sweet pepper** is popular for roasting and stuffing.

FIGURE 12-3   The tomatillo has a husk that must be removed to reveal the green fruit beneath.

FIGURE 12-4   Bell pepper colors range from green to red to yellow to orange.

Hot peppers or **chiles** (CHILL-eez) are often roasted, or may be chopped and used as flavoring. You should wear gloves when preparing them (because of the stinging chemicals), and you should remove the seeds and veins in the hottest varieties (unless you want very high heat in the finished product). The most popular types of chiles are **Anaheim**, a large, fairly mild variety; **jalapeño** (hah-lay-PAYN-yoh), a dark-green, thick-skinned type that can be fairly hot; **chipotle** (chih-POHT-lay), a smoked jalapeno; and **habañero** (ah-bahn-YARE-oh), a fiery hot variety that looks like a golf ball-size pumpkin. Peppers should be refrigerated.

Eggplants vary in size and shape. Although the most common type is purple, there is one variety that actually is the exact shape and color of a chicken egg. Eggplants should be washed and trimmed. The skin may or may not be removed. Eggplant is commonly sliced and grilled or cubed and stewed.

Plantains, although they look like bananas, are not eaten raw. When green, they are peeled, sliced, and fried in oil, like Cuban *tostones* (toh-STOHN-ayss). When ripe, especially when the skin is totally black, they are peeled and sautéd with sugar and cinnamon as a dessert (for example, Cuban *maduros* [mah-DOO-rohss]).

Avocados are rich, oily, pear-shaped fruits that grow in the tropics. They are very buttery and are normally consumed raw in salads.

Olives are the fruits of trees originally of the Mediterranean area. They must be soaked and pickled before being eaten. Olives are normally black or green, and come in several varieties, including Moroccan oil cured (Fig. 12-5) and the large Greek kalamata.

FIGURE 12-5   Wrinkly, black Moroccan oil-cured olives are very rich and flavorful.

Onions

Onions are members of the lily family and they include a wide array of pungent, aromatic plants. Common family members include the yellow onion, white onion, red onion, sweet onion, scallions, garlic, leeks, and shallots.

Yellow onions and **white onions** are chiefly used as flavoring ingredients in soups, stews, and sauces. To prep, they should be trimmed at both ends, then peeled. They should be stored in a cool, dark place.

Red onions are large, sweet purple onions. They are normally used raw in salads. They may be cooked, but, as mentioned under "anthocyanins" earlier in this chapter, they will turn blue if overcooked.

Sweet onions, such as Maui or Vidalia, are best when eaten raw or when grilled or sautéed. Sweet onions should be trimmed at both ends, then peeled. They should also be stored in a cool, dark place.

Scallions, also called *green onions*, are long and thin with white tips at the root end. Normally, the entire onion may be used, except for the roots and any wilted greens. They may be used in salads, as crudités, as garnish, or in stir-fried dishes. They should be stored in refrigeration.

Garlic (Fig. 12-6) is a bulb with a papery skin. Garlic is used around the world as a flavoring in such diverse dishes as mashed potatoes, Chinese stir-fry, Mediterranean aioli, Italian tomato sauce, and Cajun jambalaya. Cloves must be separated from the bulb, then peeled by first crushing with the flat side of a knife, then removing the peel. Whole, peeled garlic cloves are available for foodservice. Whole garlic bulbs should be stored in a cool, dark place.

Leeks look like large green onions, but they have a sweeter, stronger flavor. They may be used in soups, such as vichyssoise, or may be braised or sautéed. The roots should be trimmed, then dirt should be carefully cleaned from between the layers.

Leeks and Wales

The leek is the national dish of Wales. Centuries ago, Welsh soldiers going into battle proudly wore leeks on their headgear.

Shallots are like a cross between small onions and garlic. They have a papery skin and their flesh is purple and white. They should be trimmed at both ends, then peeled. They are normally carefully minced, so as not to bruise their delicate layers. They are excellent for flavoring sauces. Shallots should be stored in a cool, dark place.

FIGURE 12-6 An onion relative, garlic is one of the most popular spices in the world.

Crucifers

Crucifers (KRU-sif-fuhrs), also called *cruciferous* (kru-SIF-fer-uss) vegetables, are members of the cabbage family. They are so named because their flowers are cross shaped (as in "crucifix"). The major examples include cabbage, broccoli, Brussels sprouts, bok choy, and cauliflower. Cruciferous vegetables should be stored covered in the refrigerator with some air circulation.

Cabbage has a tight round head, in green, white, or red varieties. It is normally used fresh in salads, but it is very popular in Asian stir-fry or cooked in large wedges in stews. The leaves are also used to wrap meat or rice fillings. It's also popular pickled, as in European **sauerkraut** or Korean **kim chee**. (Europeans actually learned how to make sauerkraut from Asian nomadic tribes.) To prep a head of cabbage, first remove the outer discolored leaves, then remove the core. It may then be quartered and shredded.

Broccoli (BRAHK-uh-lee) forms tight clusters of tiny dark-green flowers atop a thick green stem. Broccoli may be eaten raw or cooked. To cook, wash it thoroughly, then cut the heads from the stems and cook them separately. The stems take longer to cook.

Broccoli is normally steamed or simmered briefly, but it may be sautéed in a stir-fry, as in beef and broccoli.

Brussels sprouts are like little heads of cabbage the size of golf balls. To prep them, remove the outer leaves and any tough parts of the stem. They may be steamed, simmered, or sautéed. Do not overcook.

Bok choy is a popular leafy form of Asian cabbage described in Chapter 8. For prepping, the leaves and stems should be washed and trimmed of any discoloration. The bok choy may then be chopped and the pieces steamed or sautéed.

Batches of Veggies

Cook veggies in batches that are as small as possible to maintain freshness. And, although it's tempting to do so, never mix batches of cooked vegetables together. The older batch will not match the newer and there is a danger of contamination.

Cauliflower is a white head of florets. To prep, cut away leaves and the tough end of the stem. Trim away any discoloration and wash thoroughly. Cut into florets. Cauliflower may be eaten raw, steamed, or sautéed.

Other popular members of the cabbage family include **rapini** (also called *broccoli rabe*), a leafy broccoli; **kohlrabi** (kohl-RAH-bee), a bulb that is a cross between cabbages and turnips; and **napa** or Chinese cabbage.

Roots

Roots are energy storage areas for plants. Therefore, root vegetables contain a great deal of carbohydrates and flavor. Examples of root vegetables include carrots, beets, parsnips, and cassava.

Carrots contain a great deal of sugar. As a result, when cooked, they are very sweet and pleasing to the taste. Carrots are popularly steamed or they may be sautéed and glazed with butter and sugar. To prep, cut away both ends and peel. Carrots should be refrigerated, but cut away the green carrot tops before storing to prevent moisture loss.

Beets come in several varieties, including baby beets, a small, round, red variety; red beets, very dark red, larger in size; and golden beets, small, yellow, and round. To prep, cut off the tops but leave 1 inch of the stem. Do not trim roots. Wash well. Steam before peeling. Beets may be boiled or glazed.

Parsnips look like yellow or white carrots. Before the rise of the potato, they were the most popular vegetable in Europe and the American colonies. (They were Thomas

Jefferson's favorite veggie.) They are prepped like carrots, by trimming the ends and peeling. They may be cooked in various ways, but they are excellent simply sautéed in butter.

Also called *manioc*, *tapioca*, and *yuca*, **cassava** is an important root in tropical countries. It grows about 12 inches long and has brown skin that must be removed before cooking. It is poisonous when raw. Cassava is boiled and used as a starchy vegetable, or is ground, dried, and used to make bread. Foodservice establishments normally purchase cassava meal in prepared form. Tapioca pudding is actually made from cassava.

Mushrooms

Mushrooms are types of fungi—that is, plants that lack chlorophyll and reproduce by means of spores. Mushrooms are a very popular item in today's foodservice industry. In this section, we discuss the most popular types and give general guidelines for cooking them. A safety reminder: Some mushrooms are poisonous; serve mushrooms you have obtained from a reputable vendor.

To prep fresh mushrooms, trim the ends of the stems if they appear discolored. Rinse the mushrooms in cold water. (Don't be afraid that they'll absorb excessive amounts of rinse water and become soggy; that's a popular myth. They aren't sponges.) Fresh mushrooms should be stored in refrigeration.

Mushrooms may be sautéed and eaten as a side dish, used as a flavoring in sauces and soups, or used as a garnish. They are also reduced to make a classic stuffing ingredient called **duxelle**. Some of the most common types of mushrooms are white, cremini, portobello, oyster, porcini, morel, and shiitake. Another important variety in fine cuisine is the truffle. **White mushrooms** are the generic, cultivated "button" variety commonly used to flavor soups and sauces, and are sautéed to garnish steaks. **Cremini** (kruh-MEE-nee) **mushrooms** are the same shape as button mushrooms but have a darker brown color and a stronger flavor. **Portobello** (not "portabella") **mushrooms** are mature versions of cremini. Their caps are popularly marinated, grilled, and served on buns as veggie burgers. **Oyster mushrooms** are fan shaped and grow on the trunks of trees. They have a fairly mild flavor but add an attractive visual element to dishes. **Porcini** (por-CHEE-nee) **mushrooms**, also called *cèpes* (seps) are large and brown and have a rich flavor. **Shiitake** (shih-TAH-kee) **mushrooms** are very dark brown with a large cap and they have a very rich flavor. The stems are tough; discard them before cooking. Shiitakes may be purchased fresh or dried. **Morels** (Fig. 12-7) are wild mushrooms with a distinctive honeycomb appearance that grow in North America, Asia, and Europe. They have an earthy, nutty flavor.

Truffles, very expensive fungi (hundreds of dollars per pound) that grow underground, usually near oak trees, are chiefly found in Italy and France. They have a very strong earthy flavor. Black truffles (Fig. 12-8) are chiefly used as an ingredient in cooked dishes, whereas white truffles are thinly sliced as a raw garnish on omelets or risotto. Although truffles are available packed in liquid, fresh truffles have a vastly superior flavor. Truffle-infused oil is often used to get the flavor without the expense of whole truffles.

FIGURE 12-7   Morels lend an unusual texture to a presentation.

FIGURE 12-8   Black truffles are extremely expensive, costing hundreds of dollars per pound.

In addition to the mushroom varieties mentioned, Asian chefs rely on various types of dried mushrooms such as the *cloud ear*, *snow*, and *bamboo* mushrooms.

Another unusual form of fungus used as food is found in Mexico. *Huitlacoche* (WEET-lah-coh-chay) is a fungus that enlarges corn kernels and turns them grayish black. These kernels are harvested and sautéed as a delicacy.

Potatoes

"For me, a plain baked potato is the most delicious one . . . it is soothing and enough."
—*M. F. K. Fisher, culinary writer*

Potatoes (Fig. 12-9) are tubers, the fleshy parts of underground stems. Originating in South America, they have gone on to become exceptionally popular around the world.

Cultures on every continent eat potatoes, from the *pommes frites* (pom FREETS, fried potatoes) of Belgium to the curried *aloo* (potato) dishes of India, from the potato chips of the United States to the *tortillas* (potato omelets) of Spain.

The Poutine Routine

One of the most beloved dishes in Quebec, Canada, is called *poutine* (poo-TEEN), which consists of thick French fries with cheese curds and gravy. Nearly every restaurant in Quebec features some version of poutine. Upscale establishments even feature poutine with artisan cheeses and classic French sauces. Even McDonald's® offers poutine, but the locals consider McD's fries too flimsy for the dish.

FIGURE 12-9 The potato is a versatile vegetable that may be served baked, fried, stewed, or mashed.

To maintain their quality, potatoes should be stored in a dry, cool, dark place with good ventilation. Although there are several varieties of potatoes, they really may be divided into two categories: high moisture and low moisture.

High-moisture potatoes, also called *waxy* or *new potatoes* are normally small and round. The skin may be red, pale yellow, pale brown, or purplish, like the Peruvian blue. The flesh may be white, yellow, or blue-purple. Because of their low starch content, high-moisture potatoes are suitable for salads, soups, or boiling.

Low-moisture potatoes, also called *mature* or *starchy potatoes* are larger, with a brown skin. The russet or Idaho potato is the classic type of low-moisture potato. Because their starch turns a golden brown, these are best for frying. They are also good for baking and are good mashed.

There is a third type of potato called the *all-purpose* or *chef's potato*. Higher in moisture than the Idaho, its main advantage is that it's cheaper than other potatoes because of its irregular shape. Therefore it's good for mashing and other applications for which appearance doesn't matter.

Sweet potatoes have a long, tapered, irregularly shaped body with brownish orange skin and orange or yellow flesh. They are normally roasted or boiled with the peels on, then the flesh, which doesn't hold its shape very well, is often pureed.

I Yam Not What I Yam

Although some varieties of sweet potatoes are sometimes called *yams* in the United States, that name is actually a misnomer. True yams are tropical starchy vegetables totally unrelated to the sweet potato and are hard to find in the United States.

Grains

Grains are grasses with edible seeds. The main types of grains used for food throughout the world are rice, wheat, and corn.

Rice

The most common grain used for food is rice (Fig. 12-10). Rice feeds more than half the world's population. From China to Louisiana, from the Philippines to Brazil, rice has been a staple food for many centuries. Actually, in many Asian languages, the word for food is the same as or related to the word for rice. For example, in Thai, rice is *kao* and food is *gab kao*, "with rice." To preserve its quality, store rice in a cool, dry place, tightly sealed.

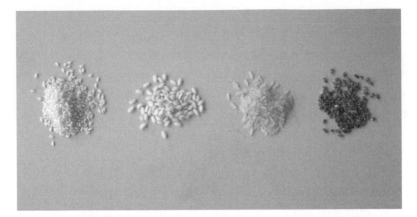

FIGURE 12-10   Some of rice's many forms: (left to right) ultrashort grain, arborio, converted long grain, and Bhutanese red rice, which grows at high altitudes in the Himalayas.

It's common practice to wash rice before cooking. It produces a less sticky product, but you may or may not decide to do so in your operation, depending on the final product you want to achieve. White rice is normally cooked in twice as much water as rice by weight. See the *Culinary Creation* CD-ROM for specific recipes.

White rice, rice that has had the outer husk and inner bran removed, is the most common type. It is divided into three categories, based on the size of the grain: **long grain**, three to five times longer than it is wide, which produces a fluffy product with separate grains; **medium grain**, shorter and slightly stickier; and **short grain**, very sticky and very short.

Converted rice is a long-grain white rice that has been partially cooked to preserve nutrients. Even though it does not have as much flavor as regular white rice, it is very commonly used in restaurants in the United States.

Arborio rice is a short-grain rice used to make Italian **risotto**, a category of creamy rice dishes. *Basmati rice* is a long-grain rice that has been fermented to produce a nutlike aroma. It is chiefly used in Indian cooking, but its popularity is growing in other cuisines. *Brown rice* has had the husk removed, but not the bran or inner covering. *Carolina gold* is one of the most popular varieties of long-grain white rice in the United States. *Glutinous rice*, short grain and very sticky, is popular in Asian cuisine because of its richer flavor and because it's easier to eat with chopsticks. *Jasmine rice* is a long-grain Asian rice that is very aromatic. *Sushi rice* is a short-grain Japanese rice that is not as sticky as glutinous rice. *Wild rice* is a type of grass seed unrelated to rice. It's a chewy grain with a nutty flavor that is native to the Great Lakes of North America. It must be thoroughly washed before cooking. Cooking wild rice takes up to three times longer (about an hour) than normal rice.

Wheat

Wheat is the major grain used in many areas of the world, especially the United States and Europe. Other than flour, which we discuss in Chapter 14, wheat comes in other useful forms.

Whole wheat is the entire grain of the wheat plant, unprocessed. It is normally **cracked** (cut into smaller pieces) before cooking, usually by steaming or boiling.

Bulghur wheat has been preprocessed—that is, cracked, cooked, dried, and ground into granules. It may be reconstituted by soaking in water. It comes in four grain sizes and is commonly used in Middle Eastern tabbouleh salad.

Wheat bran is the outer covering of the wheat and is normally removed during processing. It's often added to breads and cereals to enrich them.

Wheat germ is the tiny plant embryo at the base of the seed, which is usually removed during processing. Wheat germ is also often added to foods to enrich them.

Corn

Corn (Fig. 12-11), known in countries outside the United States as *maize* (mayz), is a tall plant that produces usually yellow seeds called *kernels* on a long cob. The kernels are consumed as a vegetable, but they are also dried and ground into various types of meal and flour. An extract, high-fructose corn syrup, is used as the primary sweetener in manufactured candies and beverages.

Corn meal is used to make such products as Italian **polenta**, a mush served creamy or firm, often served with cheese; and **scrapple**, a highly seasoned German-American product containing bits of pork.

Hominy, as we said in Chapter 6, is corn kernels that have had the hull and germ removed, usually by treating with lye. Hominy is often dried and ground to make *hominy grits*, a type of corn meal popular in the southern United States.

FIGURE 12-11   Fresh corn has been genetically modified during the past few decades to make it juicier and sweeter.

Masa (MAH-suh) is a Mexican term for dough made from corn cooked in quicklime (calcium oxide), used to make tortillas. When the dough is dried and ground, it makes a flour called *masa harina* (MAH-suh-REE-nuh).

Other Grains

Buckwheat is actually an herb, not a grain, native to Russia. From it, we get *kasha* (KAH-shuh), the **groats** (crushed seeds) of buckwheat. Kasha is used in Jewish and Eastern European cooking, especially in a dish called *kasha varnishka*, kasha with bow-tie pasta.

Oats are the most nutritious grain and they come in various forms, from groats to oatmeal. In the United States, oats are usually eaten as a breakfast food or cooked into cookies or muffins.

Barley is an ancient grain, dating to prehistoric times. It's rather chewy and is often used in soups.

Beans

Beans, also called *legumes* (LEG-yoomz), are seeds that come from pods. They have gained popularity as healthy foods during recent decades because they have been found to be the best source of plant protein. Most may be purchased as dried products, or they may be purchased in cans and sometimes frozen. Peas are also commonly available fresh.

Dried legumes should be stored in a cool, dry place, and should be used within six months. Dried legumes should be sorted before cooking to remove any dirt, stones, or discolored beans. Although they are commonly soaked overnight before cooking, supposedly to reduce cooking time, it is really not necessary to do so. Cooking unsoaked beans doesn't really take much longer.

Popular dried beans include *black beans*, brownish black medium-size beans popular in Caribbean cuisine; kidney beans, large, curved beans, solid pink to red; *lentils*, small, flat legumes that may be brown, green, or yellow; and *pinto beans*, red-and-pink speckled, medium-size, popular in Mexican cuisine.

Anasazi Beans

Some decades ago, in the 1950s, archaeologists in southern Colorado discovered, in a dwelling originally occupied by the ancient Anasazi, a clay pot hundreds of years old containing maroon-and-white dried beans. On a whim, one member of the group tried to sprout the legumes in water. Amazingly, a few of the beans were still able to grow. Today, *Anasazi beans* are a popular variety of so-called "boutique" beans available in many specialty stores in the Southwest. (Actually, the beans were also found growing wild by modern residents of the area, so not all the beans for sale are descended from those beans in the pot, but it's an interesting story.)

Peas are widely available as fresh produce, as well as dried, canned, and frozen.

Fresh legume pods are often used as whole vegetables, without removing the seeds inside, like green beans, Asian long beans, or Chinese snow pea pods. Fresh legume pods may be wrapped and stored in refrigeration for up to four days. Before use, they should be rinsed, and any tough strings or stems should be removed. If the beans are very large, they may be cut into pieces before cooking. Fresh pods may be boiled, steamed, or, if small and tender, stir-fried.

Peanuts are actually legumes. As mentioned in Chapter 1, in the southern United States they are popular boiled raw in the shell in salt water and eaten while still hot.

Edamame (ed-uh-MAH-may) are soybeans that are eaten fresh, especially in Japanese and Chinese cuisine.

Convenience Vegetables: Frozen and Canned

Many vegetables are available frozen and canned as convenience products. Although frozen vegetables are actually higher in vitamins than their fresh counterparts (because frozen veggies are chilled soon after harvest and therefore have had less chance to deteriorate), they usually have a softer texture because freezing breaks down cells. Of frozen vegetables, only frozen peas seem to be as acceptable as fresh.

Of canned vegetables, beans seem to be most accepted by the dining public, because their flavor and texture resembles the same product cooked from dried beans. As a matter of fact, some cultures prefer canned beans to fresh in some recipes, like barbecued beans.

Let's face it, sometimes chefs have to use convenience products. If so, use the following guidelines (similar to other commonsense principles discussed earlier in this book) to maximize quality and customer satisfaction:

- As with any delivery, check the product immediately on receipt to make sure it is at the correct temperature and that it is not damaged.
- Store frozen vegetables below 0°F (−18°C).
- Thaw frozen foods as described in Chapter 2.
- Don't overcook the foods. They are probably already bordering on being too soft.
- Clean can tops and the can opener before opening a can.
- Enhance the foods with herbs, spices, butter, and imagination. Garnish them attractively.

Pasta

Technically, **pasta**, Italian for "paste," refers to flour mixed with water, formed into hundreds of different shapes, then usually dried. However, the term has been broadened within the past few years to include egg noodles (flour mixed with eggs), so nearly everyone now accepts the wider definition.

The flour used to make good commercial dried Italian pasta is **semolina**, a coarsely ground hard wheat flour. However, to make fresh egg pasta (see the *Culinary Creation* CD-ROM), a lighter flour should be used.

Pasta should be cooked to the *al dente* stage in eight times as much boiling water (by weight) as the amount of pasta. Use a pot big enough to prevent boil-over, or you may add a little oil to the water to prevent boil-over. (The oil has no effect on the pasta.) Two table-spoons of salt should also be added to every 4 quarts of water. When done, drain pasta in a colander and rinse with cold water to halt cooking. Toss with a little oil to prevent sticking.

Some of the more common shapes of dried Italian pasta include *elbow macaroni*, small, curved tubes; *spaghetti*, long, thin tubes; *fettuccine* (FET-uh-CHEE-nee), thin, narrow ribbons; *lasagne* (luh-ZAHN-yuh), wide, flat ribbons; *capellini*, angel hair, very thin tubes; and *farfalle* (far-FAH-lay), bow ties. *Gnocchi* (NYOH-kee) are a popular type of fresh pasta dumpling (Fig. 12-12).

There are, however, many more pastas on the international scene than Italian types. As mentioned in earlier chapters, couscous is a tiny, granular pasta especially popular in Morocco. **Soba** is a Japanese noodle made of buckwheat flour. **Udon** is like a thick Japanese spaghetti. There are also many types of **rice pasta** (Fig. 12-13), popular in Asia, made with rice flour, including thin noodles that resemble spaghetti, Vietnamese flat rice sticks used in soups, and flat, circular spring roll wrappers. Rice pasta may be cooked by gently heating in warm water.

Summary and Conclusion

Proteins receive the most attention in the industry. However, it is important that you do not overlook vegetables and the critical role they play in the success of a foodservice establishment.

FIGURE 12-12 The characteristic gnocchi grooves may be made by rolling them with a fork.

FIGURE 12-13   Rice pasta is available in a wide variety of shapes, including thin rice noodles and circular rice paper, used to make the Vietnamese salad rolls illustrated in Chapter 1.

Vegetables are the savory edible parts of plants. In this chapter we talked about the world of vegetables and their importance in foodservice. We toured the various continents and learned about some of the styles and type of vegetables enjoyed on each. We discussed the components of vegetables and how the components are affected by cooking, as well as acidity and alkalinity. You also learned about the categories of vegetables and starches, and how they may be used in foodservice.

 ## Selected Terms for Review

Al dente

Anthocyanins

Buckwheat

Cabbage

Cellulose

Crucifer

Flavones

"Fruit" vegetables

Garlic

Grain

Leafy vegetables

Legumes

Maize

Mushroom

Onion

Pasta

Pectin

Pepper

Pigments

Potato

Rice

Root vegetable

Sweet potato

Vegetables

Wheat

Review Questions

1. Define vegetables.

2. True or false? Tempura is deep-fried in a light batter.

3. Name three major vegetables that originated in the New World.

4. Which of the following is not a way that cooking enhances vegetables:

   a. Eliminates bitterness

   b. Improves taste and smell

   c. Increases vitamin content

   d. Makes them tender

5. True or false? The more water there is in veggies, the crisper they are.

6. The fiber that gives a plant structure is the _____; the fiber that provides the glue to hold it together is the _____.

7. Match the pigment with its related vegetable.

____a. Flavones   1. Tomatoes

____b. Carotenoids   2. Beets

____c. Anthocyanins   3. Spinach

____d. Chlorophyll   4. Potatoes

8. What is the major nutritional contribution of vegetables?

9. What is a "fruit" vegetable? Name three examples of fruit vegetables.

10. True or false? A crucifer is so named because its stem is shaped like a cross.

11. Which example of a crucifer may also fall into the category of a leafy vegetable?

12. True or false? Cassava may be eaten raw.

13. The portobello is a large version of what other mushroom?

14. Truffles are found chiefly in what two countries? How should you use black truffles? White truffles?

15. Which type of potato is best for French fries? Why?

16. Define grains. What are three major types of grain?

17. In Asian nations, the name of what food is also often the word for food?

18. Name the three categories of white rice and describe each.

19. Name the Mexican dough used to make tortillas. Name the flour made by drying and grinding that dough.

20. Beans are also called _____.

21. What nut is included in the same category with beans?

22. True or false? There is no danger of contamination in canned goods because the cans are sterilized at the cannery.

23. Canned and frozen vegetables are called _____ vegetables.

24. Name three varieties of Italian pasta and describe their shapes.

Suggested Readings/Web Sites to Visit

Alden, L. *Vegetables.* Available at www.foodsubs.com/FGVegetables.html

Alford, J., Duguid, N. (1998). *Seductions of Rice.* New York: Artisan.

Bishop, J. (2001). *Vegetables Every Day.* New York: HarperCollins.

Bowers, S. *Thai cuisine.* Available at berncity.tripod.com/Thai.html

Jordan, P. (2000). *The Practical Mushroom Encyclopedia: Identifying, Picking, and Cooking with Mushrooms*. London: Southwater.

Katzen, M. (1997). *Vegetable Heaven*. New York: Hyperion.

Levy, F. (1993). *International Vegetable Cookbook*. New York: Warner.

Walton Feed: The Legumes. Anasazi beans. waltonfeed.com/self/beans.html#anasazi

Creating with Dairy Products and Eggs

Learning Objectives

By the end of the chapter, you should be able to

1. Define dairy products

2. Define and discuss lactose intolerance

3. Describe two processes that made milk more widely available

4. Describe nonfermented and fermented milk products

5. Describe how to cook milk products

6. Define butter and describe how it's made

7. Define cheese and describe, in general terms, how it's made

8. Name the two major categories of cheeses and their subcategories; name and describe examples of each

9. Describe the structure of an egg

10. Name the grades of eggs and describe each grade; name the sizes of eggs used in the United States

Chapter Outline

History of Dairy Products and Eggs

Milk Products

    Nonfermented Milk Products

    Cream

    Fermented Milk Products

    Cooking Milk Products

Butter

Dairy products include milk from various animals, as well as products made from milk. There is no other food so universally experienced by the human race as milk, because, as mammals, milk is our first meal.

Dairy products are included in a large percentage of dishes sold in the foodservice industry. Although not all cultures consume dairy products in large quantities, in the Americas and in Europe they are indispensable. Restaurants on these continents rely heavily on dairy products in every course to enrich their foods and excite their customers' palates. Cream is used in many classic sauces; cheese is served as an appetizer and as an essential ingredient in pizza and tacos; sour cream garnishes baked potatoes; butter is spread on bread; ice cream and cheesecake are served for dessert.

In this chapter we discuss the various dairy products and their uses, purchase, and storage. We'll also discuss eggs, which, although not "dairy" products, are often included in the same category as dairy, because milk, cheese, and eggs are so commonly used together in cooking. As always, related dairy and egg recipes may be found on the *Culinary Creation* CD-ROM.

History of Dairy Products and Eggs

As mentioned in earlier chapters, thousands of years ago humans began to domesticate various animals, mostly for their meat and hides. The animals they tamed were mostly mammals—that is, species that produce milk—including sheep, goats, cattle, and buffalo (not bison, as in North America, but true buffalo). Throughout the centuries, people came to realize that the milk these animals provided was a good source of nourishment. Although it isn't certain when people began harvesting and consuming nonhuman milk, the first recorded human use of milk from other mammals was about 7000 years ago, in northern Europe. Three thousand years later, it appears that animals were being milked in North Africa and that the Egyptians were even making cheese.

In India, dairy products became so important in ancient times that they play a significant role in the Hindu religion. According to some Hindu texts, many of the world's animals were created from butter. The Indian clarified butter, *ghee*, is considered to be one of the most sacred substances on earth, provided by the most divine animal, the cow. To this day, India produces milk-related products like **paneer**, a fresh cheese; and *galub jamun*, a fried-cheese dessert that are unique in the dairy world.

Gee, Ghee?

At Hindu weddings, the men engage in a contest to see who can consume the most ghee. Downing 2 pounds (1 kg) or more at a wedding is seen as a proof of virility.

Although they didn't eat butter, preferring olive oil for cooking, the ancient Greeks and Romans loved cheeses. The Roman food writer Apicius even wrote about the importance of cheese in the Roman diet.

Dairy products are virtually absent from the cuisines of many nations, most notably China. As a matter of fact, the majority of the world's inhabitants are **lactose intolerant**—that is, milk sugar (called *lactose*) upsets their stomachs (something to keep in mind regarding allergy considerations on your menu). People who are able to consume milk after infancy are in a minority on this planet. However, even those who cannot drink milk are able to consume many dairy products, like cheese, which contains very little lactose.

In the 19th century, two processes were invented that gave milk a longer storage life. First, **pasteurization** (PASS-chur-ih-ZAY-shun) was developed for the beer and wine industry (but later adapted to milk) by French scientist Louis Pasteur. Pasteur's process kills the bacteria that cause foods to spoil by exposing the product briefly to low heat

(161°F [72°C] for 15 seconds). Today, cream may be **ultrapasteurized**—that is, exposed to a higher heat (300°F [149°C]) than normal pasteurization. Ultrapasteurized cream has a longer storage life, but some chefs think it does not whip as well. Second, also in France, **homogenization** (huh-mah-jen-ize-AY-shun) was invented, a process by which milk is mixed so thoroughly that the fats don't separate. Both pasteurization and homogenization made it much easier to transport milk to markets, making it widely available for the first time to people who didn't live on or near farms.

Eggs of all sorts have always been fairly easy to acquire, especially in the spring, and some Stone Age chef undoubtedly tried cooking them at a very early stage in the evolution of cuisine. About 6000 years ago, the ancient cultures of the Middle East celebrated the spring equinox by giving gifts of dyed eggs, much as some cultures give colored eggs today at the Christian holiday Easter. The omelet, a dish also used to celebrate the equinox, was probably invented during this time in Iran.

The ancient Egyptians began using eggs in cakes to bind flour many thousands of years ago. We know from Apicius that the Romans cooked eggs in several ways 2000 years ago, including deviled (spiced) eggs and custards.

In the 19th century, the French developed hundreds of methods for cooking eggs. Supposedly, the number of pleats in a chef's *toque* (TOHK, hat) indicated how many ways a chef could cook an egg.

Today, mass production in the United States and other nations has made the chicken egg so uniform in quality and so inexpensive that it is one of the great bargains in the culinary world. But, of course, mass production has also created eggs with paler yolks and, some say, less flavor and a higher occurrence of salmonella, than those of a century ago.

Milk Products

There are many different types of milk and milk products, both fermented and nonfermented.

Nonfermented Milk Products

Fresh milk is available as **whole milk**, the pasteurized and homogenized product as it came from the cow (usually with vitamin D added); **skim milk**, milk with the fat removed; **low-fat milk**, with some of the fat removed; and **fortified milk**, with vitamin A added in addition to D. Fresh whole milk keeps in refrigeration for up to one week.

Evaporated milk is milk that has been heated to remove 60% of its water. **Sweetened condensed milk**, used in candies and desserts like key lime pie, is evaporated milk with 40% added sugar, by weight. These products are sold in cans, and have a shelf life of three to six months if unopened.

Dried-milk products—that is, milk in powdered form—are also available. Dried-milk products are often used in baking. They may be stored in a cool, dry place for up to three months.

Cream

Cream, the fat that has been removed from milk, comes in several forms. **Half-and-half**, a mix of cream and milk used in coffee, is 10 to 12% fat; **light cream**, also used for coffee as well as for sauces and soups, is normally 20% fat; **whipping cream** is 30 to 36% fat and is used for sauces, soups, and whipping; and **heavy cream** or **heavy whipping cream** is 36 to 40% fat. Other products, available mostly in England, **double cream** (48% fat) and **clotted cream** (55% fat) are spread like butter. Whipping cream is often sold in pressurized cans that can be used to apply topping directly to beverages or desserts. Reusable commercial devices are also available for this purpose.

Cream may be kept in refrigeration for up to one week. Ultrapasteurized creams keep for up to six weeks. Pressurized whipping creams keep for three weeks in refrigeration.

Nondairy creamers are also used in foodservice establishments, chiefly for adding to coffee. These have a much longer shelf life than real dairy products.

Fermented Milk Products

Crème fraîche (krem fresh), **sour cream**, **yogurt**, and **buttermilk** are all types of **fermented milk products**. These are produced by mixing bacteria into fresh milk or cream, then allowing it to sour or curdle for a few hours to give it a tart flavor and a thicker texture. Fermented milk products may be used in sauces, stews, marinades, desserts, or dips when a tangy creaminess is desired.

Buttermilk Now and Then

Modern buttermilk is not the same product as it was in the "good old days." Then, "buttermilk" referred to the leftover liquid after butter was churned. Today, the term refers to a tangy, fermented product that is sort of like thin sour cream.

Cooking Milk Products

Milk products have a tendency to curdle (separate) when heated, especially in the presence of an acid. To prevent curdling, it is best to add a roux or other starch when heating dairy products, and to use low temperatures to heat the product gently. It's also a good idea to temper a little of the hot liquid into the dairy product, as explained in Chapter 6.

Butter

"Good bread is the most fundamentally satisfying of all foods; and good bread with fresh butter, the greatest of feasts."

—*James Beard, American chef and culinary writer, 1903–1985*

Butter is indispensable in Western cuisine, not only for simply spreading on bread and melting on veggies, but also for emulsification into sauces and whipping into buttercream for dessert topping.

Butter is the product of agitating (churning) cream until it becomes semisolid. Consisting of about 80% milk fat plus some milk solids and water, butter is actually very easy to produce. It can be formed by simply shaking a jar of cream, or, accidentally, by over-whipping whipped cream.

In the United States, butter may be voluntarily graded based on texture, color, flavor, aroma, body, and salt content. Grade AA is the highest quality and Grade A is a close second. Grades B and C are not considered acceptable for foodservice use.

Butter may be purchased as salted or unsalted. Salted butter tends to keep longer, but most chefs prefer unsalted because they like to control the salt content of their dishes themselves.

Raw, whole butter burns easily and **breaks** (separates) when cooked. It should not be used for high-temperature cooking. As mentioned in Chapter 6, butter is often clarified to get rid of the milk solids and to raise its smoke point.

Margarine is a less expensive butter substitute invented (in France!) in the 1860s. It's made from vegetable and animal fats with added flavorings and color. Margarine's quality varies greatly. If you want to use margarine, you should test the various brands in your recipes before determining which one meets your needs.

Butter and margarine should be stored at 35°F (2°C). At that temperature, butter will (ideally) keep for three to five days, and margarine for five to seven days.

World Butters

Today, artisan butters from around the world are gaining popularity in foodservice. Customers are discovering that gourmet butters from Ireland, France, Italy, India, and the United States, as well as butter made from goat's or sheep's milk, have a pleasing variety of nutty flavors and floral aromas that are missing from today's overstandardized and overprocessed generic product.

Cheese

"A cheese may disappoint. It may be dull, it may be naive, it may be oversophisticated. Yet it remains cheese, milk's leap toward immortality."

—*Clifton Fadiman, American writer*

Cheese is the term for nearly any product made from milk curds. The cheesemaking process goes like this:

1. The milk (cow, goat, or sheep) is curdled by the addition of bacteria, acid, and/or rennet and/or artificial curdling substances. **Rennet** or **rennin** is a milk-digesting substance harvested from calves' stomachs.

2. The milk separates into solid, coagulated **curds** and cloudy, liquid **whey** (Fig. 13-1).

3. The curds are collected from the whey and either used fairly quickly (for fresh cheeses) or pressed into various shapes (for ripened cheeses).

4. The cheese to be ripened is injected with mold cultures (depending on the end product desired) and aged for various lengths of time.

Cheese is available in a huge variety of shapes, colors, textures, and flavors. Cheeses may be categorized according to various characteristics, such as amount of fat, age, type of milk, or texture, but we'll divide them into two essential groups: fresh and ripened.

Fresh Cheeses

Fresh cheeses are those that are only slightly aged and have no rind or mold growth. They are very moist and, for the most part, mild flavored. Primary examples include cottage,

FIGURE 13-1 Artisans use a large cheesecloth net to remove curds from whey in a Parmigiano–Reggiano factory in Parma, Italy.

feta, mascarpone, mozzarella, paneer, queso fresco, and ricotta. Fresh cheeses should be stored in refrigeration for no longer that five to seven days.

Cottage cheese is soft and moist with large, white curds and a mild flavor. It's used chiefly in salads.

Feta cheese is a very salty, soft, crumbly sheep's milk cheese from Greece. It has a rather strong, tangy flavor (unlike most fresh cheeses), and is used in salads and as an appetizer. The American version is made with cow's milk.

Mascarpone (MASS-kar-pohn) is a very smooth, creamy, tangy Italian cheese with a pale yellow color. It's classically used in the dessert **tiramisu** (teer-uh-MEE-soo), an Italian confection of coffee-flavored whipped cream and cheese.

The "Cheese" That Isn't

Even though it's extraordinarily popular for making dips and cheesecake, and for filling celery and spreading on canapés, cream cheese isn't really cheese at all. It's just milk and cream stiffened with vegetable gum. Cream cheese, invented in New York in the 1870s, was named "Philadelphia" because marketers thought that city had more appeal than New York.

Mozzarella (MOT-zuh-REL-uh) is an elastic white cheese that comes in varying degrees of firmness. Truly fresh mozzarella is very mild and tender, whereas the older cheese is firmer and chewier. The best Italian types are made with buffalo milk, but American versions are made with cow's milk. This cheese is used classically on pizza and in salads.

Paneer is a soft, ivory-color, sharp-flavored Indian cheese made from buffalo milk. It is classically cooked with spinach in the dish *palak paneer*.

Queso fresco (KAY-soh FRESS-koh), meaning "fresh cheese," is a product of Spain and Latin America. Made from goat's milk, it resembles dry cottage cheese.

Ricotta (rih-KAH-tuh) is a white, very moist, grainy Italian cheese. Meaning "recooked," it's made from the whey left over from the production of other cheeses. It's sometimes used as a filling in lasagna and ravioli, and, sweetened, to fill *cannoli*, tube-shaped pastries.

Ripened Cheeses

Ripened cheeses are those that are cured by various means. Curing may be achieved with the use of salt, special molds, or, most important, aging. Sometimes, dyes are added to give cheeses an expected, standardized look, as with cheddar, which most people expect to have an orange tint. (Many cheddars are left untinted today.) Ripened cheeses, when eaten as an appetizer or, as is the custom in many European countries, as a dessert, should always be served at room temperature.

All ripened cheeses should be stored in refrigeration. The harder varieties keep for up to three months, but the softer types should be stored for no longer than one week. Although, as we said, cheeses may be divided into many different categories and sub-categories, for our purposes we divide ripened cheeses into the following types: hard–grating, hard, semisoft, soft, and blue veined.

Hard–Grating Cheeses

As the name implies, **hard–grating cheeses**, called *grana* cheeses in Italy, are very dry, hard, and crumbly, and are used for grating over salads, rice, polenta, and pasta. This category includes **Parmigiano–Reggiano** (discussed in Chapter 8), a hard, light-yellow cheese with a sharp, nutty taste; and **pecorino**, a very sharp sheep's milk cheese, the most popular being *pecorino Romano*.

Hard Cheeses

Hard cheeses have a somewhat dry but not crumbly texture. They are moister than hard–grating types. Hard cheeses are easy to slice and grate, and are popular for use in cooked dishes. Examples include

- **Cheddar**, a white-to-orange cheese with a mild-to-sharp flavor that originated in England, the most popular cooking cheese in the United States

- **Provolone**, a light-yellow, elastic cheese with a mild-to-sharp flavor

- **Swiss**, a light-yellow rather firm cheese with a mild, nutty flavor and characteristic holes; popular for making **fondue**, a melted cheese dip

Semisoft Cheeses

Semisoft cheeses are moister and softer than hard cheeses, but they are not at all crumbly and are very easy to slice. Examples include **Monterey Jack**, a usually mild (but sometimes stronger), white cheese from the United States; **Edam** (EE-dum), a savory, mellow, all-purpose cheese from Holland with a rather elastic texture and a pale-yellow color, usually coated in red paraffin; and **Morbier** (mor-bee-YAY), a French ivory-color, mild cheese with an unusual layer of vegetable ash in the center.

Soft Cheeses

Soft cheeses may be fairly firm to liquid in texture, depending on their ripeness. They often have an edible white-mold rind. Examples include **Camembert** (KAM-um-behr), a cheese beloved by Napoleon, with a smooth, creamy pale-yellow interior and a soft powdery rind; and **brie** (bree), a similar but usually more pungent cheese (Fig. 13-2), also from France.

FIGURE 13-2   Brie is a creamy soft cheese with a white rind.

Blue-Veined Cheeses

Blue-veined cheeses have been inoculated with a blue mold that not only gives the cheese a very tart, strong flavor and aroma, but also distinctive visible blue streaks. Examples include **Roquefort** (ROHK-fert), a French sheep's milk cheese; **bleu cheese**, Roquefort-style cow's milk cheese; **Stilton**, a Welsh cheese, yellow with a blue-green marbling (Fig. 13-3); and, from Italy, **gorgonzola** (GOHR-guhn-ZOHL-uh), a soft, rather dry, piquant variety.

Eggs

"Oh, God above, if heaven has a taste it must be an egg with butter and salt."

—*Frank McCourt*, Angela's Ashes

"I can eat fifty eggs."

—*Paul Newman*, Cool Hand Luke

Eggs are often taken for granted largely because they are seemingly so simple. But they aren't (Fig. 13-4). **Eggs** are oval, hard-shelled reproductive structures produced by birds. Eggs have not only a complex structure, but diverse uses in cooking. They are enjoyed as stand-alone food items and are also used to garnish salads, thicken and emulsify sauces, and glaze baked goods.

FIGURE 13-3   Stilton is a pungent, blue-veined cheese from Great Britain.

FIGURE 13-4   The egg is more complex than it seems.

Structure of an Egg

Eggs may seem like simple, three-part things (shell, yolk, and white), but they are more intricate than they appear. As shown in Figure 13-5, eggs are made up of many individual layers and parts.

The **yolk**, which looks solid to the naked eye, is actually made up of many tiny sacs of protein and fat, enclosed in individual membranes, floating in water. That's why, when the yolk is cooked firm, it's crumbly instead of solid. The yolk contains most of the fat,

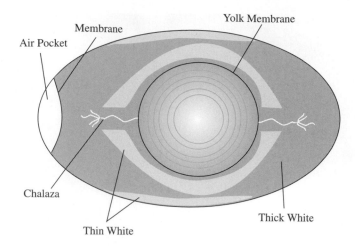

FIGURE 13-5   Structure of a chicken egg.

TABLE 13-1
Egg Sizes in the United States

Size	Weight of Egg Contents
Jumbo	2.5 oz (71 g)
Extra large	2.25 oz (64 g)
Large	2 oz (57 g)
Medium	1.75 oz (50 g)
Small	1.5 oz (42.5 g)

protein, and vitamins, as well as iron, in the egg. The yellow color of the yolk comes from the pigment *xanthophyll*, found in alfalfa and corn.

The **white** is actually four layers of thin white and thick white. The white is mostly water, mixed with a protein called **albumen** that's also found in the brain. That's why, when you cook brains, they look like scrambled eggs. (Hey! No foodism!) Despite their unappetizing appearance, the white strands, called *chalazae*, are made from the same substance as the rest of the white. They anchor the yolk inside the egg.

Grades and Forms of Eggs

In the United States, the USDA grades eggs AA, A, and B according to how well the egg maintains its shape when raw. Those with yolks that that sit highest on a plate and have the least runny whites are graded AA. Those with the flattest yolks and the runniest whites are graded B. Eggs are also graded according to size (Table 13-1).

Chicken eggs may be purchased in the following forms: fresh (in the shell or bulk, as liquid), frozen (whole, yolks, or whites), or powdered (mostly for baking). They may also be purchased pasteurized, for safety, as discussed in Chapter 8.

Cooking Guidelines

Although there are specific egg recipes on the *Culinary Creations* CD-ROM, here we'll discuss some general procedures for the basic ways to cook eggs. First of all, make certain, when cooking and handling eggs, that you practice good personal hygiene and sanitation.

Poached Eggs

To poach eggs, use the freshest eggs possible. Break the egg into a cup, then slide it gently into barely simmering water. Cook for 3 minutes, or until the white is opaque. Remove the egg from the water with a slotted spoon and serve immediately—or chill and rewarm at time of service.

"Boiled" Eggs

"Boiled" is the term often used for eggs cooked by simmering (not boiling) in the shell. For soft-cooked, medium-cooked, or hard cooked chicken eggs, bring eggs to room temperature before cooking to prevent cracking. If hard cooking, use eggs that are several days old, if possible, for easier peeling. Place the eggs into simmering water, then cook them according to the following times (for large eggs): coddled, 30 seconds; soft, 3 to 4 minutes; medium, 5 to 7 minutes; hard, 12 to 15 minutes. Submerge them in cold water to stop their cooking. Peel hard-cooked eggs under running water while still slightly warm.

Fried Eggs

To fry an egg, break the egg into a cup but do not break the yolk. Place fat in the pan. Heat the fat until it faintly smokes. Gently place the egg in the fat. For *basted* eggs, spoon some of the fat over the egg as it cooks. For *sunny-side up* eggs, do not baste the egg with fat. For *over-easy* eggs, turn the egg over and cook it briefly just at the end of cooking, leaving the yolk runny. Season to taste. Serve immediately.

Scrambled Eggs

For scrambled eggs, break two to three eggs into a bowl. Add 1 tablespoon of water. Season to taste. Whip eggs until blended. Heat a pan over medium heat, then melt butter in the pan. Heat the pan until hot. Add the eggs and cook over low heat, stirring frequently until creamy. Remove from heat and serve immediately.

Eggs around the World

Quail eggs, although very tiny, are popular in Asia for the visual delicacy they lend to a dish. **Baluts** are popular in the Philippines. They are duck eggs containing a partially formed baby duck. These are usually hard cooked and eaten as a snack. **Century eggs**, popular in China, are chicken, duck, or goose eggs preserved in quicklime, ashes, and salt for a hundred days until the shell is black, the white is amber, and the yolk is green. These are served as an appetizer with ginger and soy sauce. **Salty duck eggs** (Fig. 13-6),

FIGURE 13-6   Salty duck eggs are sometimes vacuum wrapped to preserve them for storage.

sometimes tinted red, are pickled eggs used as an ingredient in various dishes throughout Asia.

Omelets vary in size, shape, and contents around the world. In Japan, omelets are very plain and thin. They are rolled and sliced and served with sushi rice. In Spain and Italy, omelets are cooked in a large skillet, browned on the bottom, and served flat. Spanish omelets, which normally contain potatoes, are called *tortillas* (tor-TEE-yuhz); and Italian omelets, often containing pasta, are called *frittatas*. American omelets are normally well browned and folded in half, whereas classic French omelets are not browned and are rolled into a neat spindle shape (Fig. 13-7).

Omelet Stations

Many areas' health regulations do not permit, because of the risk of cross-contamination, what was once a common practice: mixing a large quantity of eggs together for use at an omelet station at a buffet. Check your local codes before proceeding.

FIGURE 13-7   (Left) Classic French omelets are rolled without browning. (Right) American omelets are normally browned and folded.

Summary and Conclusion

In this chapter we turned our attention to the wide variety of dairy products used in the foodservice industry. We learned about the versatility of such products as butter, cream, eggs, and milk. We also had a look at the wide variety of cheeses around the world.

As a foodservice professional, you must be proficient and knowledgeable in the use of various dairy products. You are encouraged, as always, to investigate this topic further, to broaden your own understanding of the world of dairy.

 ## Selected Terms for Review

Blue-veined cheese
Butter
Cheese
Dairy products
Egg
Fresh cheese

Hard cheese
Hard–grating cheese
Homogenization
Lactose
Milk
Pasteurization
Ripened cheese
Semisoft cheese
Soft cheese

Review Questions

1. Define dairy products.

2. True or false? The lactose intolerant cannot eat cheese.

3. Define pasteurization. Name two pasteurized products, including one we first discussed in Chapter 8.

4. Define homogenization.

5. What is the difference between fermented and nonfermented milk products?

6. Which of the following is not a fermented milk product?

   a. Clotted cream

   b. Buttermilk

   c. Sour cream

   d. Yogurt

7. Why is unsalted butter preferred for use in foodservice?

8. Describe the process for making cheese. What is the difference between curds and whey?

9. Match the cheese in the left column to the correct category on the right.

   ____a. Feta   1. Hard–grating

   ____b. Pecorino   2. Hard

   ____c. Cheddar   3. Blue veined

   ____d. Edam   4. Semisoft

   ____e. Brie   5. Fresh

   ____f. Stilton   6. Soft

10. Which part of an egg contains most of the fat, protein, and vitamins?

11. What protein is contained in egg whites? Where else is this protein found?

12. Describe a Grade AA egg.

13. You are cooking a recipe that requires 1 pint of eggs. How many large eggs will you need?

14. Why is the term *hard-boiled egg* technically incorrect?

15. Describe two types of eggs popular in Asian nations.

16. Describe the difference between an American omelet and a classic French omelet.

Suggested Readings/Web Sites to Visit

(April 2005). American Cheese. *Saveur.* Vol. 83 44–86.

Butter and Ghee in India: webexhibits.org/butter/countries-india.html

Harbutt, J. (1998). *The World Encyclopedia of Cheese.* New York: Anness Publishing.

Kazuko, M., Yamada, T. (1996). *French Cheeses.* New York: DK.

Marshall, M. (1968). *The Delectable Egg.* New York: Trident.

Seranne, A. (1983). *The Complete Book of Egg Cookery.* New York: MacMillan.

Teubner, C. (1998). *The Cheese Bible.* New York: Penguin.

USDA Data: Dairy and Egg Products. *Chef 2 Chef.* Available at chef2chef.net/kb/index/97-usda-dairy-egg.htm

Basic Baking Principles

Learning Objectives

By the end of the chapter, you should be able to

1. Discuss the history of baking

2. Name the functions performed by ingredients in baking

3. Define leavening and name the types of leaveners

4. Name and describe types of mechanical leavening

5. Name and describe the types of yeast

6. Name and describe the types of chemical leaveners

7. Name and describe the major types of sugars

8. Describe the role of salt in baked goods

9. Describe the role of flour and gluten in baking

10. Calculate bakers' percentages

11. Name the major fats used in baking and describe them

12. Name and describe the steps in bread making

13. Describe the phases a product undergoes when baking

14. Define quick breads, and name and describe the two major methods by which quick breads are prepared

Chapter Outline

History of Baking

The Elements Used in Baking

Leavening

Mechanical Leavening

"To sign on Adam to your crew is to buy, for a time, the best bread *I've* ever tasted. It ensures that your customers, when examining their bread baskets, will exclaim, 'Where did you get this *bread?*' . . . It also means that your life will be a waking nightmare."

—*Chef Anthony Bourdain*, Kitchen Confidential, *in reference to a sociopathic but brilliant bread baker*

Bakers are a separate breed from other chefs. There is a certain temperament required for working with flour, yeast, sugar, and fat to create ingenious, artistic, delicious works that people will remember long after they have finished their meal. Baking also requires that a certain amount of space in the restaurant's kitchen be dedicated to rolling and kneading and rising and baking—square footage that many chefs would rather use for other purposes. For these reasons, baked goods are often purchased from outside vendors, businesses with resources and employees who are completely dedicated to the baking arts.

However, many chefs, like Tony Bourdain in the opening quote, also realize that customers are very impressed when they know you are producing your own baked goods in your own kitchen (Fig. 14-1), especially if those items are exceptional. It keeps them coming back.

FIGURE 14-1   Artisan breads baked in your own kitchen can favorably impress your customers.

For this reason, it is important that, even if you do not want to be a baker, as a food-service professional you must have a basic understanding of the baking arts. This chapter is a whirlwind tour of the world of baking, outlining the principles of the various baking techniques. For students who want to pursue the subject further, there are many other books, classes, and entire curriculums available. As usual, formulas related to this chapter are included on the *Culinary Creation* CD-ROM.

History of Baking

The earliest forms of bread making occurred in prehistoric times. Grains were boiled in water to make a gruel, then were left to dry by the fire, which turned the mixture into an early type of unleavened flatbread. If the mixture was left to sit while still moist for a period of time before drying, natural yeasts in the air would cause it to ferment and rise, making it fluffier, creating (naturally) an early form of leavened bread.

Modern wheat evolved about 10,000 years ago, probably in the region of Mesopotamia (Iraq), and was being ground into flour a few thousand years later. Archaeologists have discovered a stone used for grinding grain that is 7500 years old.

The Egyptians discovered yeast as a result of their beer-brewing efforts, and were able to grow it and use it for bread baking at least 2500 years ago. Today, all yeasts used for bread are derived from those originally used for brewing beer.

Wheat arrived in ancient Greece about 600 BCE, and the Greeks became skilled at baking breads. They invented the enclosed oven, heated by wood fires.

FIGURE 14-2   The round *boule* (BOOL) is one of the earliest shapes of bread loaves.

Baking became a respected profession. The Bakers Guild, still in existence today, was founded in Rome in 168 BCE. Its members became proficient at mass producing breads for sale to the public.

Baking as a profession declined during the Dark Ages and reappeared again during the Middle Ages. When sugar and cocoa began to be imported to Europe from the New World, pastry making became a high art. During the reign of Henry the VIII in England in the 16th century, royal chefs produced spectacular, visually intricate confections to please the king. The term *banquet hall* originally referred to the room reserved strictly for serving those fabulous desserts, not the whole meal.

Yeast was the main source of leavening until the 1800s, when chemicals (for example, baking soda, discussed later) replaced yeast as the leavener in some applications, like Irish soda bread.

Flatbreads

The term *flatbread* refers to various breads used in many cultures around the world that work both as a food and an eating utensil. In Chapter 7 we mentioned various types that may be used in sandwiches.

Flatbreads may be leavened or unleavened. Leavened examples include the Middle Eastern pita and Ethiopian *injera*. Unleavened types include Mexican tortillas, French crepes, and Chinese pancakes.

Today, bread and pastry baking are much more of a tradition in the Western world than in Asian nations. Chinese confections, such as sweet buns, are normally steamed. There are some exceptions, however. Vietnam, for example, has a Western style bread-making tradition, adopted from their French colonizers. In addition, Filipinos create a sweet and savory rice flour cake wrapped in banana leaves called *bibingka*.

The Elements Used in Baking

In a way, baking is fairly simple. There are a limited number of ingredients, each fulfilling one or more functions in the baking process. These functions are leavening, sweetening, flavoring, stabilizing, thickening, and tenderizing.

Leavening

Leavening is adding air or another gas to a dough to make it lighter, improve its texture, and increase its volume. *Leaveners* are substances used to leaven dough. Leaveners may be mechanical, biological, or chemical.

Mechanical Leavening

Mechanical leavening uses physical means to create gas in the product:

- The air that is whipped into egg whites makes a soufflé rise as it heats.

- The butter that is incorporated into puff pastry makes the dough rise. This works because, as it is heated, the butter gives off steam that physically expands the dough. Steam is also the main leavener in **pâte à choux** (POT uh SHOO), also called *éclair* dough (Fig. 14-3).

Biological Leavening

Biological or **organic leavening** is yeast, a living organism that feeds on sugars and produces alcohol and, more important, carbon dioxide gas, which expands the dough. Yeasts are very sensitive to temperature. They function poorly below 70°F (21°C) and are killed at 140°F (60°C).

There are three basic types of yeast used for baking: fresh, active dry, and instant. **Fresh yeast** comes in compressed cakes. It is fully alive in the package and may be added directly to a formula. Fresh yeast must be stored in refrigeration and will keep only for one to two weeks.

Active dry yeast is granular and dormant. It should be reactivated in warm water of 105 to 110°F (41–43°C) before use. Unopened active dry yeast may be stored at room temperature for many months. It should be refrigerated after it's opened.

Instant dry yeast is also granular and dormant, but it doesn't need to be reactivated. It may be added directly to a formula. Instant yeast should be refrigerated after opening.

FIGURE 14-3   The golf ball-size profiterole (proh-FIT-uh-roll) is a cream puff made with pâte à choux dough that may be filled with sweet or savory fillings.

If you substitute active dry yeast for fresh yeast, use 40% of the amount called for by weight. If you substitute instant yeast, use 33%.

Chemical Leavening

Chemical leavening uses chemical reactions to produce gases in dough or batter. The two major chemical leaveners are baking soda and baking powder.

Baking soda is a chemical called bicarbonate of soda or sodium bicarbonate. It releases carbon dioxide gas when an acid and moisture are present.

Baking powder is a blend of baking soda and other substances, *including* acid. Single-acting baking powder begins to emit gas immediately on contact with moisture. Double-acting baking powder releases gas twice, once when it contacts moisture and again when it is heated.

Sweetening

Most **sweeteners** are some form of **sucrose**, which is extracted from sugar beets and sugarcane. **Sugar** is the general term for the water-soluble, crystalline sweetener found in fruits, honey, corn, sugarcane, and sugar beets. Common sugars include **granulated sugar**, fine, white sugar crystals, also called *table sugar*; **superfine sugar**, more finely ground than granulated; and **confectioner's** or **powdered sugar**, an extremely fine, powdery product used for frostings and decoration.

FIGURE 14-4   Challah is a rich, traditional, braided Jewish bread that uses sugar and eggs to provide richness. Bread by Ray Pisar.

Sugars help baked goods to caramelize attractively, and may be used as creaming agents when blended with fats like butter. Sugars also tend to make products more tender and moist, as in the Jewish bread challah (HAH-luh) (Fig. 14-4).

Other sucrose sweeteners include **molasses**, concentrated sugarcane juice; **brown sugar**, white sugar with added molasses; and **cane syrup**, a dark sugarcane product thinner than molasses. These contain acids, making them desirable to be used with baking soda. **Maple syrup**, reduced sap of the maple tree, is a concentrated form of sucrose.

Sucrose is actually a combination of two simpler sugars: **glucose** (also called *dextrose*) and **fructose**. Glucose is less sweet than sucrose, but fructose is 30% sweeter than sucrose.

Corn syrup, used in icing and candy, is chiefly glucose. High-fructose corn syrup is corn syrup that has been partially converted to fructose, giving it about the same sweetness as sucrose. High-fructose corn syrup is used in most manufactured sweet snacks and beverages.

Honey, secreted by bees from ingested flower nectar, is also made of glucose and fructose. Honey varies in flavor and appearance, depending on the type of nectar ingested by the bees. Some types, like buckwheat honey, have a dark color and strong flavor, whereas others, like citrus blossom honey, are light and mild flavored.

Malt sugar or **maltose** is extracted from **malt**, germinated grains. Maltose is used in brewing beer and baking bread.

About Glucose

From the human point of view, glucose is the most important sugar, because it's the body's primary source of energy. The starches and sugars in the foods you digest are, for the most part, transformed into glucose.

Contrary to popular belief, your body can't tell the difference between a "natural" sugar like honey and a "processed" sugar like white table sugar. They both are fully converted to glucose after they are eaten, and, nutritionally, they contribute only food energy (calories) to your body.

Artificial sweeteners, containing few or no calories, may be used in heart-healthy desserts on your menu. Some of them, such as **aspartame** (ASS-par-taym, sold as Nutrasweet®) break down into bitter compounds when heated, making them suitable only for cold uses like whipped cream. Others, such as **sucralose** (SOO-cruh-lohss, sold as Splenda®) remain stable when cooked and may be used in baked goods. By weight, aspartame is 200 times sweeter than sucrose, whereas sucralose is 600 times sweeter. When using artificial sweeteners, do not assume they will perform well at functions other than sweetening (for example, caramelization or stabilization or moisturizing.) Adjust formulas as necessary.

Flavoring

Flavorings in baked goods include not only things like extracts, but also nuts, chocolate, fruits, jams, and jellies. Spices, like cinnamon and nutmeg, are also important tools in adding flavor.

Salt in Baked Products

As in almost all culinary products, salt is crucial in baked goods for seasoning—that is, enhancing the existing flavors. However, salt also performs two additional important functions in baking: it strengthens dough and it inhibits the uncontrolled growth of yeast.

A word about **vanilla**. Real vanilla is a flavoring extracted from the beans of an orchid plant. Although many quality-minded pastry chefs insist on using expensive vanilla extract or even vanilla beans in their baking, a recent series of blind taste tests conducted by a prominent culinary magazine indicate this is a needless expense. Even professional bakers and pastry chefs could detect no significant flavor difference between finished products containing expensive vanilla and the cheapest imitation vanilla. In one test, the professionals even *preferred* the taste of the imitation vanilla (without knowing what they were tasting, of course).

Stabilizing

Stabilizing is performed chiefly by wheat flour and other ingredients containing protein. The protein gives the product structure and strength. The main protein in flour is gluten. **Gluten** absorbs water and, as the flour is kneaded or mixed, it forms a web of elastic strands. These strands capture gases released by the leavener and help the product to rise.

The flour with the most gluten (more than 12%) is **bread flour**. **Pastry flour** has less gluten and is used for such things as pie crust. **Cake flour** has the least gluten (6–8%) and is used for the most delicate baked products.

All-purpose flour is a middle-of-the-road blend with a moderate amount of gluten and, for the most part, is not used in professional bakeries.

 **Bakers' Percentages**

Flour plays an important part in documenting bakers' formulas. (Remember, we said that bakers call recipes *formulas*.) In a formula, bakers' percentages are often used to express the quantity of ingredients. Flour is always used as 100%, then the other ingredients are stated as a percentage based on the amount of flour. For instance, if a formula uses 2 pounds of flour and 1 pound of sugar, then the amount of sugar would be expressed as 50%. If the formula used 2 pounds of flour and 3 pounds of sugar, then the amount of sugar would be 150%. The formula for calculating the percentage is as follows:

$$\frac{weight\ of\ ingredient}{weight\ of\ flour} \times 100\% = \%\ of\ ingredient$$

To determine the weight of an ingredient if you are given the percentage of the ingredient and the weight of flour, use this formula:

$$weight\ of\ ingredient = weight\ of\ flour \times \frac{\%\ of\ ingredient}{100}$$

303

With regard to stabilizing, the protein in eggs also provides structure and strength, especially in meringues and angel food cakes. Also, although not proteins, sugars can give a product stability. Cooked sugars, for example, make a Swiss or Italian meringue more stable than common meringue.

In Asia, **rice flour** (finely ground rice) is sometimes used to provide structure in baking, although it does not form gluten like wheat flour. As we mentioned previously, Philippine *bibingka* is a major example of a product baked using rice flour.

Thickening

We discussed thickeners in Chapter 6, and much of what we discussed there applies here as well. The main thickeners used in baked goods are cornstarch and arrowroot, used for puddings and fillings; flour, used for fruit pie fillings; eggs, used for such things as pastry creams; and gelatin.

Gelatin, as mentioned in Chapter 4, is a product rendered from bones and connective tissue, especially collagen. In baking, added gelatin enables the creation of delicate desserts that hold their structure, like Italian **panna cotta**. In professional baking, gelatin is mainly used in sheet form, not as a powder. Gelatin must be softened in water or **bloomed** before adding to a formula.

Tenderizing

Fats like butter, oil, lard, and vegetable shortening provide tenderness in baked goods. They also provide moistness and richness, as well as added flavor. Fats make gluten strands shorter, resulting in a more tender product. That's why they are sometimes referred to as *shortening*. Fats may be creamed into the product, providing even distribution and a moist, cake like texture, or they may be added in coarse pieces, as in pie crust, resulting in a flaky texture. Egg yolks are also often used to provide tenderness. They contain natural emulsifiers that help to create smooth batters and dough.

Different fats have different advantages:

- Although it is expensive and highly temperamental, butter is a desirable fat in baking because of its flavor and "mouth feel".

- **Vegetable shortening** has little flavor, making it preferable for applications when the chef wants to control closely the taste of the finished product. It also tends to melt at a much higher temperature than butter. As a result, it is easier to use than butter and it provides a flakier texture.

- **High-ratio** or **emulsified shortening** is a modern development that allows a greater amount of sugar to be added to a formula by holding it in suspension more effectively than normal shortenings. It spreads evenly in a cake batter and gives the finished product a more delicate texture. The prime example of a high-ratio cake is *devil's food*, which contains 33% more sugar, by weight, than flour.

- Oils aren't normally added to baked products, but are used instead for greasing pans and for deep-frying.

- **Lard**, the rendered fat of pigs, is very easy to use and is excellent for making flaky pie crusts. However, modern shortenings have more or less replaced lard in today's bakeries.

The Bread-Making Process

"Bread is the king of the table and all else is merely the court that surrounds the king. The countries are the soup, the meat, the vegetables, the salad, but bread is king."

—*Louis Bromfield, American novelist*

Making yeast breads involves 12 steps (Table 14-1) that are universally recognized throughout the industry. These steps have been developed over centuries of bread making and each has a purpose in the process.

Bagels

The process for creating the traditional Jewish bagel differs in one major respect from baking standard breads. After proofing, the shaped dough circle is simmered in water with malt sugar for a minute or two before baking, to give the crust its characteristic chewiness (Fig. 14-6).

FIGURE 14-5 The long, narrow *baguette* (bag-ET) is considered to be the true test of the bread baker's skill.

TABLE 14-1

Steps in Making Yeast Bread

Step	Description
1. Scaling the ingredients	As we said previously, bakers always weigh or **scale** their ingredients for precision. Also, after scaling, the dry ingredients are sifted. (You can measure wet ingredients, like water or eggs, by volume; just remember that "a pint is a pound" or 1 L equals 1 kg.)
2. Mixing	There are two basic methods for mixing bread dough: the **straight-dough method**, used for basic breads like French and Italian, a one-step process in which all the ingredients are put into the mixing bowl and mixed; and the **sponge method**, used for sourdough and similar breads, for which flour, yeast, and water are mixed together in a batter that is allowed to ferment for a day or more. The batter is then used in the assembly of the bread dough.
3. Fermenting	The dough is placed in an oiled container, covered lightly, and allowed to rest in a warm area, about 80°F (27°C), until it rises to double its volume.
4. Punching	The risen dough is deflated and kneaded to redistribute the yeast and the gluten.
5. Scaling the dough	The dough is divided into portions and weighed to ensure they are of equal size.
6. Rounding	The portions are shaped into balls.
7. Benching	The portions rest and rise on the bench for several minutes.
8. Shaping	The portions are shaped into their final form.
9. Proofing	The shaped dough is allowed to rise in a warm place before baking.
10. Baking	The bread is baked.
11. Cooling	The bread is allowed to cool on racks to evaporate excess moisture.
12. Storing	The cooled bread is served within eight hours or wrapped tightly and frozen.

FIGURE 14-6 Bagels often have flavorful toppings like toasted onions or poppy and sesame seeds.

The Effects of Baking

As it bakes, dough undergoes certain changes as it reaches specific temperatures (Table 14-2). It's important that you have a basic understanding of how this process works.

Quick Breads

Quick breads are made with chemical leaveners, usually baking soda and/or baking powder. This category includes cornbread, Irish soda bread, muffins, biscuits, pancakes, waffles (Fig. 14-8), and English scones. As their name implies, these breads can be prepared much more rapidly than yeast breads. If you want to offer your customers homemade bread, these products may be created without the time and labor involved in making yeast breads.

Two major methods are used in preparing quick breads: the biscuit method, used for making dough-based products; and the muffin method, used for making batters. The major thing to remember when making quick breads is: Do not overwork the dough. You do not want gluten to develop in quick breads. The dough should be light and tender, not tough.

TABLE 14-2
Stages in the Baking Process

Temperature	Stage	Description
85°F (29°C)	Leavening	The gases in the dough expand in a controlled, gradual manner.
110°F (43°C)	Oven spring	The heating gases expand rapidly, causing the dough to swell.
140°F (60°C)	Yeast dies	The yeast is killed and is no longer able to provide any leavening.
150°F (66°C)	Gelatinization	The starches begin to solidify.
165°F (74°C)	Coagulation	The proteins (for example, eggs and gluten) begin to solidify.
212°F (100°C)	Water evaporates	The product begins to dry out as steam escapes from the dough.
350°F (177°C)	Caramelization	The sugars in the dough begin to darken and add color to the product.

FIGURE 14-7 *Focaccia* (foh-KAH-chuh) is a bread that's almost like a basic pizza. It's usually topped with flavorings and seasonings, but not sauce.

Biscuit Method

For the **biscuit method**, combine the dry ingredients, then **cut in** (mix in) the fat (butter or shortening) into the dry ingredients, either in a mixer using the paddle attachment, or by hand using a tool called a *pastry cutter* (Fig. 14-9) or your fingers. In a separate bowl, combine the wet ingredients. Add the wet ingredients to the dry ingredients and mix the

FIGURE 14-8 The waffle is a versatile form of quick bread, served not only for dessert or breakfast, but also for dinner in the southern United States with chicken and coleslaw.

FIGURE 14-9 Some bakers prefer to use pastry cutters to mix fats and flour.

dough just until combined. Knead the dough gently a few times, then cut or form into the desired shapes.

Muffin Method

With the **muffin method**, combine the dry ingredients in one bowl. Combine the wet ingredients, including the fat, in another bowl. Add the liquid ingredients to the dry ingredients and mix the batter just until combined. There will be lumps, but the lumps will disappear when the product is cooked. Cook the batter immediately by the appropriate method (baking, griddling, and so on). To minimize gluten development, pastry flour is normally used in the muffin method.

Summary and Conclusion

It is important, whether you wish to pursue baking as a career or to manage bakers as part of an overall foodservice organization, that you understand the processes and ingredients involved. In this chapter, you learned about the history of baking and about the basic ingredients involved in creating baked goods. We discussed the different types of leavening, as well as sugars, fats, and flours. You learned the steps involved in baking bread, and the changes that take place in items as they bake. We also discussed the methods used in creating quick breads.

 ## Selected Terms for Review

Artificial sweetener
Bakers' percentages
Biological leavening
Bloom
Cake
Chemical leavening
Fructose
Glucose (dextrose)
Lard
Leavening
Mechanical leavening
Quick breads
Scaling

Shortening
Sponge method
Stabilizing
Straight-dough method
Sweeteners
Vanilla

Review Questions

1. Modern bread yeasts were all originally used to produce

   a. Cheese

   b. Flatbread

   c. Beer

   d. Waffles

2. True or false? Air is a type of mechanical leavening.

3. Which type of yeast is fully alive? Which types of yeast are dormant? Of the dormant types, which type would you use if you are in a hurry?

4. What does baking powder contain that baking soda does not? What advantage does the extra ingredient provide?

5. True or false? Most sweeteners used in foodservice are a form of dextrose.

6. Which sugar is the sweetest?

   a. Sucrose

   b. Corn syrup

   c. Fructose

   d. Glucose

7. Name three functions performed by salt in baking.

8. What is the main protein in flour? How does it stabilize baked products?

9. Which flour would you use to make a crunchy Italian bread? Which flour would you use to make delicate muffins?

10. Determine the bakers' percentages for the following ingredients, for a formula containing 2.5 pounds of flour.

Ingredient	Weight	Bakers' Percentage
a. Eggs	1.5 lb	_____
b. Salt	1 oz	_____
c. Milk	1 lb	_____
d. Shortening	1 lb 4 oz	_____

11. Determine the correct weight, in grams, for the following ingredients, for a formula containing 2500 g of flour.

Ingredient	Weight	Baker's Percentage
a. Eggs	_____	25%
b. Salt	_____	2%
c. Milk	_____	40%
d. Shortening	_____	25%

12. What type of shortening would you use in a cake formula that contains 4 pounds of flour and 6 pounds of sugar?

13. List the 12 steps in bread baking.

14. List the stages in the baking process.

15. What are quick breads? What is an advantage of offering your customers quick breads?

16. What are the two methods used to make quick breads?

Suggested Readings/Web Sites to Visit

Beranbaum, R. L. (1998). *The Pie and Pastry Bible.* New York: Scribner.

Cook's Illustrated Editors. (2004). *Baking Illustrated.* Brookline, MA: America's Test Kitchen.

David, E. (1977). *English Bread and Yeast Cookery.* New York: Viking.

Gisslen, W. (2001). *Professional Baking.* New York: John Wiley & Sons.

Hamel, P. J. (Ed.) *King Arthur Flour Baker's Companion, The.* (2003). Woodstock, VT: Countryman.

History of bread. *Botham's Educational Pages:* www.botham.co.uk/bread/history1.htm

Silverton, N. (1996). *Breads from the La Brea Bakery.* New York: Villard.

Silverton, N. (2000). *Pastries from the La Brea Bakery.* New York: Villard.

Bibliography

Aidells, B., Kelly, D. (1998). *The Complete Meat Cookbook*. New York: Houghton Mifflin.

Alden, L. Vegetables. *The Cook's Thesaurus*. Available at www.foodsubs.com/FGVegetables.html. Accessed April 17, 2005.

Alderman, M., Cohen, H., Madhavan, S. (1998). Dietary sodium intake and mortality. *The Lancet*. 351, 781–785.

Alford, J., Duguid, N. (1998). *Seductions of Rice*. New York: Artisan.

(2005). American Cheese. *Saveur*. April, 44–86.

Anasazi Beans. *Walton Feed: The Legumes*. Available at waltonfeed.com/self/beans.html#anasazi. Accessed April 11, 2005.

Ancient Greece. Available at www.ancientgreece.com. Accessed June 28, 2004.

Appleby, P. A global stampede to the meat counter. *The Oven Newsletter*. Available at www.ivu.org/oxveg/Publications/Oven/Articles_General/wi_meat.html. Accessed February 24, 2005.

Audubon Institute, www.auduboninstitute.org/education/resources/wtld_info_Glossary.doc. Accessed August 2, 2004.

Balsamico di Modena. *Ottavia's Suitcase*. Available at www.ottavia.com/vinegar_consortia.html. Accessed February 12, 2005.

Basics for Handling Food Safely. *USDA Fact Sheets*. Available at www.fsis.usda.gov/Fact_Sheets/Basics_for_Handling_Food_Safely/index.asp. Accessed February 28, 2005.

Beranbaum, R. L. (1998). *The Pie and Pastry Bible*. New York: Scribner.

Binns, B. L. (2001). *Williams-Sonoma Hors d'Oeuvre*. New York: Simon & Schuster.

Bishop, J. (2001). *Vegetables Every Day*. New York: HarperCollins.

Blakemore, K. (1994). *50 Ways with Salads*. New York: Crescent.

Bluefin Tuna Data sheet. *Atuna*. Available at www.atuna.com/species/species/datasheet%20bluefin.htm. Accessed March 23, 2005.

Borghese, A. (1978). *The Great Sandwich Book*. New York: Rawson Associates.

Bourdain, A. (2000). *Kitchen Confidential*. New York: Bloomsbury.

Bowers, S. Thai cuisine. *The Thai Pantry*. Available at berncity.tripod.com/Thai.html. Accessed April 20, 2005.

Brennan, G. (2001). *Williams-Sonoma Salad*. New York: Simon and Schuster.

Brillat–Savarin, J. A. (1984). *The Philosopher in the Kitchen*. Middlesex, UK: Penguin Books.

Brown, E., Boehm, A. (1995). *The Modern Seafood Cook*. New York: Clarkson Potter.

Butter. *Web Exhibits*. Available at webexhibits.org/butter/countries-india.html. Accessed April 25, 2005.

Child, J., Bertholle, L., Beck, S. (1971). *Mastering the Art of French Cooking*. New York: Knopf.

China Cooperating on Food Safety. *Food HACCP Message Board*. Available at foodhaccp.com/ msgboard.mv?parm_func=showmsg+parm_msgnum=1010347. Accessed February 21, 2005.

Cook, S. (2003). *Salt & Pepper*. San Francisco: Chronicle.

Cook's Illustrated Editors. (1999). *The Cook's Illustrated Complete Book of Poultry*. New York: Clarkson Potter.

Cook's Illustrated Editors. (2004). *Baking Illustrated*. Brookline, MA: America's Test Kitchen.

Cook's Illustrated Magazine. Available at www.cooksillustrated.com. Accessed October 15, 2004.

Culinary Institute of America, The. (1996). *The Professional Chef*. 7th ed. New York: John Wiley & Sons.

David, E. (1977). *English Bread and Yeast Cookery*. New York: Viking.

Dim Sum Dishes. *Global Gourmet*. Available at www.globalgourmet.com/destinations/hongkong/ hkdishes.html. Accessed January 25, 2005.

Donovan, M. (1995). *The New Professional Chef*. New York: Van Nostrand Reinhold.

Drummond, K. E., Brefere, L. M. (2004). *Nutrition for Foodservice and Culinary Professionals*. Hoboken, NJ: John Wiley & Sons.

Epley, R. Aging Beef. *University of Minnesota Extension Service*. Available at www.extension.umn. edu/distribution/nutrition/DJ5968.html. Accessed February 24, 2005.

Famous Romans: Apicius. *Historia*. Available at www.dl.ket.org/latinlit/historia/people/apicius/ apicius.htm. Accessed August 2004.

FBE Species of Particular Interest. Alaska Fisheries Science Center, National Marine Fisheries Service. Available at www.afsc.noaa.gov/race/behavioral/halibut_fbe.htm. Accessed August 1, 2005.

FDA Food Code. U.S. Department of Health and Human Services. Available at vm.cfsan.fda.gov/ ~dms/foodcode.html.

Fish en Papillote. *Chef's Select Parchment Paper*. Available at www.chefsselect.com/htm/jmrecipes/ enpapillote.htm. Accessed March 31, 2005.

Food. *The Quotations Page*. Available at www.quotationspage.com/subjects/food. Accessed February 17, 2005.

Food Facts and Trivia: Condiments. *Food Reference* Web site. Available at www.foodreference.com/ html/fcondiments.html. Accessed January 30, 2005.

Food facts, food trivia. *Food Reference* Web site. Available at www.foodreference.com/html/ triviatips.html. Accessed January 30, 2005.

Food Lover's Companion. *Epicurious*. Available at www.epicurious.com/cooking/how_to/ food_dictionary/. Accessed June 30, 2005.

Food Quotes. *Food Reference* Web site. Available at www.foodreference.com/html/quotes.html. Accessed February 7, 2005.

Funk & Wagnalls. (1969). *Cook's and Diner's Dictionary*. New York: Funk & Wagnalls.

Gisslen, W. (2001). *Professional Baking*. New York: John Wiley & Sons.

Gisslen, W. (2003). *Professional Cooking*. New York: John Wiley & Sons.

Gullo, J. (1997). Looking for Kao Soi. *Saveur*. April, 88–96.

HACCP for Excellence. Available at www.haccpforexcellence.com. Accessed July 5, 2004.

Hafner, D. (2002). *A Taste of Africa: Traditional and Modern African Cooking.* Berkeley, CA: Ten Speed Press.

Hamel, P. J. (Ed.) *King Arthur Flour Baker's Companion, The.* (2003). Woodstock, VT: Countryman.

Harbutt, J. (1998). *The World Encyclopedia of Cheese.* New York: Anness Publishing.

History of Bread. *Botham's Educational Pages.* Available at www.botham.co.uk/bread/history1.htm. Accessed May 4, 2005.

History of Chicken Breeds. *University of Illinois Extension.* Available at www.urbanext.uiuc.edu/eggs/res10-breedhistory.html. Accessed March 8, 2005.

History of the Peanut. *Texoma Peanut Inn* Web site. Available at www.texomapeanut.com/inn/peanut%20history.htm. Accessed February 10, 2005.

How to Buy Meat. *Agricultural and Marketing Service Home and Garden Bulletin 265.* Available at www.ams.usda.gov/howtobuy/meat.pdf. Accessed February 20, 2005.

How to Buy Poultry. *Agriculture Marketing Service, USDA.* Available at www.ams.usda.gov/howtobuy/poultry.pdf. Accessed March 9, 2005.

How to make salade a la Russe. *Lovely Recipes.* Available at www.lovelyrecipes.com/recipe.php?recipeid=2566. Accessed February 12, 2005.

Inspection and grading: What's the difference? *Food Safety and Inspection Service, USDA.* Available at www.fsis.usda.gov/Fact_Sheets/Inspection_&_Grading/index.asp. Accessed March 9, 2005.

Institutional meat purchase specifications. *Agriculture Marketing Service Livestock and Seed Program.* Available at www.ams.usda.gov/lsg/stand/imps.htm. Accessed February 21, 2005.

Italy. *Recipes4Us.* Available at www.recipes4us.co.uk/Cooking%20by%20Country/Italy.htm. Accessed August 5, 2004.

Jaffrey, M. (2003). *Madhur Jaffrey's Indian Cooking.* Hauppauge, NY: Barron's.

Jordan, P. (2000). *The Practical Mushroom Encyclopedia: Identifying, Picking, and Cooking with Mushrooms.* London: Southwater.

Katzen, M. (1997). *Vegetable Heaven.* New York: Hyperion.

Kazuko, M., Yamada, T. (1996). *French Cheeses.* New York: DK.

Kershner, R. (1977). *Greek Cooking.* New York: Weathervane.

Key Facts: The Seven HACCP Principles. USDA Food Safety and Inspection Service. Available at www.fsis.usda.gov. Accessed April 7, 2004.

King, S. (1990). *Fish: The Basics.* New York: Simon & Schuster.

Kremezi, A. (1999). *The Foods of Greece.* New York: Stewart, Tabori, & Chang.

Kurlansky, M. (1997). *Cod: A Biography of the Fish That Changed the World.* New York: Penguin.

Kurlansky, M. (2002). *Salt: A World History.* New York: Penguin.

Labensky, S., Ingram, G. G., Labensky, S. R. (1997). *Webster's New World Dictionary of Culinary Arts.* Upper Saddle River, NJ: Prentice Hall.

Lang, S. S. Asian diet pyramid offers alternative to U.S. food guide pyramid. *Cornell University Science News.* Available at www.news.cornell.edu/science/Dec95/st.asian.pyramid.html. Accessed January 6, 2005.

Leonard, J. N. (1968). *Latin American Cooking.* New York: Time-Life Books.

Levy, F. (1992). *Faye Levy's International Chicken Cookbook.* New York: Warner Books.

Levy, F. (1993). *International Vegetable Cookbook.* New York: Warner Books.

Liebman, B. DASH: A Diet for All Diseases. *Nutrition Action Health Letter*. Available at www.cspinet.org/nah/dash.htm. Accessed April 19, 2005.

Louisiana history. *Chef John Folse & Company*. Available at www.jfolse.com/mm_history.htm. Accessed August 17, 2004.

Love it or hate it? Marmite. Available at www.marmite.com. Accessed January 29, 2005.

Luban, Y. How Do I Know It's Kosher? *OU Gateway to the Jewish Internet*. Available at www.ou.org/kosher/primer.html. Accessed January 6, 2005.

Mayhew, D., ed. (2000). *The Soup Bible*. London: Anness.

Mayonnaise: The Misunderstood Dressing. *The Association for Dressings and Sauces*. Available at www.dressings-sauces.org/pdf/mayoo.pdf. Accessed January 19, 2005.

McCourt, F. (1999). *Angela's Ashes*. New York: Scribner.

McGee, H. (1990). Beurre Blanc, Butter's Undoing. In *The Curious Cook* (pp. 89–99). New York: Macmillan.

McGee, H. (1990). The Searing Truth. In *The Curious Cook* (pp. 13–21). New York: Macmillan.

McGee, H. (2004). *On Food and Cooking*. New York: Scribner.

Meat Consumption. *Iowa State University Department of Economics*. Available at www.econ.iastate.edu/outreach/agriculture/periodicals/chartbook/Chartbook2/Tables/Table13.pdf. Accessed March 2, 2005.

Medieval to modern, the last thousand years. *Menu Magazine*. Available at www.menumagazine.co.uk/book/medievaltomodern.html. Accessed August 10, 2004.

Mediterranean diet pyramid. *Oldways Preservation and Exchange Trust*. Available at www.oldwayspt.org/pyramids/med/p_med.html. Accessed January 6, 2005.

Miller, J. E., Walker, J. R., Drummond, K. E. (2002). *Supervision in the Hospitality Industry* (p. 59). Hoboken, NJ: John Wiley & Sons.

Montagne, P. (2001). *Larousse Gastronomique*. New York: Clarkson Potter.

Morris County New Jersey Library. *Food Timeline, The*. Available at www.foodtimeline.org. Accessed August 12, 2004.

My Food Pyramid. *United States Department of Agriculture*. Available at mypyramid.gov. Accessed April 19, 2005.

New Advent. Catherine de Medici. *Catholic Encyclopedia*. Available at www.newadvent.org/cathen/03443a.htm. Accessed August 12, 2004.

Newman, C. (2004). Why are we so fat? *National Geographic*. August, pp. 46–61.

Norman, J., ed. (2002). *Herbs and Spices: The Cook's Reference*. New York: DK.

Passmore, J. (1978). *All Asian Cookbook*. Secaucus, NJ: Chartwell Books.

Pasteurized eggs: Smart thinking inside the shell. *Safe Eggs*. Available at www.safeeggs.com/markets/groceryretailer.html. Accessed February 12, 2005.

Payne–Palacio, J., Theis, M. (1994). *West and Wood's Introduction to Foodservice*. Upper Saddle River, NJ: Prentice-Hall.

Penzeys Spices Web page. Available at www.penzeys.com. Accessed June 11, 2005.

People, Places, and Things in the News: Paul Bocuse. *Southcoast Today*. Available at www.s-t.com/daily/10-97/10-05-97/zzzwnppl.htm. Accessed January 5, 2005.

Pepin, J. (1987). *The Art of Cooking*. New York: Alfred A. Knopf.

Peterson, J. (1996). *Fish & Shellfish*. New York: William Morrow.

Poultry grading manual. *Agriculture Marketing Service, USDA*. Available at www.ams.usda.gov/poultry/resources/PYGradingManual.pdf. Accessed March 9, 2005.

Quintana, P. (1994). *Cuisine of the Water Gods*. New York: Simon & Schuster.

Raichlen, S. (1993). *Miami Spice*. New York: Workman Publishing.

Reddy, S., Waliyar, F. *Properties of Aflatoxin*. Available at www.aflatoxin.info. Accessed July 15, 2004.

Regulatory Fish Encyclopedia. *U.S. Food and Drug Administration*. Available at www.cfsan.fda.gov/~frf/rfe0.html. Accessed June 5, 2004.

Romagnoli, M., Romagnoli, G. F. (1994). *The Romagnolis' Italian Fish Cookbook*. New York: Henry Holt.

Root, W. (1980). *Food*. New York: Simon & Schuster.

Ruhlman, M. (2000). "Natural-Born Keller." *Best Food Writing 2000* (pp. 194–202). New York: Marlowe & Co.

Salads. *South America for Visitors*. Available at gosouthamerica.about.com/od/salads/. Accessed February 10, 2005.

Salt Institute. Available at www.saltinstitute.org. Accessed January 15, 2005.

Santa Barbara County Public Health Department. *How Do I Prevent Bug and Rodent Infestation?* Available at www.sbcphd.org/ehs/howdoi.htm. Accessed May 6, 2004.

Schapiro, M. (1994). Muddy waters. *Utne Reader*. November/December, pp. 53–56.

Schlesinger, C., Willoughby, J. (1996). *Lettuce in Your Kitchen*. New York: William Morrow.

Schlesinger, C., Willoughby, J. (2000). *How to Cook Meat*. New York: William Morrow.

Schlosser, J. (2001). *Serving the Allergic Guest*. Scottsdale, AZ: Scottsdale Press.

Schnebel, J. J. Caesar salad. *Who Cooked That Up?* Available at members.cox.net/jjschnebel/caesrsal.html. Accessed September 2004.

Schwartz, L. (1992). *Salads*. New York: HarperCollins.

Seafood HACCP information. *U.S. Food and Drug Administration*. Available at www.cfsan.fda.gov/~comm/haccpsea.html. Accessed June 5, 2004.

Seafood information and resources. *U.S. Food and Drug Administration*. Available at vm.cfsan.fda.gov/seafood1.html. Accessed June 6, 2004.

Seafood search engine. *U.S. Food and Drug Administration*. Available at www.cfsan.fda.gov/~frf/seaintro.html. Accessed June 6, 2004.

Seranne, A. (1983). *The Complete Book of Egg Cookery*. New York: MacMillan.

Silverton, N. (1996). *Breads from the La Brea Bakery*. New York: Villard.

Silverton, N. (2000). *Pastries from the La Brea Bakery*. New York: Villard.

Silverton, N. (2002). *Nancy Silverton's Sandwich Book*. New York: Alfred A. Knopf.

Skopitz, K. (2002). Who was Catherine de Medici? *PageWise*. Available at vt.essortment.com/whocatherinede_rggi.htm.

Spier, C. (1993). *Food Essentials: Poultry*. New York: Crescent.

Stradley, L. (2004). History and legends of sandwiches. *What's Cooking America?* Available at whatscookingamerica.net/History/SandwichHistory.htm. Accessed January 25, 2005.

Sunset editors. (1991). *Sunset Appetizers*. Menlo Park, CA: Sunset.

Tallyrand. Culinary history: Origins of the names of classical dishes. *Tallyrand's Culinary History*. Available at www.geocities.com/NapaValley/6454/garnish.html. Accessed January 23, 2005.

Taylor, D. A. (March 1998) Ring king. *Smithsonian Magazine*. Available at www.smithsonianmag.si.edu/smithsonian/issues98/mar98/object_mar98.html. Accessed March 2, 2005.

Teubner, C. (1998). *The Cheese Bible*. New York: Penguin.

Tillicum Village. *Mount Rainier National Park*. Available at www.americanparks.net/ mount_rainier_tillicum.htm. Accessed June 8, 2005.

Time-Life Books Editors. (1979). *Poultry*. Alexandria, VA: Time-Life Books.

Time-Life Books Editors. (1985). *Turkey & Duck Menus*. Alexandria, VA: Time-Life Books.

Trilling, S. (1999). *Seasons of My Heart: A Culinary Journey through Oaxaca, Mexico*. New York: Ballantine Books.

Tropp, B. (1982). *The Modern Art of Chinese Cooking*. New York: Morrow.

U.S. beef gets firm foothold in the china market. *U.S. Meat Export Federation Newsletter*. Available at www.usmef.org/TradeLibrary/News02_1025a.asp. Accessed February 22, 2005.

USDA data: Dairy and egg products. *Chef 2 Chef*. Available at chef2chef.net/kb/index/97-usda-dairy-egg.htm. Accessed April 28, 2005.

USDA promotes horse and goat meat. *Horseaid's USDA Report*. Available at www.igha.org/USDA.html. Accessed February 22, 2005.

Van der Post, L. (1970). *African Cooking*. New York: Time-Life Books.

Vegemite. Available at www.vegemite.com.au. Accessed January 29, 2005.

Wallace, K. (2004). A plateful of trouble. *Reader's Digest*. August, pp. 110–117.

Weird Foods from Around the World. Available at www.Weird-Food.com. Accessed June 21, 2005.

Willett, W. C. Food pyramids: What should you really eat? *Nutrition Source, Harvard School of Public Health*. Available at www.hsph.harvard.edu/nutritionsource/pyramids.html. Accessed January 4, 2005.

Wolfe, L. (1970). *Cooking of the Caribbean Islands, The.* New York: Time-Life Books.

Yan, M. (1998). This is your knife! *Asian Connections*. Available at asianconnections.com/food/ how_to/cutting/. Accessed November 3, 2004.

Yianilos, T. (1970). *The Complete Greek Cookbook.* La Jolla, CA: Jolla.

Yuan, K. (2003). Can't get enough of umami: Revealing the fifth element of taste. *Journal of Young Investigators*. Available at www.jyi.org/volumes/volume9/issue2/features/yuan.html. Accessed April 3, 2005.

Glossary

A

à la carte menu   menu with each item priced separately

à la meunière (moon-YAIR)   cooking style using brown butter, lemon juice, and parsley

abalone (a-buh-LOH-nee)   univalve shellfish; chewy flesh

ackee   fruit popular in Jamaica

ackee and saltfish   national dish of Jamaica, ackee with salt cod

active dry yeast   dormant yeast; requires soaking in warm water before use

adipose   fat surrounding muscle; also called *deposit fat*

aerobic (air-ROH-bik)   microorganisms that require oxygen to live

aflatoxin   sometimes-fatal, fungus-produced poison found in grains

aging   allowing meat to tenderize naturally before use

aioli (ay-OH-lee)   mediterranean garlic mayonnaise

al dente (al DEN-tay)   cooking foods like rice and pasta to a slightly chewy texture

albumen   protein found in egg whites and brains

allergen   substance causing allergic reactions in some people when eaten

all-purpose flour   household flour with moderate gluten

all-purpose potato   cheap, unattractive potato; good for mashing

anaerobic   microorganisms that do not require oxygen to live

Anaheim   popular variety of chile pepper

anaphylactic (AN-uh-fill-AK-tik) **shock**   condition in which an allergy victim becomes unconscious, has difficulty breathing, or dies

angel food method   cake-mixing method in which egg whites are beaten, then dry ingredients are folded in

anodized aluminum   pan material with nonreactive electrochemically treated interior surface

anthocyanins (an-thoh-SY-uh-nins)   dark-red pigments in vegetables

AP   weight of an item as purchased

Apicius (uh-PEE-see-us)   roman gourmet/cookbook author, first century CE

appetizer   hors d'oeuvre

arborio   short-grain Italian rice

arrowroot   thickener; more expensive than flour or cornstarch

artificial sweeteners   low- or no-calorie sweeteners, including aspartame, sucralose

artisan breads   breads with a complex interior and a crusty, artistic exterior

arugula (uh-ROO-guh-luh)   peppery Italian green; also called *rocket*

asparagus   green vegetable with straight stalk and a fringe of tiny leaves at the tip

aspartame (ASS-pahr-tayme)   artificial sweetener, sold as Nutrasweet; not suitable for cooking

aspic   savory gelatin items

au gratin (oh grah-TAN)   veggies baked with cream and cheese

avocado   pear-shaped, dark-green oily fruit, used as a vegetable

B

bacteria   microscopic, single-celled animals

bagel   traditional, donut-shaped Jewish bread with a chewy crust

bain-marie   stainless steel container used to keep food warm in water bath

bake pan   rectangular pan, 2 inches deep, with folding handles

bakers' percentages   method of measuring the ingredients in baking when the weight of flour is 100%; see Chapter 14

baking   cooking a food item uncovered in dry, hot air; roasting

baking powder   blend of baking soda and other substances; the most common type, double-acting, leavens when exposed to moisture and heat

baking soda   leavens when exposed to moisture and acid

balsamic vinegar   aged, red wine vinegar of Modena, Italy

balut   duck egg, popular in the Philippines, that contains a partially formed baby duck

bamboo shoots   baby, tender bamboo stalks

bao xiang (BAU zhee-YANG)   Chinese, "explode into fragrance"; aromatic release of oils during cooking

barbecue   roast slowly with burning coals or hardwood

barding   wrapping meat in fat before cooking

barley   rather chewy grain, used in soups

base   commercially available paste used for flavoring soups, sauces; the foundation of a canapé or salad

basil   herb; soft, shiny green leaves

basmati   long-grain rice of India; fermented for aroma, flavor

batonnet   french fry cut, $2^1/_2 \times {}^1/_4 \times {}^1/_4$ inch

batter   mixture of starch, eggs, liquid, seasonings, flavorings; used to coat foods for deep-frying

beans   seeds that come from pods, including peas, lentils, and peanuts; see Chapter 12

beet   usually dark-red, edible root

bell pepper   mildest pepper, also called *green pepper*

bench scraper   see dough knife

beurre blanc (burr BLAHNK)   simple butter sauce

beurre manié (burr mahn-YAY)   paste made from raw flour and butter used for thickening

beurre noir (burr NWAHR)   butter cooked to a dark brown

beurre noisette (burr nwah-ZET)   "hazelnut butter"; butter cooked to a light brown

Bibb lettuce   delicate green, not as firm as iceberg

biological contamination   microorganisms that cause food-borne illness

biological leavening   uses living organisms, yeasts, to create gas in dough

biscuit method   quick bread mixing method in which the dry ingredients are combined, then fat is cut in

bisque   creamy, seafood-based soup

bivalve   mollusk with two-piece hinged shell (like clams, oysters)

blackening   cajun technique of coating meat, fish, or poultry with spices, then searing it over very high heat

blanch   partially precooking foods in oil or water before final preparation

blanch and shock   blanching a food item, then submerging it in cold water to stop cooking

blender   tall, narrow food processor used for sauces and beverages

bleu cheese   blue-veined, French, cow's-milk cheese

block form   table format used to organize a recipe

bloom   to soften gelatin in water or to reactivate dry yeast in warm water

blue-veined cheese   strong-flavored variety of cheese with visible blue marbling of mold

body   main part of a salad

boiling   cooking in water at 212°F (100°C)

bok choy   Asian cabbage variety with white stalks and green, glossy leaves

boning knife   used to cut flesh from bones; about 6 inches (16 cm)

Boston lettuce   delicate, buttery green; small head

bouillabaisse (BOO-yuh-base)   seafood stew from the south of France

Boulanger (BOO-lon-JAIR)   Frenchman who invented the modern restaurant in the 1700s

bound salad   salad in which all ingredients are held together with a thick dressing

bouquet garni (boo-KAY gar-NEE)   bundle of herbs tied with a string; used to flavor stocks, soups, sauces

braising   cooking a food item slowly, partially submerged in liquid in a covered pan

brazier   rondeau

bread flour   wheat flour containing the most gluten

breaking   the separation of fats from liquids and solids in an emulsion

Brie (bree)   soft, pale-yellow cheese with edible white rind

brigade system   method for organizing the tasks in a commercial kitchen

brining   soaking meat, poultry, or seafood in saltwater to improve its juiciness, flavor

broccoli   crucifer; tight cluster of green buds; thick, green stem

broccoli rabe   see *rapini*

broil   to cook with a broiler

broiler   cooks food with heat generated from above or beside the food item

broiler–fryer   poultry (chicken and duck) suitable for dry-heat cooking; up to 3.5 pounds

brown rice   husk removed but not the bran

brown stock   made from beef or veal bones; also called *veal stock*

brown sugar   white sugar with added molasses

brunoise (broon-WAH)   an eighth-inch dice

bruschetta (broo-SKEH-tuh)   Italian canapés with garlic toast as the base

Brussels sprout   vegetable resembling a tiny cabbage

buckwheat   grain native to Russia

buffalo chopper   food processor consisting of a rotating tube pan with spinning blades; also called a *food cutter*

bulghur   cracked wheat; cooked, dried, and ground into granules

butter   product of agitating cream until it becomes semisolid

butterfly   cut food item nearly in half, then unfold it; allows quicker cooking

buttermilk   term used for a drinkable, fermented milk product

C

cabbage   leafy vegetable with tight, round head; red, white, or green color

cake   In the United States, a baked, layered, frosted dessert made from a sweet batter

cake flour   wheat flour with the least gluten

calamari   Italian for "squid"

callaloo   spinach-style green popular in the Caribbean

calorie   the amount of energy to heat 1 g of water 1°C; *not* the common calorie; see Calorie

Calorie   the common food–energy measurement; the amount of energy to heat 1 kg of water 1°C; also called *kilocalorie*

Camembert (KAM-um-behr)   soft, pale-yellow cheese with edible white rind

canapé (KAN-uh-PAY)   small, open-faced sandwich consisting of base, spread, and garnish

cane syrup   sugarcane juice, thinner than molasses

caper   pickled bud of a Mediterranean shrub

capon   castrated male chicken

caramelization   browning of sugars when heated

carbohydrates   human body's primary source of energy; includes sugars, starches, fiber

carcass   whole animal minus head, entrails, and (except pork) skin and feet

Carême (kuh-REM)**, Marie Antoine**   French chef who refined culinary principals in the early 1800s

carotenoids   orange/yellow/red pigment in vegetables

carrot   root vegetable, usually orange, high sugar

carryover   temperature increase after cooked food is removed from its heat source

cartilaginous (KAR-till-A-ji-nuss)   fish with no bones or scales, such as sharks, rays

cassava   tropical root vegetable, brown skin, white flesh; also called *yuca, tapioca, manioc*

cassava flour   thickener made from cassava root

cassoulet (KASS-oo-LAY)   French dish with white beans, sausage, duck

catfish   freshwater, smooth skin, flavorful flesh; up to 8 pounds (3.6 kg)

cauliflower   crucifer; large head of white florets

celeriac   root of a type of celery; also called *celery root*

celery   mild-flavored vegetable that grows in bunches of long, pale-green stalks

cellulose   indigestible plant fiber that gives cells structure

Celsius   temperature scale used in most of the world; 0° is the freezing point of water and 100° is boiling

century egg   Asian egg that has been preserved in quicklime, ashes, and salt to give it a black color and strong flavor

cèpe   see *porcini*

cephalopod (SEFF-uh-loh-pod)   soft-bodied mollusks with internal shell or no shell (for example, octopus and squid)

ceviche (sev-EE-chay)   white fish marinated in an acid, an example of cold cooking

challah (HAH-luh)   braided Jewish egg bread

chayote (chy-YO-tay)   squashlike pale-green fruit used as vegetable, also called mirliton

cheddar   white to orange hard cheese with a mild to sharp flavor

cheese   any product made from milk curds, or similar products like head cheese or cream cheese

chef   culinary expert with management and/or training responsibilities

chef de cuisine   oversees production for an entire foodservice establishment

chef de partie (par-TEE)   responsible for a particular production area

chef's knife   versatile, large knife; about 10 inches (26 cm)

chemical contamination   any toxic substance, such as a pesticide or toxic metal, that contaminates food

chemical leavening   adding gas to dough using baking powder or baking soda

chicken   most common poultry; white and dark meat, little fat

chicory (CHIK-uh-ree)   endive with curly, firm leaves

chile (CHILL-ee)   hot pepper

chimchurri   Latin American parsley/garlic herb sauce

china cap   cone-shaped strainer, wide mesh

Chinese cabbage   long, narrow, pale-green head; also called *napa*

Chinese chef's knife   large, broad knife with square tip used in Asian kitchens

chinois (shin-WAH)   cone-shaped strainer, fine mesh

chipotle (chih-POHT-lay)   smoked jalapeño

chitlins   portions of pig intestine, popular in southern United States; also called *chitterlings*

chlorophyll (KLOR-oh-fil)   green pigment in vegetables

chop   cut into irregular pieces of roughly the same size; meat cut from lamb, pork, or veal loin

chowder   chunky seafood cream soup of the United States; a type of clam used in chowder

chutney   any of a variety of sweet/savory condiments used in cuisine of India

cilantro   green herb, tangy flavor

clam   bivalve with smooth, even shell; see Chapter 11 for a list of clams

clarified butter   butterfat from which milk solids have been strained

classification   poultry sub-type

cleaning   getting rid of visible dirt, not killing pathogens

clearmeat   materials used to clarify consommé

cleaver   heavy, square knife with broad blade

closed-top range   cooktop with a solid, heavy metal covering

clotted cream   an English product, cream with 55% fat

coagulation   stiffening of proteins when heated

cock   older male chicken

cod   lean saltwater fish, delicate flesh, up to 25 pounds (11 kg)

colander   large, bowl-shaped stainless steel strainer with handles

cold cooking   cooking proteins by marinating in an acid rather than with heat

collagen   connective tissue that dissolves and tenderizes when slowly heated

collard   cabbage relative with long stem, green leaves

combi oven   operates in three modes: steam only, heat only, or with steam and heat

concassée (KON-kuh-SAY)   peeled, seeded, and diced tomatoes; a coarsely chopped tomato (meaning varies in different kitchens)

concasser (KON-kuh-SAY)   to chop coarsely (meaning varies in different kitchens)

conch (konk)   univalve shellfish, popular in the Caribbean

condiment   flavoring, such as mustard or ketchup, added to a sandwich

conduction   transfer of heat from one object to another, as from a pan to a food

confectioner's sugar   very fine and powdery; also called *powdered sugar*

confit   method of preserving poultry in its own fat

connective tissues   proteins that join muscles and bones together

consommé (kon-suh-MAY)   rich, clear classic French soup

convection   circulation of heat in a gas or liquid

convection oven   oven that circulates hot air or steam around food

convenience product   commercially prepared, labor-saving foodservice item

conventional oven   enclosed area that surrounds food with hot air

converted rice   white rice, parcooked to preserve nutrients

conveyor oven   moves food item along a conveyor belt

cook   culinary worker with little or no supervisory responsibility (n.); to prepare a food item using heat (v.)

corn   tall plant that produces seed on a long cob, the seeds themselves; also called *maize*

corn meal   ground corn

corn syrup   glucose syrup from corn kernels; sometimes converted to high-fructose corn syrup, used in candies and soda

cornstarch   flour made from corn endosperm; used as thickener

cottage cheese   fresh cheese, mild, with large curds

court bouillon (kort boo-YAWN)   poaching liquid for fish

courtbouillon (KOO-bee-yawn)   Creole seafood stew

couscous (KOOS-koos)   granular pasta popular in North Africa

crab   crustacean with ten legs but no tail; see Chapter 11 for a list of types

crawfish   freshwater crustacean resembling a small lobster; also called *crayfish*

cream   the fat removed from milk

cream soup   thick soup made with cream or milk

creaming method   method for mixing cake batter during which butter and sugar are blended before dry and liquid ingredients are added

crème fraîche   fermented milk, thinner than sour cream

cremini (kruh-MEE-nee)   small, brown mushroom

Creole (KREE-ol)   blended culture and cuisine of the people of the Caribbean and Louisiana

critical control point   in a HACCP system, a place in the flow of food where an action can prevent, eliminate, or reduce a food safety hazard

critical limit   in a HACCP system, value to which a hazard must be controlled to prevent, eliminate, or acceptably reduce it

cross-contamination   transfer of pathogens or allergens from one food to another

crouton   toasted bread cubes used as garnish

crucifer (KRU-si-fuhr)   group name for the cabbage family

crudités (kroo-dih-TAYZ)   fresh, raw vegetables used as appetizers

crustacean   shellfish with segmented bodies and jointed legs (for example, lobster)

cuisine (kwih-ZEEN)   cooking as an art form

culture-bound attitude   belief that everything within one's culture is correct and everything else is incorrect

curdle   separation of cream or eggs into solids and liquid

curds   milk solids used in cheese making

curry   family of spice mixtures used in India and southeast Asia

cutting in   adding fat to dry ingredients

cycle menu   a menu that changes every day for a certain number of days, then repeats

D

dairy products   foods and beverages derived from the milk of various animals

dark meat   darker flesh of poultry; more connective tissue, stronger flavor

dashi   Japanese fish stock

deck oven   conventional oven with levels that may be heated separately

deep-fat fry   cooking foods totally submerged in fat

deep fryer   boxes for heating fat into which foods are submerged

deglaze   using liquid to dissolve flavorful deposits in a pan

deposit fat   adipose tissue

devein (dee-VAYN)   remove a shrimp's digestive tract

deviled eggs   hard-cooked eggs with the yolks removed, seasoned, then returned to the whites

dextrose   see *glucose*

dice   to cut into cubes; large, $^3/_4$ inch (2 cm); medium, $^1/_2$ inch (12 mm); small, $^1/_4$ inch (6 mm)

dim sum Chinese appetizers (for example, steamed buns and spring rolls)

dolma Greek grape leaves with rice stuffing

dolphin see *mahi mahi*

double cream an English product, cream with 48% fat

dough hook mixer attachment for kneading dough

dough knife square, flat metal with a handle on one edge for cutting dough or cleaning work surface

Dover sole very expensive, delicate flatfish

drawn fish gutted fish

dressed fish a fish that has been gutted, with the scales, gills, fins, and head removed

dressing flavored liquid or semiliquid for enhancing salad; a cooked mixture usually of starches, vegetables, fats, and flavorings served with poultry

dried milk milk in powdered form, often used as an ingredient in baking

dry aging storing meat in open air in controlled conditions to enhance flavor and texture

dry-heat cooking cooking without water

duck web-footed water bird with short neck and legs; dark flesh, high fat

durian large, spiky tropical fruit with objectionable odor and custardy texture

duxelles (DOOKS-ell) reduction of mushrooms used for stuffings

E

Edam semisoft cheese from Holland

eel long, narrow freshwater/saltwater fish; very oily, sweet flesh

egg oval, hard-shelled reproductive structure produced by birds

egg white clear, liquid portion of an egg; mostly water plus the protein albumen

egg yolk yellow portion of an egg, consisting of protein and fat

eggplant "fruit" vegetable, usually with purple skin and firm, white flesh

elastin connective tissue that does not dissolve when heated

emulsification forcing two unmixable liquids (like oil and water) to mix

emulsion product of emulsification

en papillote (AWN pah-pee-YOTE) from French "in butterfly"; steaming foods inside folded paper

endive family of bitter greens

endosperm largest portion of a grain's interior

entremetier (AHN-truh-met-YAY)   vegetable chef; vegetables, soups, starches, eggs

EP   edible portion weight after an item is trimmed

escargot (ESS-kar-GOH)   French for "snail"

escarole   endive with thick leaves

Escoffier (ess-KOFF-ee-YAY), **Georges Auguste**   French chef who refined culinary operations in the late 1800s

evaporated milk   milk with 60% of its water removed

executive chef   manager of a large foodservice establishment

F

fabricated cuts   pieces, such as steaks and chops, into which primal cuts are divided for consumption

Fahrenheit   temperature scale used in the United States; 32° is the freezing point of water and 212° is boiling

farfalle   bow tie shaped pasta

FAT TOM   name formed by six things needed by microorganisms to grow: food, acidity, temperature, time, oxygen, and moisture

Fats   nutrients providing energy and structure to cells

fennel   vegetable with a broad root, pale green stalks and a licorice-like flavor

fermented milk   milk to which bacteria are added to produce a tart flavor and thick texture

feta   crumbly, salty Greek fresh cheese

fiber   indigestible carbohydrates; aids in regularity of digestion

fiddlehead fern   northern green, coiled head

fillet (fill-LAY)   boneless cut of fish or meat

finfish   another term for fish, as defined in this book

fish   animals with fins and gills

fish sauce   southeast Asian seasoning made by fermenting fish

flatbread   bread, leavened or unleavened, normally used as an eating utensil or a sandwich wrap

flatfish   oval, compressed fish, such as flounder, with both eyes on the same side of its head when mature

flavones   white pigment in vegetables

flavorings   ingredients, including herbs and spices, that change the flavor of foods

flounder flatfish; up to 5 pounds (2.3 kg); delicate, flaky flesh

flow of food path a food item takes from receiving to storage, prep, and serving

foaming method cake-mixing method during which the eggs are warmed with sugar, then beaten till fluffy

folding mixing method where heavy ingredients are gently mixed into a light airy ingredient with a circular motion

fond residue on bottom of pan after meat is cooked

fondue melted cheese used as a dip for bread, veggies

food allergy condition that causes a negative reaction to certain food substances

food contamination occurs when food contains a substance that can make people ill

food cost the amount a foodservice organization pays for its ingredients

food cost percentage the percent of the menu price spent on food

food cutter see *buffalo chopper*

Food Danger Zone (FDZ) temperature range favoring growth of microorganisms, 41–140°F (5°C to 60°C)

food mill strainer with a paddle that forces food through mesh

food processor canister with a rotating blade that chops or purees foods

foodborne illness any sickness resulting from food contamination. See Chapter 2 for detailed descriptions of common foodborne illnesses

foodism prejudice against foods of other cultures

food-safety hazard biological, chemical, or physical food contamination that may cause food to be unsafe

forequarter front half of a beef side

foresaddle front half of a lamb or veal carcass

formula term for "recipe" in baking

fortified milk milk with Vitamin A added, as well as Vitamin D

fowl older female chicken

freezer insulated box for storing items at or below 0°F (−18°C) for long periods

fresh cheese slightly aged (for example, mozzarella, feta, cottage)

fresh yeast living, nondormant yeast

frijoles refritos (free-HOH-layss ray-FREE-tohss) Mexican refried beans

friseé (frih-ZAY) pale-yellow chicory

frittata Italian omelet

fructose   sweetest natural sugar; a component of sucrose

"fruit" vegetables   fruits that are used as vegetables, like tomatoes or squash

fryer–roaster   smaller, young turkey; 5 to 8 pounds

fungus   plantlike organism that includes yeasts, molds, and mushrooms

G

garbanzo   beige seed, size of large pea; also called *chickpea*

garde manger (GARD mahn-ZHAY)   pantry chef; cold foods, salads, dressings

garlic   strongly flavored bulb with a papery skin; popular worldwide

garnish   edible decoration for a plate or a food item

garum   ancient Roman fish sauce

gazpacho   cold soups of Spain

gelatin (JEL-uh-tin)   jellylike substance that forms when bones and connective tissue are heated

gelatinization (juh-LAT-in-ih-ZAY-shun)   tendency of starches to swell when added to liquid

ghee (gee, with a hard "g")   Indian clarified butter

glucose   simple sugar, a component of sucrose; also called *dextrose*; less sweet than sucrose; the human body's primary energy source

gluten   protein in wheat flour; provides strength and stability

glutinous rice   sticky rice, popular in Asian cuisine

goose   long-necked, web-footed water bird; dark flesh, high fat

gorgonzola (GOHR-guhn-ZOHL-uh)   blue-veined Italian cheese

grading   examination for quality

grain   grass with edible seed

granulated sugar   table sugar, moderately fine grain

grater   metal box with sharpened holes to shred foods

gravlax (GRAV-lahks)   Swedish salmon cured in sugar and salt

green onions   see *scallions*

griddle   large, heated, metal plates usually used for cooking pancakes, eggs, bacon, and burgers (n.); to cook on a griddle (v.)

grill   appliance that generates heat from beneath food; flavors food with smoke from fat dripping onto the heat source (n.); to cook on a grill (v.)

grillardin (GREE-yar-DAN) grill chef; broiled meats, deep-fried meats/fish

grits ground, dried hominy; similar to polenta

groats crushed grains

guinea (GIN-ee) domesticated descendant of the pheasant

gumbo Louisiana thick soup of sausage and chicken or seafood

gyros (YEER-ose) Greek lamb loaf

H

habañero (ah-bahn-YARE-oh) hottest pepper; also called *Scotch bonnet*

HACCP (HASS-up) Hazard Analysis Critical Control Point, a food safety system

half-and-half mixture of cream and milk, 10 to 12% fat

halibut flatfish weighing up to 200 pounds (90 kg); firm flesh

hard cheese somewhat dry, but not crumbly; includes cheddar, provolone

hard–grating cheese Dry, hard, crumbly cheese, including Parmigiano–Reggiano and pecorino

hazard analysis in HACCP, identifying hazards and related preventative measures

head cheese bits of seasoned meat, usually pork, set in gelatin

hearts of palm core of stem of cabbage palm tree

heavy cream cream with 36 to 40% fat

hen older female chicken

herbs flavorings using the leafy portions of plants

high-moisture potato see *waxy potato*

high-temperature oven cooks items, especially breads and pizzas, at temperatures from 600 to 1000°F (315–540°C)

hindquarter rear half of a beef side

hindsaddle rear half of a lamb or veal carcass

hoisin (HOY-sin) thick, sweet, dark Chinese sauce

hominy large corn kernels with outer hull removed

homogenization mixing milk thoroughly to prevent fat separation

honey sweetener secreted by bees; contains glucose and sucrose

hors d'oeuvre (or-DERV) finger food served before a meal

hotel pans standard-size pans in a range of sizes made to fit slots in holding tables

I

iceberg lettuce   popular green, mild flavor, firm head

immersion blender   handheld food processor that purees foods in their cooking container

IMPS   Institutional Meat Purchase Specifications; in the United States, a list of standard meat cuts

induction burner   stovetop using magnetism to heat steel or iron pans

infrared oven   cooks with a quartz tube that produces infrared radiation

infused oil   oil to which flavorings have been added

infused vinegar   vinegar to which flavorings have been added

injecting   adding a flavorful liquid to the flesh of poultry, meat, or seafood

injera   spongy flatbread of Ethiopia

inspection   examination for wholesomeness, not quality

instant dry yeast   dormant yeast that does not require reactivation

IQF   individually quick frozen, market form of shellfish

J

jalapeno (hah-lah-PAYN-yo)   moderately hot pepper, dark green

jasmine rice   aromatic Asian rice

julienne   knife cut, $2^{1}/_{2} \times {}^{1}/_{8} \times {}^{1}/_{8}$ inch

K

kalamata   pale, oval olive, 1 inch long

kao soi   Thai chicken/coconut soup

kasha   roasted buckwheat groats

katsuobushi (KAHT-soo-oh-boo-shee)   dried bonito tuna flakes used as flavoring in Japanese soups

ketjap manis   sweet Indonesian soy sauce

kilocalorie   see *Calorie*

kim chee   Korean pickled cabbage

kind   major type of poultry (like chicken or duck)

Kobe   variety of wagyu beef

kohlrabi (kohl-RAH-bee)   crucifer; a cross between cabbages and turnips

kombu seaweed used as flavoring in Japanese soups

kosher food rules related to the Jewish faith

L

lactose milk sugar

lactose intolerant term for people who react negatively to lactose in dairy products

ladle bowl with a long handle used to pour liquids

lamb meat of a sheep less than one year old

lard rendered pig fat

larding inserting fat inside meat before cooking to enrich it

lasagne (luh-ZAHN-yuh) wide, flat pasta noodle

leading sauce see *mother sauce*

leafy vegetables consist mostly of the leaves of a plant (for example, lettuce, spinach)

lean fish fish that have little body fat

leavening adding air or another gas to a dough to make it lighter

leek resembles large scallion, but has a sweeter, stronger flavor

legumes see *beans*

liaison thickener; a mixture of egg yolks and cream

light cream cream with 20% fat

lobster crustacean with ten legs and a tail; see Chapter 11 for types

low-fat milk milk with some fat removed

low-moisture potato see *mature potatoes*

low-temperature oven precisely maintains low temperatures to cook food items slowly, especially meats, to maintain juiciness

lox brine-cured smoked salmon

M

mahi mahi lean, saltwater fish; also called *dolphin*

maize see *corn*

malt grain germinated then heated to alter its enzymes and increase its sugar content; used in beer brewing and baking

maltose sugar extracted from malt

mango pine-scented, large, sweet, tropical fruit

maple syrup   sweetener; reduced sap of maple tree

marbling   streaks of fat within muscle

margarine   butter substitute made from vegetable and/or animal fats

marmite   stockpot with a tap at the bottom; brand of English yeast spread

masa (MAH-suh)   Mexican corn dough used for tortillas

mascarpone   Italian creamy fresh cheese

mature potatoes   low moisture, good for baking and mashing

matzoh (MAHT-zuh)   thin unleavened bread used during Jewish Passover

mayonnaise   thick, white sauce; emulsion of egg yolks, oil, acid

meat   in foodservice, muscle tissue of mammals

mechanical leavening   uses physical means like whipping to add gas to a product

Medici (MED-i-chee), **Catherine de**   Italian woman who introduced elements of fine cuisine to the French in the 16th century

menu   foods offered in a restaurant; the printed list of foods shown to the customer

menu price   the price of an item to the customer, calculated using food cost percentage

mesclun (MESS-klun)   mix of baby lettuces

metric measurement   system of measuring based on the number ten

mezzaluna   two-handed, crescent-shaped knife

microorganisms   microscopically small living things

microwave oven   produces radiation that heats food by exciting water molecules

milk   white fluid produced by female mammals to feed their young

mince   to chop finely

minerals   elements (like iron) and compounds (like salt) essential for bodily functions; see Chapter 4 for a detailed list

mint chutney   Indian mint/cilantro herb sauce

mirepoix (MEER-pwah)   mixture usually of carrots, celery, and onions; used for flavoring stocks, sauces, soups

mise en place (MEEZ en plahss)   having everything prepared and organized before cooking; the ingredients prepared as a result of the mise en place process

miso   clear Japanese soup

mixer   freestanding mixing appliance with various beaters, like the wire whip, the paddle, and the dough hook

moist-heat cooking   cooking with water as steam or heated liquid

molasses   dark, thick, black sugarcane juice used for sweetening and flavoring

mold   fungus used in cheese making; causes deterioration of improperly stored food

mole (MOH-lay)   rich, complex sauces of Oaxaca, Mexico

mollusk   shellfish with very soft bodies and, usually, a shell; includes univalves, bivalves, and cephalopods

monkfish   cartilaginous, lean, saltwater fish; ugly but delicious

monounsaturated fat   liquid, vegetable-based fat, such as olive or canola oil, that has beneficial effects on cholesterol

Monterey Jack   mild, white semisoft cheese

Morbier (mor-bee-YAY)   French, semisoft, ivory-colored, mild cheese with a layer of vegetable ash in the center

mortar and pestle (PESS-uhl)   grinding implement consisting of a bowl, the mortar, and a club-shaped object—the pestle

mother sauce   one of five major sauces (béchamel, espagnole, tomato, Hollandaise, and velouté) in classic French cooking; also called *leading sauce*; see Chapter 6 for a description of the mother sauces

mozzarella (MOT-zuh-REL-uh)   elastic white Italian fresh cheese

MSDS   material safety data sheet, document that explains hazardous chemicals to food workers

muffin method   quick bread mixing method during which the fat is added to the liquid ingredients, then added to the dry ingredients

muscle fiber   in meat, long, thin cells organized in bundles

mushroom   fleshy fungus used for food; see Chapter 12 for a discussion of mushrooms

N

nam pla   Thai fish sauce

napa cabbage   Chinese cabbage

new potato   see *waxy potato*

nonbony   alternate term for cartilaginous fish

nuoc mam (NOOK mahm)   Vietnamese fish sauce

nutrients   substances in food that provide energy, promote growth, or maintain the body

O

oats   most nutritious grain

octopus   cephalopod with eight legs, chewy flesh

offal (AW-ful)   edible animal parts from places other than the carcass

oils   fats that are liquid at room temperature

oily fish   fish with a high amount of body fat

old turkey   older than 15 months, 10 to 30 pounds (4.5–14 kg)

olive oil   greenish, fruity oil pressed from olives

omelet   dish made with beaten eggs and added seasonings, flavorings, and liquids

onion   aromatic bulbous vegetable; see Chapter 12 for a discussion of onions

open burner stovetop   simple metal grate over a heat source

organic leavening   see *biological leavening*

ostrich   world's largest bird; dark flesh, similar to beef, with less fat

oyster   bivalve with irregular, rough shell; see Chapter 11 for a list of oysters

oyster mushroom   fan-shaped mushroom with a mild flavor

oyster sauce   Asian sauce made from ground oysters

P

P/D   peeled and deveined, market form of shrimp

paddle   mixer attachment for all-purpose mixing

paella (pie AY-yuh)   Spanish casserole; rice, saffron, seafood, chicken cooked in earthenware dish or large steel pan

pakora   Indian deep-fried veggie fritters

pan fry   cooking in shallow fat over moderate heat

paneer   fresh cheese from India

panini   grilled Italian sandwich

panini machine   Italian sandwich grill

panna cotta   Italian gelatin-based custard

papaya   pear-shaped, tropical fruit; delicate flavor

parasite   organism that lives on or in another organism

paring knife   short-blade knife, 2 to 4 inches (5–10 cm); used for delicate cutting

parmesan   generic imitation of Parmigiano–Reggiano

Parmigiano–Reggiano (PAR-muh-JAH-noh rej-ee-AH-noh)   hard, spicy Italian cheese

parsnip   root vegetable resembling white or yellow carrot

pasta   flour mixed with water (and sometimes eggs), shaped and dried; see Chapter 12 for examples

pasta machine   stainless steel, hand-cranked machine used to roll and cut pasta dough

pasteurization   heating foods, like milk, gently to kill bacteria

pastry bag   plastic or canvas bag with tip used for decoratively applying icing or mashed potatoes

pastry flour   wheat flour containing less gluten than bread flour; used for pie dough

pastry wheel   see *pizza cutter*

pâte à choux   éclair dough, leavened with steam

pathogens (PATH-uh-juhnz)   microorganisms that produce disease

patissier (PUH-tiss-YAY)   pastry chef; bread, pastry, desserts

PDC   peeled, deveined, and cooked; market form of shrimp

peanut   legume used whole, as a paste, or grated

peanut sauce   southeast Asian sauce; peanuts, fish sauce, coconut milk

peas   legumes; available dried, frozen, or fresh

pecorino   stong, hard-grating Italian cheese

pectin   soluble fiber that provides the glue that holds plant cells together

pepper   peppercorns; "fruit" vegetable originally from Latin America, ranging from mild to spicy; see Chapter 12 for examples

perch   lean, freshwater fish

pesto   Italian basil herb sauce

pheasant   meaty game bird

pho ("foot" without the "t")   clear, rich soup of Vietnam

physical contamination   caused by foreign objects like glass or metal shavings

pigment   substance that gives color to veggies

pizza cutter   rotating blade with handle

plank   knife cut; a precise slice of a food item

plantain   bananalike fruit used unripe as a vegetable, ripe as a dessert; must be cooked

poaching   cooking gently in water at 160 to 180°F (71–82°C)

poissonier (pwah-sahn-YAY)   fish chef

poke   wild green from the United States

polenta   Italian dish made of corn meal

porcini (por-CHEE-nee)   large, brown mushroom; rich flavor

portion control   precisely measuring amount served to the customer

portion size   amount per portion; measured by count, weight, and so forth

Portobello   large version of cremini

posole (poh-SOL-ay)   Mexican hominy soup

potato   starchy vegetable, the fleshy part of underground stems; see Chapter 12 for discussion

poultry   domesticated bird used as food

poultry grading   assigns a grade according to quality

poultry inspection   inspection for wholesomeness, not quality

powdered sugar   see *confectioner's sugar*

prawn   confusing term for various crustaceans, including large shrimp and small lobsters

pressure steamers   tightly sealed unit that cooks food quickly with steam at high pressure

pressureless convection steamer   convection oven that circulates steam around food

primal cuts   largest portions into which a carcass is cut

professionalism   an attitude that emphasizes responsible behavior and self-control

proteins   basis of animal life; provide the structure of tissues, especially muscle, and regulate bodily functions

provolone   pale-yellow, elastic hard cheese; mild to sharp flavor

pullman loaf   long, rectangular bread used in foodservice

puree   to pulverize softened fruits and vegetables into a smooth semiliquid

Q

quail   smallest bird used as poultry

quail egg   tiny egg popular in Asia for its visual delicacy

queso fresco (KAY-soh FRESS-koh)   fresh cheese from Latin America and Spain

quick bread   bread made with chemical leaveners

R

rack ovens   large conventional oven with a single enclosed area

radiation   heat generated by waves, as from an electric broiler element

radicchio (ruh-DEE-kee-oh)   endive with red leaves, white ribs

raft   clear meat structure that forms on consommé

range   cooking appliance with surface burners

rapini (ruh-PEE-nee) leafy broccoli

ray cartilaginous, saltwater fish shaped like a stealth bomber; sweet flesh; also called *skate*

reach-in smaller freezer or refrigerator

ready to cook most common style of poultry sold to foodservice institutions

recipe written description of creation of a food item

reduction liquid thickened by simmering to evaporate its water

refrigerator insulated box for short-term storage below 41°F (5°C)

rennet milk-digesting substance from calves' stomachs used in cheese making

restaurant foodservice operation that offers a selection of foods from a menu

revolving oven oven with shelves that revolve like a Ferris wheel

rhubarb vegetable with red stalks similar to celery, and large green leaves

rice most common grain used for food; see Chapter 12 for discussion

rice flour rice ground to a fine powder

rice pasta Asian pasta made of rice flour; see Chapter 12 for examples

ricotta (rih-KAH-tuh) moist, grainy Italian fresh cheese

rigor mortis stiffening of meat after slaughter

ripened cheese cheeses cured by using salt, mold, and/or aging

risotto Italian creamy rice dish made with Arborio rice

roaster poultry (chicken and duck) suitable for dry-heat cooking; up to 5 pounds

roasting cooking a food item uncovered in dry, hot air; baking

roasting pan large bake pan for roasting large meat cuts

rock Cornish hen small chicken for roasting/broiling

Romaine lettuce dark green, loose, long head

rondeau (RON-doh) large, shallow pan for braising

rooster older male chicken

root energy storage area for plants; root vegetables are high-starch and flavorful

Roquefort (ROHK-fert) blue-veined, French, sheep's milk cheese

rotating oven oven with shelves that rotate around an axis

rotisserie broiler that cooks food rotating on a rod called a *spit*

rotisseur (ROW-tuh-SUR) roast chef; roasted/braised meats, gravies

rouille (roo-ee) spicy garnish for bouillabaisse

round fish   thick-bodied, symmetrical fish

roux (roo)   mixture of flour and fat used to thicken, color, and flavor sauces and stews

RTE   acronym for "ready to eat," foods that are to be served without further cooking

S

sachet (sa-SHAY)   herbs and spices wrapped in a cheesecloth bag added to a liquid

salad   usually cold dish of leafy green vegetables and other foods, with dressing

salamander   open-front, easy-access broiler, usually installed above a range

salmon   oily, saltwater/freshwater fish; orange-red flesh; up to 25 pounds (11.4 kg)

salsa   Spanish word for "sauce"

salt   human body's most important mineral; required for water absorption and nerve function; the primary seasoning used in the kitchen

salty duck eggs   pickled eggs, dyed red, popular in Asia

sambal   Indonesian sauces, ranging from mild to spicy; most popular is sambal ocleck

sandwich   bread with a filling, or flatbread wrapped around a filling

sanitizing   washing with enough heat or chemicals to kill pathogens

sashimi (sah-SHEE-mee)   slivers of raw fish with condiments

satay   southeast Asian grilled meats on skewers

sauce   liquid or semiliquid used to enhance the flavor and appearance of food

saucepan   small pot, straight sides, single handle

saucepot   similar to stockpot, but smaller, 6 to 60 quarts/liters

saucier (SAW-see-YAY)   sauce chef; sauces, stews, hot hors d'oeuvres, sautéed foods

sauerkraut   European-style pickled cabbage

sauté (saw-TAY)   cooking very quickly on high heat with little fat

sauteuse (saw-TOOSS)   slope-sided sauté pan

sautoir (saw-TWAHR)   straight-sided sauté pan

scaling   measuring an item by weight, especially in baking

scallions   long, thin onions with white tips

scallop   bivalve with tender, sweet flesh (see Chapter 11 for a list, n.); to cook foods in a cream sauce (v.)

scoop   bowl-shaped utensil with a quick-release lever for quickly measuring items; various sizes

Scoville scale   used for measuring the heat of peppers

scrapple   German-American product of corn meal and pork

seafood   fish and shellfish consumed by humans

sear   form a brown crust on meat using high heat

seasonings   ingredients, like salt and sugar, that enhance existing flavors without changing them

selective menu   offers choices in every category

semisoft cheese   moist, easy to slice; includes Monterey Jack, Edam

semolina   hard wheat used for pasta

ServSafe   National Restaurant Association's food safety program

sesame oil, toasted   flavoring used in Asian cuisine

shabu shabu   Japanese beef hotpot

shallot   small, onion relative; flavor between onion and garlic

shark   cartilaginous, oily, saltwater fish; sweet, firm flesh

sharpening   removing material from a blade to create an effective edge

sheet pan   large flat pan used for baking, transport, storage

shellfish   animals with an external shell or internal cuttlebone (except for the octopus)

shiitake (shih-TAH-kee)   dark-brown mushroom, large cap, rich flavor

shortening   fats used to make gluten strands shorter in dough

shred   cut into thin strips

shrimp   most popular crustacean; small, ten legs, with a tail; various sizes

side   first division of a beef carcass, cut in half along the spine

sieve (siv)   round screen with solid frame for sifting flour

simmering   cooking in moderately hot water at 185 to 205°F (85–96°C)

skate   see *ray*

skim milk   milk with the fat removed

slicer   long-bladed slicing knife; electrical appliance with circular blade for slicing meats, cheeses

small sauce   spinoff of a mother sauce; see Chapter 6 for a list of small sauces

smoke point   temperature at which a fat breaks down

smoker oven   gently heats wood to produce smoke to flavor food

snail   mostly land-dwelling univalve

soba   Japanese buckwheat pasta

socle (SAH-kul)   food (like mashed potatoes) placed beneath another food on a plate to elevate it; a structural unit placed beneath a container on a buffet to raise it for greater visual interest

soft cheese   firm to liquid, very soft, with edible rind; includes Camembert, Brie

soft-shell crab   crab harvested soon after it sheds its shell; nearly completely edible

sour cream   fermented milk, thick and tangy

sous chef   supervises kitchen employees; reports to the chef

soy sauce   Asian sauce made from fermented soybeans

spaghetti   pasta in long, thin stands

spatula (SPAT-choo-luh)   utensil with straight handle and unsharpened blade, used for scraping bowls, flipping fried items, and folding

spices   flavorings using the nonleafy portions of plants (for example, seeds and bark)

spinach   mildly bitter, tender green, dark green leaves

spiral shredder   hand-cranked machine for shredding vegetables into long decorative strips

sponge method   bread-mixing method where a prefermented batter is added to the dough

spread   smooth paste used as a filling

squab   small pigeon

squash   "fruit" vegetable; several varieties, including summer squash, with tender skin, mild flavor (for example, zucchini) and winter squash with tough skin and strong flavor (for example, acorn squash)

squid   cephalopod with 10 legs and tender flesh; also called calamari

sriracha (sree-RAH-juh)   Thai thick red pepper sauce

staling   in breads, loss of moisture and change in starch

standard breading procedure   method for preparing an item for frying: seasoning, flouring, dipping in egg wash, coating with breadcrumbs

standardized recipe   set of instructions for preparing a product in a foodservice establishment

starches   usually nonsweet carbohydrates found in flour, potatoes, and beans

starchy potato   see *mature potatoes*

state of refrigeration   specification of whether a food item is to be purchased frozen or chilled

static menu   offers the same items every day

station chef   see *chef de partie*

steak cross-section of fish; or, fabricated cut of meat

steam an invisible gas that forms when water is heated above the boiling point. See also *water vapor*

steam cooker oven that cooks by bringing food into contact with steam

steaming moist-heat cooking by surrounding a food item with steam

steam-jacketed kettle freestanding pot with a hollow body through which steam circulates to heat food

stem vegetables vegetable in which only the aboveground stems are used as food

stewing cooking foods slowly, covered in liquid

stewing chicken larger, older bird for moist-heat cooking

Stilton Welsh blue-veined cheese

stock clear liquid used as base for soups, sauces; extracted from beef, fish, or poultry bones plus vegetables and flavorings

stockpot largest pot, 8 to 200 quarts/liters

straight-dough method bread-mixing method during which all ingredients are added to the mixer at once

strainer utensil used to separate solids from liquids

style classification of poultry according to how much processing it has had

sucralose (SOO-cruh-lohss) low-calorie sweetener, sold as Splenda; may be heated without negative effects

sucrose sweetener extracted from sugar beets or sugarcane

sugar water-soluble, crystalline sweetener found in fruits, honey, corn, sugarcane, and sugar beets

sukiyaki (skee-YAH-kee) Japanese dish of beef, mushrooms, onions, with soy-based sauce; prepared tableside

summer squash thin rind, delicate flavor

superfine sugar fine-grained sugar

sushi (SOO-shee) seasoned rice usually eaten with other items such as vegetables and fish (cooked or uncooked)

sushi mat bamboo mat used to roll sushi

sushi rice moderately sticky Japanese rice

sweat soften without browning

sweet potato long, tapered body; brownish skin; orange-yellow flesh

sweetbreads veal thymus gland

sweetened condensed milk evaporated milk with added sugar

sweetener any substance used to add sweetness to foods or beverages

Swiss chard vegetable; large, glossy green leaves; red or white ribs

Swiss cheese pale-yellow hard cheese, mild nutty flavor

sylta Swedish head cheese

T

table d'hôte (TAHB-luh DOHT) menu with full meal at set price

table sugar see *granulated sugar*

tagine (tah-JEEN) Moroccan stew; earthenware dish for cooking it

tamari thick Japanese soy sauce

tandoor very hot oven used in India

tapas (TAH-puhs) appetizers in Spain

tartar sauce mayonnaise sauce for fish

tempering mixing a little hot liquid into eggs to prevent curdling when they are added to a large amount of hot liquid

tempura (tem-POOR-uh) Japanese light batter for deep-frying

thermometer used to measure the temperature of meats, candies, fats; see Chapter 3

tilapia lean, freshwater fish; firm, mild flesh

tilting skillet griddle with high sides with a hinged top, from which food can be emptied by tilting

tiramisu (teer-uh-MEE-soo) coffee-flavored creamy italian dessert

tofu soybean curd, white, mild flavor

tomatillo green berry with husk, resembling a tomato

tomato berry used as a vegetable

tongs attached handles that allow handling foods without touching them

tortilla Latin American flatbread made with cornmeal or wheat flour; a style of potato omelet in Spain

tournant (toor-NAHN) chef who works wherever needed; swing chef

tourné (tor-NAY) knife cut, seven-sided 2-inch oblong

tourné knife paring knife with hooked tip

trencher early type of sandwich

trichinosis (TRIK-in-OH-sis) disease caused by roundworms in the muscle tissue of pork

tripe   beef stomach

trout   mostly freshwater; somewhat oily fish; delicate, rich flavor

truffle   expensive underground fungus, strong, earthy flavor

truing steel   long rod for realigning the edge of knives

trussing   tying a bird to make it more compact for cooking

tuna   oily, saltwater fish; firm flesh; up to several hundred pounds

turkey   large North American bird; large breasted, low in fat

U

udon   thick Japanese spaghetti

ugli (UHG-lee)   citrus fruit, cross between grapefruit and tangerine

ultrapasteurization   heating a product to 300°F (149°C) to deter bacterial growth

ulu (OO-loo) **knife**   one-handed, crescent-shaped Native Alaskan knife

umami (oo-MAH-mee)   Japanese for "savoriness" or "richness"; the fifth taste bud on the human tongue

univalve   shellfish with a one-piece shell, like the conch and the snail

U.S. measurement   system of measuring based on various units, including colonial measurements, British units

utility knife   narrow-bladed, 6–8 inches (16–20 cm)

V

vanilla   flavoring extracted from beans of an orchid

variety meats   see *offal*

veal   meat of cattle less than 3 months old

veal stock   see *brown stock*

vegetable   savory edible parts of plants, including leaves, roots, stalks, flowers

vegetable shortening   bland vegetable fat with high smoke point

vegetarian   one who eats chiefly plant products; variations include vegans, who strictly eat vegetables only; ovo-lacto, allowing milk products and eggs; pesco, allowing fish; lacto, allowing milk products

venting   technique for quickly cooling large amounts of liquid

vertical cutter   large food processor

vinaigrette (VIN-uh-GRET)   dressing, usually vinegar and oil emulsion

vinegar   acetic acid solution made by fermenting fruits or grains

virus   simple, very tiny life form with no cells; grows only inside living cells

vitamins   substances in food essential in small quantities to regulate bodily processes. See Chapter 4 for a detailed list

volume measure   measuring utensil used for liquids

W

wagyu   Japanese black cattle; most tender beef

walk-in   large freezer or refrigerator

wasabe (wah-SAH-bee)   Japanese condiment, green horseradish

water chestnut   crunchy tuber of Southeast Asia

water vapor   the fluffy white clouds that form when steam cools to just below the boiling point and forms tiny water droplets. See also *steam*

waxy potato   high-moisture; good for salads, soups, boiling

wet aging   storing meat in liquid in a vacuum package

wheat   major grain used for bread, pasta

wheat bran   outer covering of the wheat grain

wheat germ   plant embryo at the base of the wheat grain

whey   cloudy milk liquid separated from the curds

whipping cream   cream with 30 to 36% fat

white meat   light-colored flesh of poultry; less connective tissue; milder flavor

white rice   outer husk and inner bran removed

whole fish   intact, as caught, with no cleaning

whole milk   milk with all its fat, usually pasteurized, homogenized, and with vitamin D added

whole wheat   entire grain of the wheat plant

wholesome   term for food that is fit to eat

wild rice   North American grass unrelated to rice

winter squash   thick shell, dense, stronger flesh

wire whip   handheld utensil or a mixer attachment typically used for incorporating air into cream or eggs

wok   deep sauté pan with rounded bottom and curved sides

wok burner   Large, hot gas units for woks

working chef   cooks and supervises others in a smaller establishment

Y

yearling   turkey 8 to 15 months, 10 to 30 pounds (4.5–14 kg)

yeast   type of fungus used to ferment bread and beer

yield   amount produced by a recipe, measured by weight, pans, servings, portions, and so on

yogurt   fermented milk product popular in Middle Eastern cooking

young goose   younger than 6 months, up to 10 pounds (4.5 kg)

young turkey   5 to 7 months, 8 to 22 pounds (3.6–10 kg)

Z

zester   small tool for removing zest (colored part) of citrus peel to use for flavoring

Index

velouté sauce, 134

venting, 43

Vietnam, 14, 136

vinaigrette dressing, 175

vinegars

in dressing, 177

viruses, 31

vitamin

A, 88

B1, 88

B12, 88

B2, 88

B3, 88

B6, 88

C, 88

D, 88

E, 88

vitamins, 88

in vegetables, 254

volume

measure, 75

measurement, 104

metric, 107

US, 107

W

wagyu cattle, 196

walk-in, 66

wasabe, 157

water

chestnut, 167

in cells, 253

vapor, 58

waxy potatoes, 266

weighing ingredients, 106, 306

weight

AP, 104

EP, 104

metric, 107

US, 107

wet aging, 196

wheat, 268

whey, 283

whipping cream, 281

White Holland turkey, 209

white

meat, poultry, 213

mushrooms, 263

of eggs, 288

onions, 260

Pekin duck, 209

rice, 267

whole

fish, 239

milk, 280

wheat, 268

wholesomeness, meat, 187

wild rice, 267

winter squash, 257

wire whip, 74

attachment, 66

wok, 68

burner, 54

Worcestershire, 136

work surface sanitizing, 41

working chef, 19

workplace safety, 44

world

cuisine, 6

sauces, 134

Y

yams, 266

yearling turkey, 212

yeast, 299

yellow onions, 260

yield of recipes, 103

yogurt, 281

yolks, 287

young turkey, 212

yuca, 133

Z

zabaglione, 8

zester, 75